BREADCRUMBS FOR BEGINNERS:

Following the Writing Trail

DR. SHERRY L. MEINBERG

BALBOA.
PRESS
A DIVISION OF HAY HOUSE

Balboa Press books may be ordered through booksellers or by contacting:

Balboa Press
A Division of Hay House
1663 Liberty Drive
Bloomington, IN 47403
www.balboapress.com
1-(877) 407-4847

Because of the dynamic nature of the Internet, any web addresses or links contained in this book may have changed since publication and may no longer be valid. The views expressed in this work are solely those of the author and do not necessarily reflect the views of the publisher, and the publisher hereby disclaims any responsibility for them.

The author of this book does not dispense medical advice or prescribe the use of any technique as a form of treatment for physical, emotional, or medical problems without the advice of a physician, either directly or indirectly. The intent of the author is only to offer information of a general nature to help you in your quest for emotional and spiritual well-being. In the event you use any of the information in this book for yourself, which is your constitutional right, the author and the publisher assume no responsibility for your actions.

Any people depicted in stock imagery provided by Thinkstock are models, and such images are being used for illustrative purposes only.
Certain stock imagery © Thinkstock.

Printed in the United States of America.

ISBN:978-1-4525-7166-9 (sc)
ISBN: 978-1-4525-7168-3 (hc)
ISBN: 978-1-4525-7167-6 (e)

Library of Congress Control Number: 2013905916

Balboa Press rev. date: 04/19/2013

ALSO BY

DR. SHERRY L. MEINBERG

Diabetes ABC

Imperfect Weddings Are Best

Recess is Over!
No Nonsense Strategies and Tips
for Student Teachers and New Teachers

It's All Thought!
The Science, Psychology, and
Spirituality of Happiness: Teacher's Guide

Autism ABC

The Bogeyman:
Stalking and its Aftermath

Toxic Attention:
Keeping Safe from Stalkers,
Abusers, and Intruders

Be the Boss of Your Brain!
Take Control of Your Life

Chicken Soup for the Kid's Soul (Story)

Into the Hornet's Nest:
An Incredible Look
at Life in an Inner City School

AUTHOR'S NOTE

This is a highly personal book, chock full of my experiences, opinions, and biases. It is intended solely for education and information purposes. Not being a *New York Times* best-selling author, I realize that I've got a lot of nerve writing about the act of writing. And although critics have honored me with over 70 awards to date, I have yet to be a financial success. Even so, this is a book, not of rules or commandments, but of breadcrumbs freely thrown, which you have the choice to follow, or ignore.

Human beings,
who are almost unique
in having the ability
to learn from the experience of others,
are also remarkable for
their apparent disinclination to do so.
—Douglas Adams

DEDICATION

To all my former students,
present students,
and those yet to come.

*I greet you at
the beginning of a great career.*
—Emerson

*If you are invested in a writing life—
as opposed to a writing career—
then you are in it for the process
and not the product.*
—Julia Cameron

I greet you all!

*Your big opportunity may be
right where you are now.*
—Napoleon Hill

CONTENTS

The Publishing Process

The Promotion Process

Writer's Helpers

Final Words

PART 1

THE WRITING PROCESS

WELCOME

I know, I know. The world doesn't need yet another book about writing. There are seemingly tons of books telling the would-be author how to write. I ought to know, having bought well over one hundred through the years. My problem was that I read them with interest, and happily highlighted and underlined to my heart's content, but I never did the suggested activities, nor did I actually put pen to paper. Afterward, I stashed the books on a high shelf for easy reference (next to the ceiling, where I couldn't even see them, much less read the titles), where I promptly forgot them. And there they sat, undisturbed, gathering dust, for decades.

Every morning, I take my meds and vitamins (15 pills in all), along with my orange juice and toast, after which I throw all the crusts and breadcrumbs to the birds. In the same manner, I am offering you the experience of a trail of breadcrumbs to follow, as a beginner writer.

*The future belongs to those who believe
in the beauty of their dreams.*
—Eleanor Roosevelt

Breadcrumbs for Beginners: Following the Writing Trail is for those individuals (like me), who have long dithered about their big, fat, juicy, writing dreams, but somehow, life always got in the way. It is written for young students, who yearn to write, but haven't a clue as to how to start, as well we those individuals who are young at heart, but slightly older in other places, who have learned something of importance over the years, and want to share that hard-earned knowledge with others.

*True teachers use themselves
as bridges over which
they invite their students to cross;
then, having facilitated their crossing,
joyfully collapse, encouraging them
to create bridges of their own.*
—Nikos Kazantzakis

We older people are living treasures—a part of history—who need to tell our stories. As a student teacher supervisor, visiting in a history class, I was dumbfounded to see my entire lifetime included in high school history books. On one page, the text said that the Women's Movement was over. Standing up, I begged to differ, showing my membership cards to

NOW—the National Organization of Women—and the Feminist Majority Foundation. Both groups still work for educational, social, political, and economic equality. We need to share what we know.

My breadcrumbs are meant for those who have the dream of a book inside them, and are now ready to make the decision to actually write it.

If we wait for the moment
when everything,
absolutely everything is ready,
we will never begin.
—Ivan Turgenev

It is said that a doctor is a shortcut to health, a coach is a shortcut to peak performance, and a teacher is a shortcut to knowledge. So I am here to share with you some things I have learned over the decades.

This book is a practical and entertaining once-over-lightly glimpse into the World of the Writer. It is intended to cover the writing *process*—from first just *thinking* about writing, to actually putting pen to paper, and then, much later on, a discussion as to what to do with your completed manuscript to get it published. I am here to give you the gift of my experience, providing an overview, some practical advice, and a few useful tips along the way. Before we get started, let me remind you:

There is no perfect teacher . . .
The point is to make a sincere effort
to become a perfect student
of an imperfect teacher.
—Issho Fujita

Let me also warn you up front, that some of what I say might be considered *provocative, controversial,* or even *off-the-wall.* So, just use what you agree with, and drop-kick the rest. For, as Todd Michael says, "Expressing reasonable skepticism is the mark of someone who is thinking clearly." Consider the following words by a well-known writer:

If I had to give
young writers advice,
I'd say don't listen to writers
talking about writing
or themselves.
—Lillian Hellman

On the flip side, however, are the words of another famous author, whose words have lasted since the days of Ancient Rome:

Believe one who
has tried it.
—Virgil

Take your pick.

You shall listen to all sides
and filter them for yourself.
—Walt Whitman

TIP: The first tip I offer you is: Writing is just talking on paper. Write the way you talk.

Writing is a way of talking
without being interrupted.
—Jules Renard

It is often said that everyone is unique, everyone is creative, and everyone has something to say. That bears repeating: Everyone is *unique*. Everyone is *creative*. And everyone has *something to say*. You can do this! (Don't think you're too scared, too self-conscious, too proud, too embarrassed, or too shy. You can do this!)

Aspire to inspire
before you expire.
—A church newsletter

TIP: The second tip is that you make it a point to *not* talk to others about wanting to be a writer. Everything is easier said, than done. You can *think* about writing all day and all night, but keep your longing to yourself. It will simply *bore* your friends and family, and the subject will soon become *tiresome* to them. Instead of being supportive of your goal, they may simply ignore you, or you may receive negative remarks, and outright laughter. Or they may simply dismiss you, with discouraging words about "pipe dreams." It will sap your energy, your will, and your faith. You have to *believe in yourself* when no one else will. Surround yourself with a serenity shield of some sort, and let their comments easily roll off your back, or bounce harmlessly off your armor. Understand that most of the population is content to just snooze along, simply going through the motions, operating mostly on autopilot. Stay away from those naysayers who belittle your ambitions (those who say, "What you're doing is five-star dumber than dumb," or "You're just wasting your time." You must become your own cheering section.

We must not allow
other people's limited perceptions
to define us.
—Virginia Satir

And know that, if you are born into a family of nonreaders, they will not *appreciate* your efforts in this regard. Even when you finally start writing a book, keep the details to yourself. To do otherwise, is to weaken your work. Professional writers know that the more you *talk* about something you're planning to write, the less likely it is that you'll ever write it. Keep in mind: Less talk, more action.

Jane Austin secretly wrote while she sat on a sofa in the drawing room. She always kept some sewing material nearby, to toss over her writing, just in case someone came in unannounced. (So you, too, can start writing on the sly, if need be.)

Gertrude Stein became most upset upon hearing that one of her brothers was critical of her work. In response, she announced, "Very well, then, I will write for myself, and for strangers."

Your writing needn't spark a family squabble. Don't worry about what others think (especially family and friends who may be concerned about seeing themselves—with all their warts—in print). Protect yourself by keeping your work close to your vest. Don't allow anyone to step on you're dreams, or clip your wings.

*I think it's bad to talk about
one's present work,
for it spoils something
at the root of the creative art.
It discharges the tension.*
—Norman Mailer

PREPARATION

<u>ELIMINATE THE WORD "CAN'T":</u>

When someone tells you that
you can't do something,
perhaps you should consider that
they are only telling you
what they can't do.
—Sheldon Cahoon

At the outset, you are to *erase* the word "can't" from your vocabulary. Don't run yourself down, thinking that you can't do this, that, or the other. Dispel the idea that you can't write, because you're so different from everybody else. Get rid of the herd mentality. Stop trying to walk in lockstep with the majority, with everyone thinking, saying, and doing the same things. Anybody can be "normal." As Jody Foster says, "Normal is not something to aspire to, it's something to get away from." Count your blessings that you're a little off-center. Be yourself.

Know that you're never too old, and it's never too late. Besides getting older, you've been getting better, and you've been getting wiser. Liberate yourself from old patterns and behaviors that hold you back.

Don't try so hard to fit in,
when you were born to stand out.

PEN NAMES/PSEUDONYMS:

Pen names are masks
that allow us
to unmask ourselves.
—Terri Guillemets

So, moving on, with names in mind, let's take a minute or two at the outset, to think about pen names or pseudonyms:

Authors sometimes use assumed names to disguise who they are. You may find it useful to have a pen name, and often it is a smart thing to do for privacy purposes (strangers knocking on your door at all hours of the night, stalkers, and so forth), but be sure your reasoning is sound, to offset any drawbacks.

Thousands of authors throughout history have used aliases. Check out the Internet for particulars. It's mind-boggling. Theodor Geisel had three. Lawrence Block had six. Ray Bradbury has had many (three published in the same magazine issue). At last count, Dean Koontz had eleven. Then again, Samuel Clemens had only one, but it's among the most famous (Mark Twain).

If you decide to use a pen name, pick one that suits you. You should be called what you want to be called; one that feels comfortable and right. You might choose a pseudonym because:

- You may dislike your name, like the man who was named James J. James. (Can you guess what his middle name was? Right: James.);

SIDEBAR: The population of Iceland stands at 320,000 now, and Lawrence Block says, in *Hit Me* (2013) that they all descended from five Viking men and four Irish women. (All?) That makes me wonder if perhaps, with such a small population to begin with, their last-name conventions made sense: the boys take their father's first name and add "son" to it, and the girls do the same with "dottir." The traditionalists give their sons both the father's first name and last name, such as Magus Magnusson (author, translator, journalist, and TV presenter). How interesting.

> *I'm not my name.*
> *My name is something I wear,*
> *like a shirt.*
> *It gets worn.*
> *I outgrow it, I change it.*
> —Jerry Spinelli

When my son was born, we named him Jerald Jon, but within a couple of hours, we realized that it took too long to say his name. So we tried Jerry Jon, which still took too long. Then we started calling him J.J., and it stuck, right from day one. We called him J.J. throughout his infancy, and I never thought to inform him that he had a different legal name. When he entered kindergarten, it became a major problem. His teacher was old-school, demanding that he answer to his *formal* first name Jerald—which he didn't even know about, and thus, never responded to. As such, he was always in trouble, and experienced an identity crisis of sorts, which negatively affected his attitude toward school for the next twelve years. When he was in high school, he decided to legally change his given name. I informed him that he had a whole world of names to choose from, and he gave it a couple of weeks consideration. He finally decided to move from Jerald and J.J. to just plain Jay. Whew! We filled out the forms, paid the money, and it was finally official. And, he's been called Jay ever since.

My friend absolutely *hated* her given name, and refused to tell anyone what it was. She only whispered it once to me, and I wasn't sure what she said, as she mumbled it so fast (something on the order of Hildegard), but she refused to repeat it. Once was enough. When she was a youngster, and for years thereafter, she idolized a high school girl, by the name of Pat Joseph—who was beautiful, smart, and talented. She wanted to be just like Pat Joseph. When my friend was in kindergarten, her grandfather always walked her to school. He affectionately called her Pet, but the children misheard him, thinking that he called her Pat, so that's what they called her. As such, she was known as Pat to everyone throughout her school years. After graduating from high school, and moving to California, she became a hairdresser in Long Beach, working for the prestigious Bob Joseph Salon. In time, she married her boss, and she legally became known as Pat Joseph—who was beautiful, smart, and talented. Talk about obtaining a long-term goal!

- Maybe your name doesn't match your personality, and you want a closer representation;

I have known three women named Barby, and none were blonds. They paid no attention whatsoever to their bodies, clothes, or appearance. In addition, I know two women named Joy, and a colleague named Gay, who were also obviously unhappy with their given names, and worked hard to distance themselves from them—with perpetual frowns and constant negativity. On the flip side, a woman named Mona Lisa was always smiling and laughing;

- Perhaps a well-known politician, actor, sports star, TV personality, or historical figure has the same name as you have (John Wayne/Marilyn Monroe/Tom Cruise/Peter Jennings/George Washington);

- It may be that a well-known comic book or cartoon character has the same name as you (Clark Kent/Pebbles/Ziggy);

- Consider a change if your name is hard to pronounce.

One high school teacher had such a long and difficult name that he went by Mr. K. The nameplate on his desk announced him as Mr. What'shisname);

- You may have an unusual or foreign sounding name (Evan Hunter was born Salvatore Lombino);

> Lolita *is famous, not I.*
> *I am an obscure, doubly obscure, novelist*
> *with an unpronounceable name.*
> —Vladimir Nabokov

- If your name is a huge distraction, you may see the need to change it:

> One couple had the same last name—Morrison—so they didn't have to make any name changes once they became married. However, both were police officers, and both were detectives, in the same city. Confusion reined, until they moved to another city, where he became the Chief of Police. It is now easy to tell them apart.

> When my neighbors got married, her first name was Averil, and his last name was Averil, so she became Averil Averil. And then, of course, there are other names similar to Johnny Cash's song, "A Boy Named Sue."

> The famous Olympic skier Picabo Street (Pee-ka-boo), is now a nurse working

at an Intensive Care Unit (ICU) in a large metropolitan hospital. She is not permitted to answer the hospital phones any longer. It caused too much confusion when she would answer the phone and say, "Picabo, I.C.U."

• Another person or author may have the same name as you;

A blues artist named James Milton Campbell dropped his first name entirely, upon learning that he had a half-brother with the same name. He took the stage name Little Milton, so there would be no mistaking who was who.

My brother has the first and last name, and middle initial as another author, and they both wrote similar books. He thought he'd fix the problem by simply omitting the period after his middle initial, but everyone just thinks it is a printing error. That little change didn't help matters. Now he has left out his middle initial altogether. I still don't see that as much of a change.

• You may write two different kinds of books: serious books under one name and comedies or romance novels under another name; or maybe children's books under one name, and shoot-'em-up thrillers, soft core sex, or horror books under another name. (Like Evan Hunter who wrote serious books under that alias, and the police procedurals of the 87th Precinct series, using the name Ed McBain);

- You might have a lackluster or common given name (Tom, Dick, or Harry), or a surname (Smith, Jones, or Brown—which is most common surname beginning with the letter B), and want to use a more unforgettable name;

- Maybe you don't want to use your married name because it might tarnish your spouse's good name or family business reputation. (A Blues artist, Bobby Rush, changed his name—from Emmit Ellis Jr.—because his father was a preacher);

- Or perhaps you are married to a published writer, and prefer have your own identity (like the Kellerman family: husband, Jonathan Kellerman, and wife, Faye Kellerman. They have four children; the oldest son, Jesse Kellerman and the youngest daughter, Aliza Kellerman, are also writers). Consider the fact that if you ever got a divorce, your names would forever link you together;

- You might want to disguise who you are because of your day job.

> Alice B. Sheldon, took the nom de plume, James Tiptree, Jr., because she was a CIA agent and doctor of experimental psychology, who was writing SciFi books. She wrote, "At last I have what every child wants, a real secret life. Not an official secret, not a Q-clearance polygraph-enforced bite-the-capsule-when-they-get-you secret, nobody else's damn secret but MINE.").

> Dr. Todd Michael, the author of twelve books, who served as a medical director of an emergency room and Level III trauma center, used the pen name Michael Abrams to protect his patients and personal life.

- Your boss may conclude that you aren't working hard enough, if you have extra time to write a novel (and pile on a heavier workload), or could see him or herself within the pages;

- You may have a specific reason to avoid recognition. You could be writing a no-holds-barred whistle-blower, and don't want anyone to know your status in the business or corporation; or you may be in the witness protection program, or you could have IRS problems; you may be a stalking victim, or are involved in a nasty divorce, or have alimony issues, and so forth);

- You are too prolific (using different publishing houses for different series, like some Blues artists of long ago, and some authors of today). My girlfriend and I used to argue over whether Stephen King or Richard Bachman was the better writer. It turned out that they were both the same author.

- You want to look like an expert. Legally, you can add an M.D. or a Ph.D. to your name, as long as you don't actually write prescriptions or counsel others;

Joe Vitale has published many books, and suddenly he published one that emphasized *Dr.* Joe Vitale, above the title. It was clear that he didn't have the time to put forth to take classes and write a dissertation (judging from his schedule and other known hobbies). His degree is in Metaphysics, from the University of Sodona. It was a one-year home study course, that is worth less than five total college credits, giving him both a Masters degree and a Doctorate, at the same time! The school is *not* accredited. Then I read that he had a Doctorate in Marketing from Belford University in Texas (where he lives). So I thought that sounded better; perhaps I had misjudged him. Not so. The Belford University is an online college, charging $300 for unaccredited degrees for life experience. No classes, no books, no attendance, and no learning was involved. The diploma mill was found to be operated by a young man, in an apartment in Pakistan, who had become an instant millionaire, since he was running 14 such schools. They were shut down by legal action, for "fraudulent Ph.D.s," and the U.S. Federal Court fined him $22.7 million. Eek! As a result, various states have passed laws prohibiting the illegal use of credentials from unaccredited schools (Oregon, Missouri, Maine, North Dakota, New Jersey, Washington, Nevada, Illinois, Indiana, and Texas), with other states considering following suit. People with top jobs have since been fired because such schools were listed on their resumes.

It took me a straight four years of heavy coursework at BYU (not to mention time, money, and inconvenience), *beyond* my already earned Masters degree and various certificates. It offends me, that anyone can use the same initials without doing the work, and to know that it is still legal in some states. I now have some 30 units beyond my doctorate, so it's like a double doctorate. As such, it's easy to see my bias.

> The Los Angeles School District Superintendent, John Deasy, first represented himself as having a doctoral degree, until numerous newspaper articles questioned his resumé, suggesting that he bought his title. He later dropped the Dr. in front of his name.

- Perhaps you are not proud of what you write (trashy romance novels/graphic sex);

> Carolyn See says that she has written only one of what she terms "lady novels," titled *Mothers/Daughters*, and she is embarrassed by it. But she is proud of the rest of her work.

- You may feel the need to hide your gender within a male-dominated industry. Or vise versa.

> Consider Mary Ann Evans (1819-1880, Novelist, Journalist, Translator, and assistant editor), who changed her name to George Eliot, to ensure that her writing would be taken seriously. She

wanted to escape the stereotype that
women only wrote only silly, trivial, simple
light-hearted romances, with ridiculous
plots. She wrote seven popular novels,
which are known for their realism and
psychological insight.

More recently, Joanne Rowling was
advised by her publisher, to consider
taking a pseudonym, because of
prejudice against women writers.
Thinking that boys were less likely to buy
her books, she opted for the pen name of
J.K. Rowling, for her Harry Potter series.

- And, like J.K. Rowling, you may opt for initials
instead of names, although for different reasons
(J.A. Jance, J.D. Robb, R.L. Stine, J. Paul Getty,
J. Edgar Hoover, F. Scott Fitzgerald, M. Scott
Peck, M.D.).

- Or, you may want to keep your private life
hidden from the public, to avoid a glaring
spotlight on your scandalous behavior, thereby
keeping your lifestyle from reflecting upon your
family. Again, consider the life of George Eliot
(She certainly meant her quote: "It's never too
late to be what you might have been.")

According to various sources, Mary Ann
was not considered to be beautiful by any

stretch of the imagination. As such, her father thought she didn't have a chance of marriage, so he invested in a private education for her (several boarding schools), as she was quite intelligent, and a voracious reader. And, since her father was the manager of a large estate, she was allowed access to the estate library. She also was in a position to observe the extremely wealthy, and the destitute. At sixteen, her mother died, and she came home to be a housekeeper for her father. When she verbally questioned prevailing religious views, her father threatened to throw her out, so she continued to respectfully attend Sunday services, keeping her thoughts to herself. Later, when her brother, Isaac, married, and took over the family home, MaryAnn and her father moved into town, where her free-thinking connected with those of like mind. She was introduced to more liberal theologies, and both progressive and radical views. As her writing progressed, she took the pen name, George Eliot. Her father died when she was thirty, whereupon it was common knowledge that she embarked upon a number of rather embarrassing, unreciprocated, emotional attachments. Later on, she settled down, and lived with a married man for *twenty* years—during which time, Isaac refused to speak to her, because she wasn't married. Shortly after her partner died, she formed another liaison, then later married a man who was *twenty* years her junior (Isaac sent congratulations!). During their honeymoon, her new husband either jumped or fell from the hotel balcony, but he survived. So they carried on together, with her dying a few years later, at 61, from a throat infection, coupled with kidney disease. Even in death, she generated controversy, and caused a sensation, by not being buried in Westminster Abbey, because of her denial of the Christian faith, and her (monogamous) twenty years spent with a married man (but *not* her various affairs—which were common in society during that era).

Oddly, after she had become a leading writer of the Victorian age, keeping her private life under wraps, a man claimed that *he* was George Eliot ("a pretender to authorship" it was called), so she finally admitted to being the author of the popular books. She was not considered to be a member of polite society until

> Princess Louise asked for a meeting, and her mother, Queen Victoria, commissioned a painting of her.

- You may be considered "too old" or "too young" for the readers you are targeting;

- You are a single female writing as a married man (or vise versa);

- Maybe you don't want a drastic name change, and just want to change the *spelling* of your name, such as Dav Pilkey (Dave Pilkey).

> When a teen, he once worked at a Pizza Hut, and wore a nametag that misspelled his name as Dav. Apparently, he got used to it. Unfortunately, many new readers think of him as being of East Indian or foreign heritage, because, in the English language, a silent e stands to show that a long *a* is sounded. So, without the ending e, his first name is often pronounced with an ahhh sound (Dahhhv). Until, that is, someone tells them that his name is *really* just plain ol' Dave;

- You may like your middle name better, and simply switch your first and middle name, as did Henry David Thoreau (from David Henry Thoreau);

- Two or more authors may collaborate on a series (Ellery Queen was actually two cousins, Frederic Dannay and Manfred Lee. Both Franklin W. Dixon of the *Hardy Boys*, and Carolyn Keene of the *Nancy Drew* series, were actually written by a group of writers), so you might invent a name between you; or,

- You may consider the length of your name, and find it too long. Janet Evanovich said that her last name is a lot to write when signing books. She said that she wished she had kept her first name, and had chosen a shorter last name. At one lecture, my hand went numb from signing so many books—Dr. Sherry L. Meinberg—and I lost control, as my pen flew across the table onto the floor. After that, my handwriting looked like chicken-scratchings. And I was embarrassed. Oh, woe.

TITLES & WORKING TITLES:

There are few things in this world
more desperate
than a writer with no title
to stick on his cover.
—Robert Masello

You might want to start thinking of a possible working title for your manuscript. Ask yourself, "What shall I *name* my book?" Play around with titles: outrageous, funny, repulsive. *Who cares?* Have fun with it! You have plenty of time to decide.

Just know that some titles will turn off buyers: There are dozens of books with the word *poop* in the title. Yuck! And others, such as *Sh*t My Dad Says*, by Justin Halpern, and *Assholes Finish First*, by Tucker Max. *Go the F**k to Sleep*, by Adam Mansbach, was changed the following year to *Seriously, Just Go to Sleep*. Consider your readership.

IN 1972, the children's book, *Alexander and the Terrible, Horrible, No Good, Very Bad Day*, by Judith Viorst, was first published. I read a review about it in a *Psychology Today* magazine. When no bookstores had it in stock yet, I tried to order it. The owner of a bookstore laughed in a very unpleasant way, and told me there was no such book with that ridiculous title. I argued with him, and a crowd of teachers formed around us, listening to our conversation. I was well-known in the district as an expert in Children's Literature, as I was always presenting show-and-tell speeches in schools and conventions. I finally convinced him to order one. He was amazed to find that there actually *was* such a book (it is still selling!). And because I was ordering it, others did also. Later, when I went to pick it up, he told me that every time I ordered a new title, he would order a dozen copies, because he knew they were going to sell. We established a good relationship thereafter, over the unusual title of the book. How weird is that?

*An attention-grabbing title
can be the difference between
blah-blah-blah and a best seller.*
—Michael Larson

Titles sell. A good title is vital. It is considered to be *half* of your sales package. Note that your title is the first thing that an editor, publisher, and readers will see, and it should tell them something about your book. It's important that your title *stands out*, and makes a good first impression. Make it interesting and bold, or colorful and clever, or provocative, mysterious, or controversial. Anything but boring! Experts suggest using one to three words, if possible (although there are many lengthy titles on the market, that are best sellers). You can even take an oppositional approach to published books, such as *The Antidote: Happiness for People Who Can't Stand Positive Thinking*, by Oliver Burkeman, or *How to Win Friends and Influence People*, by Dale Carnegie, versus *How to Lose Friends and Infuriate People*, by Jonar C. Nader.

TIP: Begin a list of titles for yourself, and add to it, over the months and years. (I had a laundry list of 30 possible titles for my first book.) Peter Benchley claims to have tried more than 100 titles, before settling on *Jaws* twenty minutes before going to press. So you might as well get started on possible titles for your books. No rush.

> The working title during the entire writing of my first book was *Humpty Dumpty was Mugged*. The publisher didn't like it. He suggested what I thought to be horrible titles, such as *White Teacher in a Black School*. I didn't like any of them, as I considered all to be racist and divisive. So I suggested a compromise: "I'll give you a different title, and you can write the subtitle." There was a pregnant pause, and then he agreed, and *Into The Hornet's Nest: An Incredible Look at Life in an Inner City School* was the result. (A number of years later, eight books came out with the title *Humpty Dumpty was Pushed*, with different subtitles, so I felt vindicated. I *still* like *Humpty Dumpty was Mugged* better than *Pushed*, since a rough inner city school was involved, at least in my case.)

ASIDE: The average American child (2003) had seen 100,000 images of violence on TV, movies, and video games *before* entering the first grade. In addition, those children living in inner cities, had already witnessed violence first hand. So the word *mugged* would actually be considered tame to them.

Third grade Ambrosia was inconsolable. Her daddy had been shot and killed on her front porch, by his *girlfriend's* boyfriend. "Blood all over *everywheres!*" she wailed.

The working title for *Gone with the Wind*, by Margaret Mitchell, was *Tomorrow is Another Day*. The former is original and memorable, whereas the latter is stale and humdrum. We've heard it before. J.K. Rowling's first adult book, *The Casual Vacancy*, had the working title: *Responsible*. All agree that she made a wise choice.

Working titles are used mainly because the official title has not yet been decided upon. In films, however, a working title is often a ruse, used to disguise a high-profile movie or television series, helping to keep the project secret. Such working titles are meant to prevent theft, and price gouging by suppliers, as well as undesirable attention. (Check out the Internet for movie code-names. Interesting.)

TIP: Your title should be eye-catching, but it should fit the story. Deliver on your title's promise; you don't want your readers to feel suckered.

> *Making It With Mademoiselle* at first glance was thought to be a titillating romance story, whereas it was actually a book of how-to sewing patterns from the now defunct *Mademoiselle* magazine; *The Secret Lovers*, by Charles McCassy, is a spy book, not a romance novel; and although *Gunfight at Eco-Corral*, by Robin L. Murray & Joseph K. Heumann, sounds like a Western, it is about movies and the environment; *The Bride Wore Scarlet*, by Liz Carlyle, is also misleading, in that the heroine doesn't become a bride until the epilogue, and she doesn't even wear red; and the original 1953 title, *A House is Not a Home*, by Polly Adler, is about a brothel and prostitution (a memoir—covering 1920 to 1940—regarding a social club for celebrities and New York gangsters). *Who knew?* Later, the same title has been used for two decorating books, and a children's book.

TIP: Make sure your title is honest: *Writing Your Dissertation in 15 Minutes A Day*, by Joan Bolker, could only happen if you want to take years to write it. Granted, it's an enticing title, but, not likely to be believed. Then, again, *Writing Your Journal Article in 12 Weeks*, by Wendy Laura Belcher, seems a tad longish time-element, to me.

TIP: Let me give you some friendly advice: get rid of any titles that are mouthfuls or tongue-twisters. Make sure your title is easy to pronounce. Robert Ludlum wisely changed *The Wolfschanze Covenant* to *The Holcroft Covenant*. Even *The Search for Zarahemla*, by Terry L. Neal, gives some people pause to ponder, until they say the word several times, to become comfortable with it.

> If your book or movie title is difficult to spell or pronounce, and you have to add pronunciation in your ads, you're in trouble:
>
> - *Koyaanisqatsi* (1982)
> - *Powaqqatsi* (1988)
> - *Gigli* (2003) (GEE-lee)
> - *Zzyzx* (2006)
> - *Zyzzyx Road* (2006)
> - *Raatatouille* (2007 (rat-a-too-ee)
> - *Synecdoche, New York* (2008)

TIP: Here's a fact you might find of interest: There is no copyright protection for titles. So twenty books, or more, might have the same title. It is the subtitle, or the author's name, that differentiates them. Check out Amazon beforehand, to see if any (or how many) other books have your title of choice.

Anyway, the title of your book is nothing to stress over at the beginning of your journey, just keep the idea percolating in the back of your mind.

ACTIVITY: And, since we're still on the topic of titles, if you were to write your biography, what would you title it? What would you name the chapter in which you are now living? What would you hope to call your next chapter?

HOW-TO BOOKS, CLASSES, & SEMINARS:

First of all, if you have read other books about writing, or have taken other writing classes, you might find some of the things I say to be diametrically opposite to that of other teachers. So run everything I say through your BS detector. Your reasonable skepticism is the mark of someone who is thinking clearly. Just use what appeals to you—and let the rest go.

I'm here to tell you that: You don't really *need* seminars, writing classes, or How-To books. You learn best by *reading* a lot and *writing* a lot. Every book about writing, tells you to read, read, read. Top authors, like Lawrence Block and Sue Grafton, all encourage you to read, to get a sense of what works, and what doesn't. Understand that the most valuable lessons are the ones you teach yourself.

Even so, creative writing class discussions can be stimulating, fun, and you get to meet people with the same interest. Rubbing shoulders with like-minded individuals can provide reassurance, encouragement, support, and validation. And, if you are surrounded by nonreaders at home, it doesn't help your situation, or feelings of alienation, so classes, book signings, book fairs, and writing conferences, *can* help you resist the feeling of being the Lone Ranger.

For instance: My friends are either nonreaders, or they read only one type of book (Sherlock Holmes, the bible, cozies, and so on). My sons only read about sports, cars, or hobbies. They haven't read any of my ten published books. They proudly stack them all together—to show their friends that *someone* in the family is literary—but that's about the end of it. My husband only reads the newspaper. He checks out sports events and top fuel dragster races on the Internet, so he knows who's won, even before the game or race is on TV. So he reads my books *slowly*—during commercials. I'm not sure how much he gets out of it, but, at least, he makes the effort, and is proud of me. (Actually, he has committed the page numbers of his favorite stories to memory, so I shouldn't make fun of him).

Know that many classes often stray from the nuts-and-bolts business of the subject matter, in favor of theory. It has been my experience that universities are into teaching theory, with little or no practical input. My position is: This is what you need to know; this is what works.

Decades ago, as a university student, I checked in on the second day of an elective class, so I missed the directions, and no printed syllabus was then provided. It was a class on how to teach various construction skills to students. So, I merrily spent my time building as many items as possible to use in my classroom (This was before Teacher Supply Stores were operating.) Although I made the most items in the class, I received a poor grade, because I didn't use *every* tool in the toolbox (screwdriver, wrench, pliers, or a miter box). I knew how to use each tool, and could teach about the handling and safety measures of each and every tool, but I only constructed items that I would actually *use* in my own classroom. It cost me a decent grade, but I thought it was a great class

> anyway, as I made so many items I could
> actually put to use.

So it is my intention to supply you with some *practical* knowledge. Keep in mind that How-To books on writing can keep you focused on the subject, but may actually keep you from *practicing* writing, unless you follow through with all the suggested activities and suggestions (which I always skipped!). In much the same manner as many seminar junkies are perpetual students, who often have no follow through. (I'd *still* rather read than write, and I'd rather read a book *about* walking, than actually walk. So I understand.) Realize when you are just going through the motions by keeping your finger in the pot.

> *For God's sake, don't do it*
> *unless you have to . . .*
> *It's not easy.*
> *It shouldn't be easy,*
> *but it shouldn't be impossible,*
> *and it's damn near impossible.*
> —Frank Conroy

NO MAGIC FORMULA:

So I'm here to burst your bubble. I'm here to tell you that there are *no* magic wands, magic beans, or magic formulas. There is no pixie dust, or crystal ball involved; there is *no* Secret of Writing, or a decoder ring, and there is certainly no Dumbo's magic feather to hang onto. "Learning to write is not a linear process," says Natalie Goldberg. "There is no logical A-to-B-to-C way to become a good writer."

The only real secret is
that everything works—
for somebody.
—Robert Masello

You can only find what works for you through trial and error.

The magic bullet for everything is
spelled *intentional effort.*
—Eldon Taylor

But there are some things that you can learn sooner than later. I will present what I've learned, observed, and experienced over the years, and I will share examples, and that's a good thing.

Smart people learn from their mistakes.
But the really sharp ones
learn from the mistakes of others.
—Brandon Mull

RULES:

If you obey all the rules
you miss all the fun.
—Katharine Hepburn

Lee Child tells us, in *Jack Reacher's Rules*, that "Some rules are official. We form clubs and societies and associations and give them procedures and bylaws more complex than government bodies." And, granted, there are rules of etiquette, rules of physics, rules of grammar, traffic rules, rules of board games, sports, and such, but, there are no such rules for writing.

> *There are three rules*
> *for writing a novel.*
> *Unfortunately, no one knows*
> *what they are.*
> —Somerset Maugham

Having said that, let's cut through all the phony baloney. There is only one rule you should concern yourself with: **There are NO rules!** There are no laws, no blueprints, no maps, and no specific prescriptions for the creative process.

> *Any fool can make a rule, and any fool will mind it.*
> —Henry David Thoreau

To be creative is to break out of the straightjacket of rules. For instance, some experts say that authors should never use the words *however, in addition, et cettera,* or colloquialisms, clichés, and adverbs (*-ly*), or overuse exclamation points and italics in their writing, whereas I use them *all,* and in my daily speech, as well.

*If you're going to
kick authority in the teeth,
you might as well
use two feet.*
—Keith Richards

I was standing at the bank teller's window, and overheard a man at the next window. He was loudly complaining about his teenage daughter who knew *everything*, and thought he knew nothing of consequence. I started laughing, and he said, "Oh, you heard that, did you?" I responded with: "Been there, done that, bought the T-shirt, and am *still* wearing it! Don't think you're the Lone Ranger." We laughed, and then carried on with our business. Driving home, I thought to my utter dismay: *Just how many clichés can I fit into one short response?* At least, I didn't add, *"Twas ever thus,"* as I am wont to do.

*Rules make good servants
and poor masters.*
—Proverb

There is no One Special Way to write your story. There are no rules to follow, or break, for writers. It is not a "one size fits all" situation. It's not even a "one size fits the same person forever and ever" situation. (Each of my eleven books were written in a different way.) "Each time is a new journey, with no maps," Natalie Goldberg assures us.

The shoe that fits one person
pinches another;
there is no universal recipe for living.
—Carl Jung

There is more than one way to get published, and there is no right way to get there. Do not berate yourself for "not doing it right." The phrases "different strokes for different folks," "whatever floats your boat," "whatever rings your bell," or "whatever pops your cork," hold true here. I am simply sharing some *suggestions* to explore, to improve your writing, and make it more efficient. You need to find the process that works best for you. As philosophers and mystics have been saying for centuries:

There is more than one way to the mountaintop,
and there is no right way to get there.
—Neale Donald Walsch

There is no need to run yourself ragged, turning from book to book, class to class, speaker to speaker, workshop to workshop, seeking the *right* way to write. True, teachers and books have their value, but don't forget your inner wisdom. Trust your own gut instincts and intuition. As in life, there is no one single way to do anything. Many have come to understand that:

like our faces, our personalities, our attitudes and experiences, our individual responses to life, love, liberty, and the pursuit of happiness are many and varied.

TIP: Write to please yourself. Adapt my advice or scrap it, and follow your heart. Write your book your own way. (As Shakespeare continues to remind us: "To thine own self be true.") Writing, like virtue, is its own reward. Writing is a *personal* process. Do what *feels* right, not what's expected.

> *Start where you are.*
> *Use what you have.*
> *Do what you can.*
> —A Plaque

You can pick up bits and pieces from each other, and follow some breadcrumbs left by authors along the way, but, at its base, writing is a solitary act, a Do-It-Yourself experience. Your intuition, or gut feeling, should be the primary position in your decision-making.

> *The most essential gift*
> *for a good writer*
> *is a built-in*
> *shock-proof shit-detector.*
> —Ernest Hemingway

DR. SHERRY L. MEINBERG

When I started to write,
I was relatively old, and lived in CA.
So I was the wrong sex, wrong age, wrong coast.
Luckily, I was too ignorant to know it.
—Carolyn See

When I read the above quote aloud to my students, one asked: "What did she mean by too old, the wrong sex, and California?" Others in the class nodded. They weren't aware of the built-in bias, either.

She didn't know it couldn't be done,
so she went ahead and did it.
—Mary's Almanac

Everyone makes his or her own path. (Think of Frank Sinatra singing, "I did it myyyyy way.") In fact, I have a wooden sign, that has a painted green arrow, with the words MY WAY printed on it.

Having said that, however, writing a screenplay is a different animal altogether. There are plenty of rules, as Mary Lloyd shows us: "To be commercial, a screenplay must be between 95 and 120 pages long. It must be formatted the way people in the industry are accustomed to reading them. Certain happenings have to be set up in the script, and you have to write predominately in images." (Believe it or not, the dialog is secondary.)

PLACE TO WRITE:

The best place to write
is by yourself
because writing then becomes
an escape from the terrible boredom
of your own personality.
—John Kenneth Galbraith

You don't need a special space in order to write, anywhere will do (a desk, a private room, a library study carrel, a patio). *Don't be a victim of place.* Curl up in any ol' nook, cranny, or closet. Write wherever you are (floor, couch, lounge chair, rocking chair, against the wall, or the back steps writing on your knees, or at the kitchen table with kids running amok all around you. (A former third grade student lived in such a crowded space—several multi-generational families living in one small apartment—that the only place she could do her homework was sitting on top of the refrigerator. Another student, in the same situation, did his homework in the family's parked car, while a third used a picnic table at the park, and a fourth sat in the crotch of a tree.) Use the time wasted on transportation: write while a passenger on buses, trains, and planes. (Dr. Richard Carlson wrote his popular self-help book, *Don't Sweat the Small Stuff,* during a 12-hour transatlantic flight.) Or write in the dead and dark of night, with scribbled notes to decipher in the morning).

Ray Bradbury is known to have written *Fahrenheit 451* in a UCLA library basement, in a room full of typewriters, one of which he rented for ten cents an hour. He spent nine days pounding on the keys, for a total cost of $9.80.

I was amazed to read various newspaper accounts stating that J.K. Rowling wrote the first Harry Potter book in a restaurant, with her baby daughter parked in a buggy next to her. It was warmer than her apartment. Nathalie Sarraute (a French lawyer and author of many books), also chose to write in a neighborhood café, at the same time and at the same table, each morning.

Decades ago, I read a book by Irma Bomback, who said that long after she was a successful newspaper columnist and author, her husband cleared out a section of their *garage*, and moved in a rug, a desk, a chair, and a lamp, so she would have a writing space of her own. If she could do without for so long, so can the rest of us.

There are some writers, however, who feel the need for total isolation (the leave-me-alone crowd). They need peace and absolute silence. It is said that Jack

Kerouac wrote *Doctor Sax* in the bathroom of a friend's apartment. And although Agatha Christie could write anywhere, she often wrote in the bathtub, as did Edmond Rostand (*Cyrano de Bergerac*). Benjamin Franklin liked to take, what he called, "air baths" where he'd sit around naked in a cold room, while he wrote. Oddly, D.H. Lawrence (*Lady Chatterley's Lover*) would sit nude in a mulberry tree, before coming down to write. (Ouch!) Victor Hugo (*Les Miserables*, and *The Hunchback of Notre-Dame*) would have his servants take away his clothes, so he'd have nothing to do but write. In a similar fashion, James Whitcomb Riley (America's "Hoosier Poet") would have his friends take away his clothes, and lock him in a hotel room, so he would write, instead of going down to the bar, as did Harlan Ellison (multi-award winning American fantasy author) who, while sitting naked in a Las Vegas hotel, writing (*Pretty Maggie Moneyeyes*), contracted pneumonia as a result. Corinne Gerson wrote her children and teen novels while under the hair dryer in a beauty salon. Some rent offices, while others prefer public parks or private beaches. William Zinsser (*Writing Places*) once wrote in a crude shed in Connecticut, as did Anne Dillard (*The Writing Life*), in a tool shed on Cape Cod. Peter Benchley (*Jaws*) worked by winter in a room above a furnace company in New Jersey, and by summer in a converted turkey coop in Connecticut. Terry L. Neal (*The Search for Zarahemla*) writes on his yacht while it is moored, and Frank McKinney (*The Tap*) writes in his tree house.

Wherever you are is always the right place to write. Use whatever space is available, that feels good for you.

> *The best place to write*
> *is in your head.*
> —Ernest Hemingway

TIME TO WRITE:

> *Know the true value of time;*
> *snatch, seize, and enjoy*
> *every moment of it.*
> —Philip Dormer Stanhope

As an author, you will make a writing schedule to suit your lifestyle, which may change as your life evolves. Although most authors have a specific schedule for writing, you do not need a special time. You are not a hamster on a treadmill. Urgency is not an issue.

All you need to do is to write down a phrase or a sentence whenever it comes to you. Grab time in dribs and drabs, here and there, now and then—five to fifteen minutes at a time. Enough stolen moments and you will have completed a book—and without the luxury of a specific time element. Make the time. Write anytime, morning, noon, afternoon, evening, midnight, whenever you can squeeze it in. Get aggressive. Steal time.

You may find that having a specific period of time to write works best for you. Marcel Proust wrote from midnight to dawn.

*I write when I'm inspired
and I see to it
that I'm inspired
at nine o'clock every morning.*
—Peter De Vries

In the middle of the night, I will jump out of bed, and scribble a note in the dark, or race down the hall to the computer room, to record a phrase or sentence. Even while driving, I have been known to pull over, to jot a short note, to remind myself of an example I want to include in my books. Other authors are known to record notes to themselves on their cell phones. Every tiny, little, itty-bitty bit helps. *Don't be a victim of time.*

How we spend our days is, of course,
how we spend our lives.
—Anne Dillard

Wendy Hornsby, the Edgar Award winning author of the Maggie MacGowen mysteries, is a great example of stealing time: Over decades, as an adjunct teacher at Long Beach City College, she continued her own schooling, while raising two children to adulthood, and received a full-time tenured position at LBCC, and somehow, between school, sports, and plays, she managed to get seven books, and many short stories published. She clearly shows that *NOW* is always a good time to write.

The great dividing line
between success and failure
can be expressed in five words:
I did not have time.
—Anonymous

HOW TO WRITE:

Nor is there a special how involved in writing. You can handwrite (using printing or cursive, in shorthand or code), or typewrite, keyboard, dictate, and collaborate, or have your story ghost written. Now there is even speech recognition software, whereby you can talk into a headset, and your computer will automatically type the words for you. [$99.99 <givedragon.com> 1-888-297-2040]

Ernest Hemingway was known to type while standing, due to a bad back (and often in the nude), as did Thomas Wolfe (due to his 6'7" height), whereas Marcel Proust, Mark Twain, and Truman Capote preferred to write while lying in bed. Henry Ford's formula for success was: "I never stand up when I can sit down, and I never sit down when I can lie down." Both Charles Dickens and Philip Roth wrote while strolling or walking. A very famous female writer of racy books once said that she preferred to write in the nude. Who knows if that's still true? While Carolyn Wonderland, a blues artist, says she *feels* naked when she writes love songs. There are other well-known authors who are said to write in the buff, but I need confirmation before I mention them.

Any way in which you choose to write your drafts, is just fine. Most of us perch ourselves on a chair, bench, or wall, from which, as Stephen King says, "to shovel shit from a sitting position." Suit yourself.

TOOLS:

Before beginning,
prepare carefully.
—Cicero

Certainly, there are things you may need to use in your writing efforts beyond a pencil and paper, or a computer. Think of them as the tools of your trade, like a hammer and nails to a carpenter, or paint and a canvas to an artist. Cheap or expensive, it doesn't matter. Suit yourself.

> *Thou Shalt Be Organized.*
> —Clip Sign

TIP: To help you be more efficient, you may decide to buy:

- a large desk calendar (Kenneth Atchity says that your plan won't be productive until a working calendar has been set up. After you fine tune your calendar, it will be "effective and self-reinforcing.")

- a 3-hole notebook

- 3-hole dividers

- 3-hole paper or a 3-hole punch

- 3 tab files or accordion files

- a small memo book for your pocket or purse (use only one side of the paper to record a turn of phrase, or a witty remark, or something significant that comes to mind.)

- possibly a pack of 3x5 blank cards

- Post-it notes

Betsy Lerner tells us: "In a world threatening to go electronic, our pencils and Post-its and erasure shavings sometimes seem as antiquated as the letterpress and quill pens of yesteryear." No truer words were ever spoken.

> At a Christmas Grab-Bag party, among the presents I took was a set of fancy 3-tab file folders (with colorful graphics and fun quotes), that I thought would be a great gift for students or budding writers. Not so. They sniffed with distain, explaining that computers had all the files they needed. Talk about a put-down! (I am currently using my fifth computer for word processing and research, but I *still* need file folders, to hold all the information that I gather from other sources. I am clearly out-of-date. Not only that, but I found that my vocabulary is old-fashioned, as well: apparently, the words penmanship and cursive writing are obsolete, as the word *script* is now preferred. When did I become quaint?)

Consider the words of Natalie Goldberg: "When I am writing something emotional, I must write it the first time directly with hand on paper. Handwriting is more connected to the movement of the heart. Yet, when I tell stories, I go straight to the typewriter." She advises, "Choose your tools carefully, but not so carefully that you get uptight or spend more time at the stationary store than at your writing table."

Some simple writing implements can run from a dollar or so, to a thousand dollars each (for those pens with fabulous designs and engravings). Don't spend your valuable writing time trying to decide on a brand (Bic, Papermate, Mont Blanc, Parker, Lanier, and such).

No special tools are required (fountain pen, ballpoint pen, rollerball pen, Sharpie, precision pen, colored ink, typewriter, computer, or laptop). You can also key your first drafts in any font that pleases you. Who cares? Suit yourself.

> The daughter of a famous writer asked her father, upon beginning her college career, if she could have a computer. He replied, "If a pencil was good enough for Charles Dickens, it's good enough for you."

A short pencil is better than a long memory.
—Unknown

> On the application form for the doctoral program at BYU, one of the questions was:

Do you own a computer? I went right out and bought one, so, in all honesty, I could check the word yes. I was accepted into the program. But no one ever asked me if I knew how to *use* a computer. Yikes!

Nor is a special kind, color, or quality of paper (size, brightness, weight, color) required for your rough drafts. You can write with toothpaste, lipstick, or with a crayon on toilet paper. *Who cares?* (I jot ideas and words to myself with any writing tool that happens to be at hand, on a legal pad, scratch paper, the backside of envelopes, or Post-It notes, before I approach my computer. I use the flip side of my throw-aways, in an effort to conserve paper, and recycle. Some writers are known to use cut squares from paper grocery bags, while others write on faded construction paper, or use those cleaners thin shirt cardboard inserts to write on. Anything will do. Saying you don't have the proper paper is no excuse to stop writing.

"The dog ate my homework" excuse doesn't work, even though in some cases, it may actually be true. Consider Jack Kerouac (1922-1969): He cut strips of tissue paper to fit his typewriter, and taped them all together, into a 120 foot roll. This allowed him to type continuously without stopping. He wrote nonstop, with his first draft of *On the Road* completed in three weeks. So fast and furious was his writing, that no chapter headings or paragraph breaks were included. *Can you imagine?* His final draft took three weeks, with his wife bringing him pea soup and coffee to keep him going. His writing was considered too explicit for the times (drug use, homosexuality, sympathy towards minorities, religion, and foul language), which resulted in obscenity charges. As such, it was hard to find a publisher, and even then, major revisions followed before printing was allowed. No one actually knows what the final ending lines of the original manuscript were, because a cocker spaniel belonging to his friend, had eaten the last lines. Even so, the original scroll was bought for $2.43 million (which included the real names of the people involved, as well as doodlings and sketches of crosses on each page.) It was bought by Indianpolis Colts owner and CEO, Jim Irsay, who said that the scroll "belongs to the people," and has allowed it to be displayed in various exhibitions and museums.

QUESTION: Consider the question posed by Mihaly Csikszentmihalyi: "How many of our demands could be reduced if we put some energy into prioritizing, organizing, and streamlining the routines that now fritter away our attention?"

To sum up: You can write anywhere, anytime, anyhow.

COLLABORATION:

> *I always believed in writing*
> *without a collaborator,*
> *because when two people*
> *are writing the same book,*
> *each believes he gets all the worries*
> *and only half the royalties.*
> —Agatha Christie

And while we're on the subject of collaboration, let me say this about that: People usually enter into such a partnership by thinking two or three heads are better than one, or they do it largely as a way to avoid all the work, or they think it will be less time-consuming, or they think such shared work will be less lonely. According to Stephen King, "What often ends up happening in a joint effort is that one person ends up with five times the work, for about a quarter of the fun, for half the money (or less), with bruised feelings all around." I can testify to that. I hated team reports in college, as I ended up doing most or all of the work.

There are successes, however, such as Janet Evanovich (with her daughter, Alex, and her friend,

Inya Yalof), and, of course, the monumental success James Patterson has had, with several different individuals, which enable him to publish several books a year. Just know in advance what you could be getting yourself into. You don't want to lose a friend, or become estranged from a family member, if things don't work out.

I'm not talking about the kind of collaboration in which each person writes a short story or poem, and all are gathered together and published, in which the sale of the book is donated to charity. I was one of 101 authors chosen—out of 7,800 entries—who were ultimately published in *Chicken Soup for the Kid's Soul*, (edited by Jack Canfield, Mark Victor Hansen, Patty Hansen, and Irene Dunlap). We just sent in our work, dusted off our hands, and simply hoped for the best. This requires no face-to-face interaction.

Nor am I talking about a specific subject in which many authors contribute to one book, writing one chapter each, according to their expertise. These books present a comprehensive, up to date, scholarly review, such as *The Psychology of Stalking: Clinical and Forensic Perspectives* (edited by J. Reid Meloy), wherein I was interviewed, and quoted in the book, but not mentioned by name. I imagine that any proceeds from this kind of book would be split evenly amongst the authors. This also requires no real face-to-face interaction.

Nor are we discussing the kind of collaboration in which many authors are involved, who pool their expertise for a specific cause. There may be some face-to-face interaction, but certainly not all, and not at the same time. *No Rest for the Dead* (2011), was the result of 26 *New York Times* bestselling mystery authors, who wrote one chapter each. The proceeds were donated to the Leukemia and Lymphoma Society. Those involved in the project were: Jeff Abbott, Lori Armstrong, Sandra Brown, Thomas Cook, Jeffery Deaver, Diana Gabaldon, Tess Gerritsen, Andrew F. Gulli, Peter James, J.A. Jance, Faye Kellerman, Raymond Khoury, John Lescroart, Jeff Lindsay, Gayle Lynds, Phillip Margolin, Alexander McCall Smith, Michael Palmer, T. Jefferson Parker, Matthew Pearl, Kathy Reichs, Marcus Sakey, Jonathan Santlofer, Lisa Scottoline, R.L. Stine, and Marcia Talley, with an introduction by David Baldacci. What a line-up of talent! "Too many cooks spoil the broth," does not seem to apply in this case, as the book is still selling.

The collaboration I'm talking about is that of two or three writers who work together, either in the same room, or daily by phone and email. Some collaborate by coming up with the storyline together, then one writes a chapter, and the other edits it, adding and deleting as need be. And then, vice versa. And whatever money comes from the sales of the published book, is split evenly.

A committee of three
gets things done
if two don't show up.
—Herbert V. Prochnow

JUST DO IT:

Writing only happens when you do it,
so plant your butt in a chair,
and get busy. Keep busy.
—James V. Smith, Jr.

It is said that one of the most powerful objects you can ever have is a blank sheet of paper. Put your thoughts and memories in writing. Keep your words positive. Use this as a perfect beginning. You don't have to do it right, or use big or fancy words. As the famous Nike ad commands, "Just do it!" Hang out on the page. It doesn't matter how you write. You can do it by time, you can do it by word count, you can do it by number of pages, or by scheduling. *Who cares?* JUST DO IT. The *act* of writing makes you a writer.

Forty thousand wishes
won't fill your bucket with fishes.
—Fisherman's Saying

Pam Bartlett (*WomenConnected*) says that she *thought* about writing a book for *eight* years, but nothing happened. The bottom line was that she didn't *do* anything about her idea. Her dream got stuck.

You'll never plow a field
by turning it over in your mind.
—Irish Proverb

As noted by Dan Millman, "The gap between *knowing* and *doing* remains a weak link in most of our lives . . . Find the will to *follow through*." A teacher complained about yet another meeting, by saying, "I already *know* how to teach better than I do." Yikes! Recognize that recipes don't make cookies. Just sit down and write something. Catapult yourself into action!

People who deliberate too long
before they take a step
may spend their lives
on one leg.
—Anthony de Mello

Your thoughts are fleeting, like clouds floating by. You cannot simply think about writing. You cannot simply read books about writing. You cannot simply listen to authors talk about writing. You have to act, by actually writing something, in order to leave your mark.

We can either die in the bleachers,
or die on the field.
We might as well come down on the field,
and go for it!
—Les Brown

GOALS:

You need to stop thinking that you're going to write someday, and actually write *now*. Your goal is to put pen to paper in a meaningful way: Practice.

> *If I miss three days of practice,*
> *my audience knows it.*
> *If I miss two days, my critics know it.*
> *If I miss one day, I know it.*
> —Ignace Paderewski

Practicing writing is not a waste of your time and energy. Writing is an ongoing, expanding process. Think of it as practice shots, or an investment. There is no free pass in life. As Neale Donald Walsch tells us: " . . . what occurs occurs as a result of the energy you give it. That is true in all ways. It is true about physical energy, mental energy, emotional energy, and spiritual energy. Where are you putting your energy right now?" Each revision will show an improvement.

> *Writing is the only thing that,*
> *when I do it,*
> *I don't feel I should*
> *be doing something else.*
> —Gloria Steinem

Keep practicing. "Do it every day for a while," Kenneth Lamott kept saying to his daughter, Anne. "Do it as you would scales on a piano. Do it by prearrangement with yourself. Do it as a debt of honor. And make a commitment to finishing things."

Keeping your commitment
to your purpose
does not depend on
other people keeping theirs.
—Alan Cohen

Set some bite-size goals for yourself: one paragraph at a time, then one page at a time, then one day at a time. If you have determined that you can do this, and you're in it for the long haul, start making some long-term goals for your manuscript. Grab your calendar, and start making plans.

DOUBTS/JUDGMENTS:

A person who doubts himself
is like a man
who would enlist in the
ranks of his enemies
and bear arms against himself.
—Alexandre Dumas

Don't waste one minute of your time and energy fussing and fretting over the fact that you are having a doubt. Doubts are normal, and they mean nothing. Don't fight it, or suppress it. Acknowledge it by simply saying something on the order of, "Oh, that's interesting. A doubt is running across my mind." Don't use doubts as an excuse. Stay focused on your writing goal.

*The only limit to
our realization of tomorrow
will be our doubts of today.*
—Franklin Roosevelt

Don't be dismayed, depressed, or despaired upon reading some of your former work. Remember, your rough drafts are written with no restrictions, no limitations, and no boundaries. Be thrilled with how far you have improved! If you are committing your special thoughts, feelings, or perceptions to paper, then you can consider yourself to be a success. Understand that the more you write, the more you learn about writing, the better writer you become. And the more you practice, the easier it is to deal with interruptions—without temper tantrums, brain strains, or drains. Stay on your chosen path, and follow the breadcrumbs wherever you find them.

The worst enemy to creativity
is self-doubt.
—Sylvia Plath

Your job is to write—not to judge your writing. Embarrassment is a pointless experience. Abandon it, as it's not worth your time. Self-doubt impedes your progress. Substitute a carrot for the stick. Make your writing an enjoyable challenge. Jot down the dribs and drabs. Make a wild and wooly first draft. Write for the heck of it; for the fun of it. When in doubt, put it all in! You can pare it, shape it, polish it, and switch it around, later. Simply catch the thought—embellish it later. Don't minimize. Don't judge. LOVE everything you write. VALUE all of it. Set your judgments aside. You are simply laying down track. Remember: rough drafts are not to be published, and shouldn't be shared.

> *Doubt is not a pleasant condition,*
> *but certainty is an absurd one.*
> —Voltaire

See yourself as progressing one step at a time. Give yourself credit for what you have accomplished each day. You are improving. Take pride in that. Know that comparisons and judgments will stop you dead in your tracks. As Martha Graham suggested: "It is not your business to determine how good it is, nor how valuable, nor how it compares with other expressions. It is your business to keep it yours clearly and directly—to keep the channel open." Don't let your emotions shut you down! Write it out. Take heart from the words of Lawrence Block: "If you are gaining satisfaction from writing, if you are exercising and improving your talent, if you are committing to paper your special feelings and perceptions, then you can damn well call yourself a success."

Use what talents you possess:
the woods would be very silent
if no birds sang there
except those that sang best.
—Henry van Dyke

PERMISSION:

Constant effort
and frequent mistakes
are the stepping stones
to genius.
—Elbert Hubbard

Give yourself permission to be a beginner. Give yourself permission to be a poor writer. Or, as Natalie Goldberg says, "Give yourself permission to write the worst junk in the world." Rome wasn't built in a day. Progress—not perfection—is what you should be asking of yourself. Consider the delegates who signed our Constitution: the Preamble reads "to form a *more* perfect union"—not a perfect union. Besides, as Salvador Dali put it, "Have no fear of perfection— You'll never reach it." Stretch yourself, make mistakes, and learn from them. Start with a sentence, here and there. Then move on to short paragraphs. Record one tiny memory, one small scene, one quick conversation. Baby steps. No high jumping. Remember, no one will see your first attempts, but you. Mistakes and stumbles are necessary and normal.

To live a creative life we must first
lose the fear of being wrong.
—Joseph Chilton Pearce

In order to be a good writer, you must first be willing to be a bad writer. According to Anne Lamott, "All good writing begins with terrible first efforts. Start by getting something—anything—down on paper." If failing as a writer is your greatest fear, David Deleon Baker (award-winning editor) has a few words for you: "Look, if you are doing anything remotely worthwhile, you will suffer a dozen failures. So start failing right now, so you can start succeeding." Or, to paraphrase Ralph Waldo Emerson: All great writers were bad writers at first. Be courageous: write boldly and badly.

If you write one story, it may be bad;
if you write a hundred,
you have the odds in your favor.
—Edgar Rice Burroughs

You don't need to write well, you just need to write. You can always sort it out later—good, bad, or indifferent. (That's why it's called a *rough* draft.)

The possibility of making an error
should never, ever stop you
from doing anything.
—Neal Donald Walsch

So, no more messing around! It's time to become the writer you want to be. Grant yourself the emotional permission to live the life you want, and be a writer.

I am not discouraged,
because every wrong attempt discarded
is another step forward.
—Thomas Edison

Mistakes are the
portals of discovery.
—James Joyce

If you are only worried about
not making a mistake,
then you will communicate nothing.
You have missed the point . . .
which is to make people feel something.
—Yo-Yo Ma

According to Anne Lamott, "Writing is getting something down, not thinking something up." Keep your writing casual. Don't try to make it perfect. Write something down on paper, and start things moving, and changing. Don't be a lint-picker, focusing on your imperfections. Save the lint-picking for your revisions. Value everything you write. You are in practice mode.

Writing is like sex;
you don't have to wait
until you're an expert
to begin doing it.
—Anonymous

NEVER SAY NEVER:

You fail only if you stop writing.
—Ray Bradbury

Don't be a naysayer. Don't limit yourself. Break past your self-imposed mental boundaries. Be open to all genres. Value your efforts. Julia Cameron says that "Too many times, torn up pages are merely a reflection of our mood, and not a reflection of merit."

In my youth, I used to write stories at home. While in the third grade, my teacher let me read them to the class, while she took the roll. I enjoyed writing about the twins, Tizzy and Izzy, and their exploits. (I was shocked, decades later, to find three men with the name Izzy, because I thought I made up the name! And later, I found a girl called Izzy, who was named Isabelle.) Even though I was always the youngest in my classes (no California laws were in place when I was registered), I could read at a much higher level than my current grades. When I began reading adult books, I would compare my beginner writing efforts to that of adult professionals, and would moan, "I could *never* do that!" And I stopped writing. So it took me some 46 years later, before my first book, *Into the Hornet's Nest: An Incredible Look at Life in an Inner City School,* was published. I lost all of that time (when I could have been practicing!), because of a decision I made when I was around seven years old.

Years later, after writing several books, I continued to tell myself that I could *never* be a short-story writer. When I finally took a good look at my books, I saw that they were actually a bunch of little stories all cobbled together. My later *Imperfect Weddings are Best,* features close to 300 wacky wedding stories.

Similarly, for years, I loved reading mysteries, but thought I could *never* write them. When I finally took a good look at my unpublished nonfiction children's series, which I considered all revolved around *science* subjects, I saw that each book was also a science *mystery* that my students solved. (The first book in that series is titled *The Cockroach*

Invasion, the subject of which adults can't abide, but children love, due to the ick factor.) So I *can* write mysteries after all!

Learn from my mistakes, and stay open to all forms of writing. Don't set limits on yourself.

> *We should learn*
> *from the mistakes of others.*
> *We don't have time*
> *to make them all ourselves.*
> —Groucho Marx

WRITING CLUBS:

> *Snowflakes are one of nature's*
> *most fragile things,*
> *but look what they can do*
> *when they stick together.*
> —Vista M. Kelly

Writing is such a solitary experience, you may feel the need to be with those of like-mind. Widen your social circle. Hanging out with other writers is a good way to get attention, acceptance, validation, and respect. Join a writing club (such as Sisters in Crime—both local and national—for those interested in mysteries), for fun, encouragement, and support. You learn faster in social groups, if you really engage and connect with people.

It is well to remember that
the entire population of the universe,
with one trifling exception,
is composed of others.
—John Andrew Holmes, Jr.

According to Dan Zadra (who has written many self-help and inspirational books), "People who share a common direction and sense of community can get where they're going quicker and easier, because they're traveling on the strength of one another." Be on the lookout for new friends, as well as for networking purposes. In the Sisters in Crime Orange County, CA Chapter alone, authors Wendy Hornsby, Earlene Fowler, Jan Burke, Patricia McFall, Marisa Babjack-Wiggins, and myself, all became published when I was a member, with other members published afterward. We encouraged, supported, and helped one another. Such meetings may cause opportunities to knock on your door. (I was also able to give speeches at the SinC San Diego and SinC Los Angeles club meetings, which had large, supportive memberships.)

Writers must stick together
like beggars or thieves.
—Ernest Hemingway

TIP: Check each writing group out *first*, before paying any dues. See if you are a good fit. If not, keep searching.

I once sought out a book club. In the dead of night, in a scary section of town, it was an adventure just finding a parking space, and then finding the place itself, as the building had no visible address. At length, I went up a slender, creaking, shadowy set of stairs, to meet a bunch of total strangers. I found it odd to see so many men involved, and thought it might be because it was a night meeting, rather than an afternoon time, due to work schedules. It seemed to me that no one appeared to be that interested in books, and I wondered why the emphasis on choosing books to read of less than 130 pages. (*These can't be book lovers!* I complained to myself.) By the end of the second visit, it finally became apparent that this club was set up simply as a way to meet prospective dating material. What a waste!

TIP: Make sure you're not *ignoring* your own writing by belonging to writing groups. Keep in mind, as Stephen King says, that "the hours we spend talking about writing is time we don't spend actually *doing* it." Knowing and *doing* aren't necessarily the same thing. (Support other women authors by attending their speaking and signing events, buying their books, or checking their books out from public libraries.)

And it is still true,
no matter how old you are,
when you go out into the world,
it is better to hold hands,
and stick together.
—Robert Fulghum

INTERRUPTIONS/DELAYS:

Everything you put in your way
is just a method of
putting off the hour
when you could actually be doing
your dream.
—Barbara Sher

"There will always be something else to do, so if you really mean to write, you have to ignore that something," advises Ellen M. Kozak. You have to want it bad enough. There will always be interruptions, frustrations, and delays. Don't let them throw you off track. Get back to your writing with a glad heart. Don't let delays or frustrations surprise or discourage you. Exercise patience. Deal with snags, stumbling blocks, and mental inertia. Keep going. Keep your eyes on your goal, and keep moving towards it. Know that the determined writer enlarges his/her tolerance for disappointments and interruptions, and gets back to work. Success belongs to the persistent.

When I am totally focused, I can ignore the neighborhood noise (airplanes droning, dogs barking, babies crying, kids playing, sirens blaring, garbage trucks rumbling, street sweepers, and so forth), as well as indoor interruptions (phone ringing, door bell buzzing, my husband popping in for a chat, and so on). I may not like it, I may get irritated, but I can deal with it. I quickly regroup, return to my writing, and move on.

> *In truth, I've found that any day's interruptions and distractions don't much hurt a work in progress and may actually help it in some ways. It is, after all, the dab of grit that seeps into the oyster's shell that makes the pearl.*
> —Stephen King

AVOIDANCE/PROCRASTINATION:

> *Writers are notorious for using any reason to keep from working: over-researching, retyping, going to meetings, waxing the floors—anything.*
> —Gloria Steinem

Don't be lured by other distractions. Recognize television ("Bubble gum for the eyes," Steve Allen called it), surfing the web, cell phones, talk-radio, Facebook, twittering, and tweeting, for what they are: seductive distractions. Think of them as your very own Sirens. The hardest, most difficult part of writing, for many, is the act of actually sitting down to write. Writers often get sidetracked; their attention is easily diverted.

> *Everything you put in your way is just a method of putting off the hour when you could actually be doing your dream.*
> —Barbara Sher

Take to heart the words of E.L. Doctorow: "Planning to write is not writing. Outlining, research, talking to people about what you are doing, none of that is writing. Writing is writing." Understand that procrastination is the enemy. You must fight the problem of avoidance. Writers are known to take any opportunity to keep from writing. That's why it is said that many authors pick fights with their spouses, or others, as a distraction. Or why so many male writers have affairs, and so many female writers have clean houses. Consider each day a fresh start. We are advised to just hold our noses and leap into the deep end of the pool.

> *I can take forever sharpening pencils, dusting the windowsills, or rearranging the contents of my desk drawer, before I get down to writing.*
> —Ellen M. Kozak

ACTIVITY: As such, Ellen M. Kozak asks, "Will your Tombstone read: 'She always meant to write'"?

(The following is an adaption of her contract.) A few students have refused to sign it, because they recognize that they aren't yet ready to commit. Good on them to know themselves.

CONTRACT

I,_____, commit to being a learner rather than a student. Learners apply what they know; students just keep going back for more knowledge. I commit to writing.

Your future depends not upon what you know, but how well you *apply* what you know. Never forget: There is no substitute for action.

PRACTICE

HAVE TO/MUST:

Habit is either the best of servants
or the worst of masters.
—Nathaniel Emmons

Many experts say that you *must* do such and such before you can call yourself a writer. One says you *must* write three pages of stream-of-consciousness in *longhand* each morning. Several say that you have to write 1,000 words a day, *every* day, for the rest of your life. Jack London is known to have slept for four hours a night, and wrote for twenty hours a day. And so forth.

I wholeheartedly disagree. I take a more leisurely approach: I write when I am moved to write. I say, get off your invisible treadmill, and write when it pleases you.

SIDEBAR: And speaking of writing in longhand, classic penmanship is going the way of the quill. Cursive writing is becoming a lost art. (Although I am not a Luddite, I still want to live in a paper-and-pen world.) Students may no longer be able to sign their John Handcock on the dotted lines of contracts, registrar forms, college forms, reimbursement forms, bank forms, and so forth. New education standards (The Common Core State Standards for English) no longer include learning cursive writing. Some 45 states (by 2012) have adopted the QWERTY keyboard instruction, and use of digital tools for writing, instead, leaving out cursive altogether. Students can write faster than they can print. And since not everyone owns a computer or cell phone, such schools are putting those students at a disadvantage. How will all children (when grown) be able to sign such documents? We'll be reverting to Xs once again.

So my question is: How badly does 15 minutes a day—for one third grade semester—impact on other subjects? Not much. Why all the controversy? My third graders loved to practice handwriting, because I always wrote funny poems and silly sayings on the board, for them to copy. Practicing was fun, and it also gave them something absurd to read to others at home. Practicing cursive writing doesn't have to be drudgery. And, too, we know that most parents will not have the time or inclination to teach their own children how to write in longhand.

Granted those children with specific disabilities (ADHD, Dysgraphia, Executive Function Disorder, delayed motor skills, and such) will need extra practice, or simply keyboard, as they were doing so, anyway. To my way of thinking—as a teacher—doing away with longhand is a disservice to students.

SIDEBAR: Anthony Robbins asked and answered his own question, "Why have we clung to the QWERTY keyboard for 120 years?" The arrangement of the letters QWERTY on your computer keyboard (on the top left-hand row) was devised in 1882. The original configuration for typing was considered too fast for the typewriters in those days, as the parts kept jamming. So the QWERTY method was invented to *slow down* the typist. Other methods have since been developed (Dvorak, for instance) that are much more efficient, and radically increase the speed. So another question is: Why is the now 131 year old QWERTY method perpetuated?

DIARIES:

One advantage in keeping a diary
is that you become aware
with reassuring clarity
of the changes which
you constantly suffer.
—Frank Kafka

Diaries are recording the daily happenings in one's

life, arranged by date, like the events recorded in a ship's log. It is more to do with important personal events, transactions, and factual information, although some also record their observations, as well as reflections. Below are a few entries by the author, Chuck Palahniuk, in his *Diary: A Novel:*

- Just for the record, the weather today is calm and sunny, but the air is full of bullshit.

- Just for the record, the weather today is partly suspicious with chances of betrayal.

- Just for the record, the weather today is bitter with occasional fits of jealous rage.

- Everyone's in their own personal coma.

Although over the years I had been given beautiful diaries as gifts, I never got the hang of actually using them. I was too busy out in the world *doing* things, rather than taking the time to write about them (which I considered rather wearisome and boring). If something exciting happened, it was way too long to fit in my limited diary space anyway, so I wrote about the experience instead, sending cards, letters, or emails, to friends and family. I simply saved many stories, to place in my future books.

I never travel without a diary.
One should always have
something sensational to read
in the train.
—Oscar Wilde

Personal diaries are considered to be private, and for the writer's own use. Long after my mother died, I found her college diary, and read it. Her family was totally shocked that I had done so, saying it was an invasion of privacy. I didn't think so, as I had learned more about her, and felt closer to her. It was a glimpse of history.

Another day, another dollar;
fourteen hours on snowshoes,
and I wish I had a pie.
—From a Maine Trapper's Diary

As Sir Walter Scott said: "What is a diary as a rule? A document useful to the person who keeps it. Dull to the contemporary who reads it, and invaluable to the student, centuries afterwards, who treasures it." History clearly shows that official government records, military records, and political diaries, alongside business and institutional ledgers, play a role in how various civilizations are now viewed. Some of the oldest diarists were from ancient Middle East and Asian cultures, the earliest surviving from the 11th century.

In Hollywood now when people die,
they don't say,
"Did he leave a will?" but
"Did he leave a diary?"
—Liza Minnelli

Many diaries have turned into published autobiographies, biographies, and memoirs. Famous writers have kept impressive diaries, like those of Anne Frank, Charles Darwin, Buckminster Fuller, Frank Kafka, and Lewis Carroll, Queen Victoria, Harry S. Truman, George Bernard Shaw, Andy Warhol, Virginia Woolf, Anais Nin, and Sylvia Plath, to name a few.

I always say, keep a diary
and someday it'll keep you.
—Mae West

People have often kept diaries, but some were totally unaware—and unprepared—to find that their spouses, girlfriends, or boyfriends, also keep hidden diaries, which offer surprising facts about them. Consider Johanna Fantova, Albert Einstein's last girlfriend, and Anna Dostoyevsky, the second wife of Fyodor Dostoyevsky. Explore a list of diarists via Wikipedia and other websites.

Although diaries have historically been considered private, many people are now posting their daily thoughts and reflections on the web. For instance, my friend, a globe-trotter, keeps wonderful, detailed daily travel diaries, to which she adds photographs in her scrapbooks, leaving a creative legacy for her family. She shares her logs with friends, via the Internet.

Still, you may want to keep your diary private. The Oakland University, in Detroit, Michigan, is being sued (2013) for $2.2 million by an A student, who was suspended after he wrote diary entries about his attraction to his teachers. He is seeking damages for mental anguish and embarrassment. He says the English 380 class was told that no topics were off limits on the assignment; that the students could write "raw things, a personal diary that maybe you wouldn't want anyone to read." Officials said that his writings violated a policy against intimidation or harassment, and he was barred for three terms, and must undergo counseling, if he wants to return as a student. He is fighting for his civil rights. "When you get past the titillation, you've got to look at what's really going on here," he said. "It's academic freedom or no academic freedom. We're all collectively dumbed when speech is suppressed or challenged." (Stay tuned.)

There are many kinds of diaries: travel diaries, diet diaries, health and fitness diaries, dream diaries, war diaries, business diaries, and such.

JOURNALS:

*The key to a journal's effectiveness is
that you simply put pen to paper
and see what you get.*
—Victoria Moran

Another name for the journaling process is "free writing." Journaling only works when you do it freely, unfettered by conscious expectations. It is a private place in which to record your thoughts, dreams, ramblings, and diatribes. This is hardest for writers, who want everything to sound good, and don't want mistakes to show (spelling, punctuation, content, flow, penmanship, neatness, and so forth), even though journaling isn't for sharing or communication. It is not an obligation to schedule. You only journal when you feel like it.

*Keeping a journal will change your life
in ways that you'd never imagine.*
—Oprah Winfrey

Journaling is personal and private, which explores your thoughts, moods, and feelings in detail. Some call it confessional writing, as it is a self-exploration tool, kind of like discussing topics in therapy sessions, using both your conscious and subconscious minds. It is valuable for self-knowledge, self-improvement, and self-healing. It is used for problem-solving, and is considered to be a powerful tool for self-growth. Researchers found that journaling is good for stress management, as it provides both emotional and health benefits. The benefit of keeping of a journal is the process.

I will write myself into well being.
—Nancy Mair

I happen to take another view, however. I only use my journals to jot notes to myself, or record quotes, or write affirmations, and such. To my way of thinking, if you want to be a writer, journaling is a waste of both time and paper. I agree with Robert Masello, when he rants, " . . . knock off the hours of journaling and do the grunt work that real writing requires." He further raves that such stream-of-consciousness writing " . . . is just a stall, a waiting game, a way to tell yourself that you are working, when you're not." You are just going through the motions of being a writer. Anyone can fill a paper with words, at any time. He concludes: "If you're serious about writing, burn the journal and get to work."

It is not enough to be industrious;
so are the ants.
What are you industrious about?
—Henry David Thoreau

I suspect that published authors would agree that the hard part of writing isn't scribbling stream-of-consciousness on a page. The hard part is recording words that *mean* something, that make sense. Writing should have a *purpose*; it's meant to *communicate* something specific. It requires you to think before you write, and then to edit, revise, and amend, as you go along.

TIP: For a specific kind of journal, check out the various Inner-Truth Journals by KnockKnock at <knockknockstuff.com>. Each journal has thought-provoking quotes and prompts to encourage your written response. Alongside *My Pet Peeves*, and *It's Gonna Be Okay* journals, try these:

- *I Can't Sleep* (a journal for passing the time when insomnia strikes . . .);

- *In My Humble Opinion* (a journal to vent about why . . .); and,

- *My Dysfunctions* (a journal for chronicling your immeasurably fascinating dysfunctions, neuroses, emotions, . . .).

LETTERS:

> *Letter writing is the only device for*
> *combining solitude with good company.*
> —Lord Byron

So I suggest that you write letters for communication, as well as practice. Letters have staying power, much longer than a phone call. For three and a third years, I wrote 1,000 letters in 1,000 days in a row. I sent them to relatives, friends, authors, and total strangers. I limited myself to one page *only*, so recipients would actually take the time to read them. I learned to whittle, condense, and tighten up my writing. I was writing to interest others, entertain them, and share bits of newly-learned information with those of like-minded interests. I hoped for a reaction of some sort, although I didn't expect it. Happily, return letters, emails, and phone calls followed, with even a few books, CDs, and gifts. After writing 1,000 letters in a row, I knew I could do it, and didn't need that kind of commitment anymore. So, I stopped.

Apparently, I was in good letter-writing company, as the poets, Elizabeth Barrett and Robert Browning exchanged 574 love letters over a 20-month period, before eloping to Italy. It is estimated that H.P. Lovecraft wrote an estimated 100,000 letters in his lifetime, of which some 20,000 survive. Yikes! (If they lived in an email world, things might have been different.) And Jack Kerouac wrote long rambling letters to friends and family.

Understand that writing a letter *is* a form of publication. You don't know how many people will read your letters. My letters were shared with many individuals, I later found out, especially those letters of complaints, or support, and encouragement. Several letters were placed on various websites and blogs, unbeknownst to me, until long after the fact.

Decades ago, a letter that I sent to an organization in Florida, landed in a newsletter for an entirely different group in the Great Lakes region. I still wonder how that had happened.

Several years ago, a letter I had written to a husband and wife team—about their book on synchronicity—landed on their website (unbeknownst to me), and almost three years later, a producer emailed me, asking to be interviewed about my story. You just never know how far your words will go, and who they will impact.

My stalker (according to the FBI, I am the longest-stalked person in the nation) wrote numerous letters to me, over a half-century period. They were mostly written on yellow legal paper, in tiny, cramped handwriting, with no margins. They were generally eight to ten pages long. He used the old sandwich approach: starting out by saying something nice, then saying something threatening, and ending with something nice. Family, friends, psychologists, and the police all read them—and got the creeps.

TIP: If you are writing a fan letter, make sure you include a SASE, if you want a return message.

Know that if you happen to become famous, your letters may be printed in books! Whereas, no one will read your stream-of-conscious pages or journal entries (much less you), others *will* read your letters. Just commit to writing letters for the long haul, no matter what, and see what feedback it brings.

> *One line on a postcard*
> *has great impact—*
> *certainly more than*
> *no letter at all.*
> *—Alexandra Stoddard*

POETRY:

> *Poetry has never brought me*
> *enough money*
> *to buy shoelaces.*
> *—William Wordsworth*

Some say that writing poetry is a science, while others say it is an art. Some basic tips for beginner poetry writers: First, you must choose whether your poetry will rhyme, or not. Your poetry will need to rhyme if you are writing song lyrics or greeting card messages. Of course, you can choose both forms:

IF POETRY SHOULD RHYME

In the park the children playing
Leader swears he will not peek
He'll count slowly to one hundred
They will hide, then he'll go . . . find them
(Hide and Seeks a favorite game
When ending words can sound the same.)

Fishing in the silvery stream
It's awfully hard to wait
I hope those ripples mean some fish
Will soon snap up my . . . worm
(Bait was once on snaggled hooks
When rhyming words filled poem books)

Clear water ripples softly
Over pebbles in the brook
Frolicking and bubbling
In each cranny and each . . . crevice
(Each nook contained a sound sublime
When poetry could rhyme)

With undulating muscles
Snail makes its tedious climb
It leaves a shiny, silvery trail
A gooey sort of . . . excretion
(It's slippery and a lot of slime
But poetry should never rhyme)

Music of a small town band
A special summer treat
Through the ground you feel the sound
Of all those marching . . . boots
(Their feet were beating four/four time
But poetry can't rhyme)

Fluffy ice cream from the freezer
Peach in color and in flavor
Worth the long, hard job of cranking
Now a tasty treat to . . . enjoy
(We savored it in olden time
When poetry could rhyme)

The sun is sinking slowly
In a sky of darkening blue
The red and yellow blend to make
A luscious golden . . . orange*
(And orange can be the perfect hue
In poems when rhyming words won't do)

Summer breezes humming gently
Coax the tired babes to rest
Wake to treasure summer pleasure
Of all time, these days are . . . good
(They used to be the best of times
But that's when poetry had rhymes)

*It's said there is no rhyme for orange

—Audrey Sosoka

Next, after choosing whether to rhyme or not, you will choose the style that appeals to you. There are over fifty types of poetry (Haiku, Limerick, Cinquain, Ode, Sonnet, and so forth). Most are structured, with specific rules. Others are "free verse" poetry without too much form. Some are more difficult to follow than others, taking a lot of thought. Poetry can be serious, unexpected, or humorous, but all should be meaningful.

> My mother-in-law used to write long personalized poems for family member's birthdays and special occasions. They are treasured by all recipients, as they now have her special hand-written poetry to remember her by.

If you like to play around with words, if you have words running through your mind all the time, you may be a poet in the making. Find a local poetry group in which you can learn about poetry definitions and techniques, express yourself, and share your poems. The leader will often give a homework assignment (which you are free to follow or ignore), which will give you experience with the different styles. There are also poetry communities online.

Betsy Lerner says, "Perhaps poets have to push that much harder because the world is generally indifferent to their work." Lawrence Block reminds writers that,

"Poetry, like virtue, is its own reward." You must get a sense of accomplishment from your efforts.

Publishing a volume of verse
Is like dropping a rose–petal
down the Grand Canyon
and waiting for the echo.
—Don Marquis

BLOGS:

Whereas diaries are considered personal, blogging is intended for an audience. A blog is a discussion or informational site, consisting of posts by individuals, small groups, and larger organizations. Most blogs are interactive, allowing readers to provide commentary, or leave personal messages. It is a form of social networking and publishing at the same time. You might find that blogging is a way to practice, and keep your skills up, while you're searching for ideas for a novel!

Do not START a blog.
You will begin with ZERO readers.
Instead, find blogs on your subject
and contribute to them.
Be a "guest blogger."
You will reach a multitude of readers
who are already sold on what you do.
—Dan Poynter

THANK YOU NOTES:

Feeling gratitude
and not expressing it
is like wrapping a present
and not giving it.
—William Arthur Ward

Carolyn See maintains that you *must* write a Thank You note every day. I disagree. I say that you only need write Thank You notes, or heartfelt compliments, for no other reason than to convey a feel-good message. And whenever the situation warrants it, not every single day. Otherwise, it's like a homework assignment, something that is *required*, something you *have* to do, not necessarily what you *want* to do. Unlike phone calls and emails, handwritten personal messages are often saved as keepsakes, long after an occasion has passed. Thank you notes should be from the heart, something that you truly *feel*, and are *meaningful*.

TIP: As such, I recommend: *365 Thank Yous*, by Judge John Kralik (2010), which is now titled: *A Simple Act of Gratitude: How Learning to say Thank You Changed My Life* (2011). (I liked the first cover and title better!)

TIP: Read the tiny book, *Thank Your Wicked Parents: Blessings from a Difficult Childhood*, by Richard Bach (2012), for a fascinating slant on gratitude and forgiveness. He is the author of 17 books, to date.

WORK HABITS/SELF-DISCIPLINE:

Discipline has always been
a cruel word.
—Natalie Goldberg

Just keep asking yourself: "What have I written lately?" Take your own work habits seriously. Anne Tyler says, "The one ironclad rule is that I have to try. I have to walk into my writing room and pick up my pen every weekday morning." Often, simply showing up is enough. Your greatest obstacle is said to be procrastination. Practice regularly.

Being busy is not the same
as being challenged,
just as change is not the same
as progress.
—Brendon Burchard

To me, the military discipline—your inner sergeant—that many authors say is *required* of an author, is an unnecessary chore. I say, "Don't be a slave to routine!" Writing can then become drudgery, instead of a joy; something you *have* to do, instead of *want* to do. Besides, such discipline can be addictive.

Habits are at first cobwebs,
then cables.
—Spanish proverb

As such, it becomes *the discipline itself*, and not the *creative outflow*, that becomes the point. I used to keep track of how many books I read on a yearly basis. After a number of years, I realized that it had become a race to read more each year, rather than the enjoyment involved. So I stopped recording titles, and feel happier for it.

The loss of routine,
the more of life.
—Amos Bronson Alcott

It's not about how many pages you can type, or how many you can cover in ink each day. I write spontaneously, whenever the spirit moves me. And then I barely come up for air. When I'm on a roll, I will write up to 14 hours straight. Time loses all meaning. As such, my husband often yells "Breathe!" down the hall, and will quietly bring me water, when I've been at it, too long. Later on, he will bring me a mug of soup, or a toasted cheese sandwich, when I'm in the zone. On occasion, I awake at 2:00 AM, and write for nine hours straight. Other days, I do not write at all. And I don't feel guilty about it. A healthy balance is all that's needed.

When I'm writing, I write every day.
And when I'm not working,
I'm not working at all.
—Stephen King

Truman Capote imposed upon himself a strict ritual, requiring him to produce two full revisions in *longhand*, before he ever even approached his typewriter, and then, he had to use a special yellow paper. (It seems extreme to me, as well as limiting, but then, it worked successfully for him.)

(Mary) Flannery O'Connor said that she went to her room every morning, from 9:00 to 12:00. She would sit there, with a sheet of paper, waiting for an idea to come to her. She was ready for it, if something imagined or pictured came to mind. (I would be bored silly, just twiddling my thumbs. But it worked for her, as she wrote two novels and 32 short stories, as well as numerous reviews and commentaries.)

One author maintains that he works very hard for a couple of hours at a time, before he goes out to a restaurant, the bars, casinos, or to the track. (Now that's more like it!) Others say they write four to six hours each day, rain or shine. William Styron's goal is to write one page a day, but then he rewrites it, and rewrites it, and rewrites it, throughout the day, until it is deemed perfect. Yikes! (I would still be working on the first page of my first book, if that were the case.)

Janet Evanovich says, "Discipline is what separates the men from the boys. Stick to the freaking first idea, and *make* it work." All you need to do is remember Stephen King's words on the subject: "Work your ass off."

A WRITER'S DATE:

> *Growth means change,*
> *and change involves risk,*
> *stepping from the known*
> *to the unknown.*
> —Author Unknown

Dance with the idea to get out and about, to mingle, and pay attention to the world around you. You need to be *living* life, not just observing it, not just passing through it, or withdrawing from it.

> *The knowledge of the world*
> *is only to be acquired in the world,*
> *and not in a closet.*
> —Lord Chesterfield

If you are disengaged from what is happening in the real world, take yourself out of the house, and off your beaten track. Carve new pathways. Drive a different way to your job. Push your boundaries. This is your excuse to go places, explore, and do things you wouldn't normally do. It is often said: The bigger your world, the richer your life.

We are always getting
ready to live
but never living.
—Ralph Waldo Emerson

It is dangerous to live only in your mind. As is often said: Life begins at the end of your comfort zone. Your life is not meant to be spent safely at home, sitting on the sidelines, watching the world go by. Refuse to isolate yourself. Take John Donne's famous phrase, "No man is an island," to heart. Desire more color, variety, and creativity in your life. Develop new interests, engage with others, and make new friends. Your mental health—and your skill as a writer— requires interaction and change.

Allow yourself to soak up
images and impressions.
—Julia Cameron

Scientists say that you can actually increase your creative abilities, through stimulating your brain, simply by incorporating new experiences into your life. Neuroscience shows that what engages the most neural activity is novelty, challenge, connection, and expression. Brandon Burchard says that what makes us feel engaged, energized, and enthusiastic, are things like choice, contribution, and creative expression. Allow yourself to be frequently amazed!

When your creative energy
seems to be flatlining . . .
get out of the house and go
engage with the world again.
—Brendon Burchard

Step away from your passive stance in life. Many of us function exclusively in our heads (talk radio, television, movies, surfing the net, and social media, such as Facebook and YouTube). Let go of these *substitutes* for living, drop that emotional baggage, and actively participate. Engage yourself in the process of exploring new territory via direct experience, instead of a second-hand one. Dabble in a variety of activities. Break the control of your left brain. Brendon Burchard encourages us to *"want and hunger* for the challenges that will stretch our abilities."

New thoughts create new connections. See through different eyes. Pay attention. What you see depends upon where you choose to look. Get out of your head, and see life from a whole new angle.

Slow down and open up to new experiences. Live *in* the world. Soak up the atmosphere. Know that the simple act of getting outside is therapeutic. Make your escape. As your parents may have told you from time to time, "Go outside and play."

Relearning how to play not only increases
your creativity, imagination, and intuition,
it also brings more joy into your life.
—Dr. Ellie Katz

Dean Sluyter's advice is to keep your awareness wide open, whether you are " . . . walking down a forest path or a supermarket aisle, singing in the choir or slamming in the mosh pit, tooling down Pacific Coast Highway on your Harley or crawling through the Lincoln Tunnel in your Chevy." Be a people watcher, and an eavesdropper. See yourself as a writer who *notices*, rather than *judges*.

All genuine knowledge
originates in direct experience.
—Mao Tse-tung

ACTIVITY: Take an outside excursion, once a week. Make a date with yourself—a writer's date—to go someplace that you've never been before: an antique mall, an outdoor nursery, an aquarium, a train station, a museum, a new store, a flea market, an art gallery, or a New Age, witch, or voodoo shop (you never know what you will use as a scene setting in your future stories). Of course, you may prefer to attend a lecture, a conference, or a privately-owned specialized bookstore, instead. Check out any upcoming meet-and-greet authors' signings in your local newspaper. Where you go isn't important, as long as it's off your beaten path. See it as an adventure.

By introducing a change of scenery, the experience will revive your interest and energy. Soak up the atmosphere, conversations, colors, textures, sounds, and impressions. They may trigger memories. You need to *live* in the world to write about it. Notice yourself, and notice the new environment, and notice yourself *in* the new environment. Be aware of your body, your feelings, and your perceptions. Watch for new ideas and connections flooding in. Brendon Burchard reminds us that neuroscience proves that what engages the most neural activity is novelty, challenge, connection, and expression.

In this way, your writer's eye won't grow cold. Stimulate your senses. Look for the new, novel, and noteworthy. Opt for the unusual and exotic. Make a different date with yourself each week, or, if your schedule is too limited, at least once a month. If you do have strict time restraints, a writer's date will give you something to look forward to. As Julia Cameron says, "Regular Artist Dates, like regular exercise, allow us to maintain both our stamina and our tone."

While you're waiting for your Writer's Date, you might discover alternate routes for where you routinely drive. At other times, shake things up a bit by taking a different mode of transportation somewhere (train, bus, subway, cab, helicopter, plane, boat). Explore, discover, and create. Then you can begin to expand the events, people, and experiences that shape your life and your stories.

Everyday life is an
endless resource.
—Janet Evanovich

NOTE: If you are walking during your Writer's Date, it is an added bonus, both energizing and creatively productive. Walking is low-impact. Begin with a stroll for a few minutes a day, and gradually lengthen the distance or time. Remind yourself that unless you try something new or encourage different experiences, your life will continue to be the same.

However you fit walking into your day,
choose an appealing route,
wear shoes so comfortable
Mercury would trade his wings for them,
and fuel your walks with water . . .
Water, like walking, is basic,
grounding, and healing.
—Victoria Moran

MUSIC:

Focus on the music around you. Listen to other types of sounds and song lyrics. Get out of your rut. (I still receive as many comments on the music titles or phrases I spread throughout *The Bogeyman*, as I do on my stalking experiences.) Broaden your musical tastes.

I know, I know, we're all of "an age" here, and our generational music is decidedly different, but make the effort. You might surprise yourself. (During a lecture, when one adult asked me about my choice of music, I replied that although I grew up on classical music and show tunes, my favorites were the blues, next was rock 'n roll, and then jazz. I stated that I could stomach just about any music for a short period time, as long as it wasn't blasting out the windows, didn't rail against women or minorities, and I could actually *hear* the lyrics. As an afterthought, I added that I wasn't fond of polka music or yodeling, to which I received blank stares from all students. No one knew what I was talking about! Of course, I was aware of the generation gap, but I didn't realize how wide and deep it was.)

Francis enrolled as a third grader late in the year. She did the work expected of her, and took part in daily activities in a robot-like way, with no emotion involved, but she wouldn't speak. She had not uttered a word to anyone, not even me. She and her beloved sister had recently been separated, taken away from abusive parents, and placed in separate foster homes. She was having a hard time adjusting to the loss of her *total* family, as well as a new family, a new neighborhood, a new school, a new teacher, and new classmates. She followed directions well, making no trouble for anyone, but took part in school activities with all the joy of a wind-up toy. She had definitely been traumatized by her experience. Since we didn't know what would work, we did what we could, feeling our way, by guess and by golly. The class tried new things to interest her every day, hoping to find the combination that would open Francis like a safety-deposit box, to no avail. Finally, after three weeks, she became one with the group—during music, of all things. I was teaching the class to sing a two-part melody, titled, "White Choral Bells." We were doing a grand job of harmonizing, when her voice joined ours in song. It was immediately apparent to all. I could see the youngsters' bright eyes and matching smiles, and they continued to happily sing. Francis had finally decided to become a full-fledged member of our class family. She later confided, shyly and hesitantly, that her big sister used to sing that song, and it reminded her of the good times they had shared together. We made it a point to sing it often.

EVERYTHING IS A STORY:

Some people think we're made of flesh and bone.
Scientists say were made of atoms.
But I think we're made of STORIES!
When we die, that's what people remember,
the stories of our lives
and the stories that we told.
—Ruth Stotter

The poet Muriel Rukeyser agrees: "The world is made up of stories, not atoms." Know that everything that happens to us, and everything we do, is story fodder. Things are always changing. Good and bad things come and go. As a popular bumper sticker said, "Shit happens." So, as you face each condition, write about it. Like Julia Cameron preaches: "If you dump drama into my life, I will put it, and you, onto the page." She adds, "I use hurt feelings to write." Whenever anything negative happens to me, I always say—*while it is happening*—"This will make a *great* story!" It takes the edge off, and lessons the fright factor. I have been involved in a number of accidents, robberies, weddings, fires, divorces, funerals, and weird experiences, many of which I have written about.

Telemarketers are the bane of our existence, so nowadays, when they call, I just save my time, energy, and breath, by hanging up. One day, however, a man called, introducing himself as Kelly Robinson, a producer for the *Extreme Makeover* series on ABC, Channel 7. Normally, I would have dismissed the call, but I had recently worked with three TV producers on the Investigation Discovery Channel, so I thought the call might be related.

He said that the show was looking for rooms to remodel, and asked if I had a room that needed to be changed. I said, "No," adding that I was happy with my house. He was shocked, saying, "You're telling me that you don't have *one* room that could be remodeled? It's FREE!" (Now, I had told the last TV crew to stay out of my kitchen, because it hadn't been redone since 1956, and was sadly out of date. So, of course, everyone congregated there, much to my chagrin. As such, I thought that those producers may have mentioned it to other producers, even though different channels were involved. Friends, and all that.) With such in mind, I admitted that the kitchen needed remodeling. I smelled a rat—as any normal person would—but again, I was thinking of my recent filming experience.

So, we set up a date for the measurement process. In the meantime, I searched the web for his name in connection with ABC's *Extreme Makeover*. There were seemingly hundreds of names on their roster, and dozens upon dozens of producers, but his name was nowhere to be seen. So I determined to ask him about it.

But on our scheduled day, a *different* man called, giving his name as Carlos (who didn't sound like any Carlos I'd ever met). He called to change the measurement schedule to an earlier time. We quibbled over it, when I refused. The last thing he said was, "And you'll be getting a ten percent discount!" (like it was a big deal.)

Say, what? I questioned him, explaining I was told that it would be FREE, and he responded that the *estimate* was free. Riiiight. I further questioned him about the TV show, and he finally said, "We've done work for them." Which isn't the same thing, and probably an untruth, anyway. I got him to say that he worked out of Carson, and later, that the business name was Mega Builders. (When I checked the Internet, Mega Builders is affiliated with the Discovery Channel—not ABC—and though it has local sites, it is not listed in the city of Carson. Needless to say, by *misrepresenting* themselves, I didn't want any of them anywhere near my house.

So I called the Fraud section of the Long Beach Police Department. I was politely listened to, and was told that they had never heard that scam before, and thank you very much. Click. Frustrated, I contacted our local KABC, Channel 7, thinking they might want to get their lawyers involved, to at least send a "cease and desist" letter, since these people are fraudulently saying they are representing their TV series, *Extreme Makeover*. But I was instructed to write a response on the web-site. All I received was an automatic Thank You return email, about five seconds later. I doubt anyone of consequence would ever see my message, much less, read it. And no one at the ABC Network will know that someone is pulling scams in their name.

I was upset. After a two-week stay in the hospital, my six-month-old son was scheduled for release that morning, but his temperature had elevated *one* degree, and the doctors decided to keep him an extra day, just to be on the safe side. I couldn't believe that one little degree was cause for concern, and I was unhappy about it, in the extreme. I missed him.

Nursing heart-sick feelings, I was driving home on the freeway, at a fairly fast clip. The traffic was lighter than usual, and I was traveling a number of lengths behind a large moving van, with an open back door. I wondered if the bosses knew that a motorboat was being hauled therein. I figured that the workers had already delivered furniture that morning, and on the QT were moving a privately-owned boat, *without* their boss's knowledge.

I no more than considered that scenario, when the untied boat took flight out of the back of the moving van, sailing straight for me. I began swerving back and forth across the wide open lanes, trying to avoid the boat, while leaning on my horn at the same time, in an effort to alert drivers behind me. The boat hit the pavement, with sparks flying, as it bounced erratically, then skidded over to the middle divider, ricocheted off the cement wall, and then flew in an arc back across three lanes, for a perfect crash landing on the front of my car. It proceeded on its way in bumper-car fashion, back down the freeway, damaging vehicles left, right, and center. When the California Highway Patrol finally arrived, there was a scraggly line of ten or so vehicles stretched along the side of the freeway—with various amounts of damage—alongside the many freaked out drivers. It took a long time getting home. Few people believed me when I said, "A boat fell on me on the freeway."

I was so thankful and relieved that my son hadn't been released from the hospital that day. The elevation of a mere one degree temperature may have saved his life. (This happened at a time before seatbelts and children's car seats were mandated, and my son would, most likely, have violently landed on the floorboards.)

I have always wondered what happened to the two workers that were driving the van. And, I have pondered, as well, about just how much damage was caused, by not taking the time to tie down the boat, or simply close the van door.

Around 9:30 one morning, I turned onto Woodruff, a large four-lane street, to find not one vehicle on the road, coming or going, which was highly unusual. And spooky, as the fog was very dense, and much lower than usually experienced. Portions of it was swirling about, which I had never witnessed beforehand. I was mesmerized by the soundless atmosphere, as it appeared that I was the only person left in the whole wide world. Very weird. So as I'm staring at the low-hanging fog, I was shocked to see the nose of a blimp piercing through the fog bank. I couldn't believe my eyes, as it slowly materialized, and seemed to be heading down, at an angle, straight for me. I figured that the pilot didn't realize the fog was so low, and was looking for landmarks. As I white-knuckled the steering wheel, scenes of police and hospitals instantly filled my mind, even as I recognized that neither the driver nor I would survive the crash. Seemingly, at the last minute, the blimp jerked up and slowly moved across the street in front of me, barely skimming across the rooftops, as it headed for the nearby airport. In large letters, on the side of the blimp, it said: GOOD YEAR. I happily decided that this sign, this symbol, this *omen*, meant that my books were going to do well this year, and I would live to write another day.

ATTITUDE:

Our attitude is the crayon
that colors our world.
—Allen Klein

Attitude is everything! Know that what you assume, expect, or believe, is what you will experience. You get what you look for. "Your attitude is a primary catalyst both to what you magnetize and what you manifest," says Sandra Anne Taylor. "You choose how you approach every day." There is no need for painful rope burns in your writing life. No matter any difficulties involved, see your writing efforts as exciting and rewarding. The more positives you see and project into your writing, the better your experience.

A positive attitude
may not solve all your problems,
but it will annoy enough people
to make it worth the effort.
—Herm Albright

Not all challenges are negative, difficult, or painful. Look at them as interesting or stimulating problems to be considered and worked out. An exciting challenge is one thing; a struggle is quite another. Just because you have heard of the trials and tribulations of some famous authors, does not mean that you must travel the same route. Your writing journey does not have to be a strenuous effort against opposition. Opt for the easiest path, or the simplest path, or the fastest path. Take the most joyous path for you.

> *If writing is not to become a chore*
> *more dismal than dishwashing,*
> *not only must you want to write,*
> *you must need to write,*
> *and you must love to write.*
> —Ellen M. Kozak

Use your positive attitude to meet and overcome the obstacles of your day-to-day writing life. Dr. Wayne Dyer suggests that you: "Imagine a sort of pit-bull kind of resolve or determination—a never give up attitude," adding, "Recognize the super-achiever within." Acceptance, patience, and a determined attitude will keep you involved. Know that you are responsible for the things you choose to mentally dwell upon. Your writing will become a pleasure and a joy, once you reframe the whole idea of work. Live as if your writing is easy, all your readers love your stories, and fame and fortune is now coming to you. Live with a grateful heart.

*Our greatest freedom is the freedom to
choose our attitude.*
—Victor Frankl

My husband and I were standing in line before the polls opened, waiting to vote. A man, and his young son (about ten years old), were quietly standing behind us. At length, the boy turned to his father, and asked, "Dad, are you mad at me or something?" The man slightly smiled, and said, "No, son. I'm trying to exercise patience." His simple demonstration sure helped me.

I could never write slash and burn thrillers, or horror novels, because I know that dwelling on unpleasant things merely perpetuates their existence in my life. Think how depressing it would be to only write graphic action books—surrounded by guns, knives, explosions, and a high body count, every single day. (A sweet, gentle teen, whose two novels I have edited, was constantly staging gruesome, detailed fights—seemingly a blood-bath per page, with body parts flying every which way, while blowing up iconic buildings—in each chapter he wrote. I worried about his frame of mind. But that was probably why he was so well-balanced. He got it out of his system.) To me, however, the potential fame and fortune gained would never offset the perpetual gloomy atmosphere that such authors have to live with on a daily basis.

Granted, not all writing is rainbows and lollipops. Sure Virginia Woolf and Sylvia Plath were depressed. Just as Keats, Poe, and Hemingway were depressed. But that doesn't mean that you as a writer must follow in their footsteps. Leave those mindsets at the door. Don't cave in to setbacks. Get out of your funk by doing something different, and come back to your writing refreshed. Refuse to use depression as an excuse not to write.

Any mood is a good mood to write, regardless of what Dorothy Parker said, in *The Collected Dorothy Parker:* "If you have any young friends who aspire to become writers, the second greatest favor you can do them is to present them with copies of *The Elements of Style.* The first greatest, of course, is to shoot them now, while they're happy." (Keep in mind that even though she was considered to be the most talked-about woman of her day—the 1920s and 1930s—and even though she was known to be a "masochist whose passion for unhappiness knew no bounds," she continued to write. So don't let her sway you.)

Don't waste your time worrying and fretting over circumstances you can't control. Understand that you keep your *worries* and problems alive by giving them your attention and energy, letting them live rent free in your head. Understand, too, that worry is like a rocking chair. It is moving, but getting nowhere. Know that what you do each day is important, because you are trading a day of your life for it.

Man is fond of counting his troubles,
but he does not count his joys.
If he counted them up, he would see
that every lot has enough happiness
provided for it.
—Fyodor Dostoevsky

Don't make writing so serious (moan, groan, whine, sigh). Don't make it such a Big Deal. That tends to make creative writing difficult to do. Write for the sheer *joy* of it! Change your mindset to that of having fun, *fun*, FUN! Make writing something you *want* to do, not something you *have* to do. Don't make it a chore. (I had the most fun of all, writing *Imperfect Weddings Are Best!*) Trust the process of your writing. You've heard of Sunday painters, Shade Tree Mechanics, weekend photographers and musicians. Be thrilled that poets and writers can find any time during the week to write. EASY DOES IT! Conduct yourself with concrete confidence.

All of life is a chance. So take it!
The person who goes the furthest
is the one who is willing
to do and dare.
—Dale Carnegie

CHOICE:

> *Life is change.*
> *Growth is optional.*
> *Choose wisely.*
> —Karen Kaiser Clark

You have choices and voices, it is said. You can choose if and when to write, you can choose what to write, and you can choose how truthful you care or dare to be. Will you speak with anger, or with gentleness and love? Will you be the author of your changes, or merely be impacted by outside forces?

> *The minute you choose to do*
> *what you really want to do,*
> *it's a different kind of life.*
> —Buckminster Fuller

Your choice, on this very day, could set the tone, or set the stage, for an entirely different year for you. As Neale Donald Walsch says, "Funny how things work. Sometimes the smallest choice, one that you might make within the next 24 hours, can set into motion huge energies, bringing you great good and enormous joy." On this five-star day, choose to get your stories on paper.

Today I will do
what others won't,
so tomorrow I can accomplish
what others can't.
—Jerry Rice

"Every choice has consequences that can teach us something," says Dan Millman, adding, "Whatever decision you make is perfect for you at the time."

Choose feelings over logic,
adventure over perfection,
here over there,
now over then,
and always love, love, love.
—Mike Dooley

Choose happy and successful thoughts, and send them out in all directions. You can make writing a chore, or you can have a good time. Choose to be positive and enthusiastic about your writing!

You are free to choose,
but the choices you make today
will determine
what you will have, be, and do
in the tomorrow of your life.
—Zig Ziglar

People always ask me what I'm going to do each weekend, and when I cheerfully say that I'm going to be writing, they don't understand why I'm so thrilled about it. When you love to write, or when you're inspired to write, " . . . work becomes play, perspiration becomes inspiration, and it doesn't matter what others may say," adds Mike Dooley. I can testify to that.

> *Remember, happiness doesn't depend on*
> *who you are or what you have;*
> *it depends solely on what you think.*
> —Dale Carnegie

ACTIVITY: Quickly list 10 things that make you happy. What makes you feel thrilled, and on top of the world? Do you know that experts say being happy adds nine years to your life?

> *When one door of happiness closes,*
> *another opens;*
> *but often we look so long*
> *at the closed door*
> *that we do not see*
> *the one which has been opened for us.*
> —Helen Keller

WRITE A BOOK IN A YEAR:

> *Get a good idea and stay with it.*
> *Dig it, and work at it*
> *until it's done right.*
> —Walt Disney

If you are really serious, and will commit to writing *something* each day, like *one* page, you will have a solid book within a year. Lawrence Block asks, "Don't you figure you could produce one measly little page, even on a bad day? Even on a rotten day?" It is said that Walt Disney built Disneyland in 222 day (about 7 and a half months). So you might keep that in mind. If he could accomplish that much in a mere 222 days, you could use that as your target end date.

Many of what I thought to be my own private revelations, I've since found in other books. I thought that I had an original observation about the birthing of a book. Not so. It appears that several authors have come to the realization that producing a book is a lot like having a baby: First there is the *conception* period (ideas, intention, research), then there is *gestation* period (writing, alongside worries, frustrations, and concerns), and finally there is the *delivery* period (completed manuscript, publishing). You can't skip steps. There's no rushing the process, like a flower from its seed, as no stage can be ignored or achieved out of order.

> *Like a farmer*
> *eager for a new crop,*
> *any rush to harvest*
> *would spoil the yield.*
> —Mike Dooley

You don't control the timetable, as each process takes as long as it needs—there is really nothing you can do about it—around nine months, give or take. (So you might want to set your target date as nine months.) And then, of course, after the birth, most writers act like parents who endlessly pace up, down, and around the neo-natal care unit, worrying: Is my baby going to make it? Will readers like my book? Will they understand it? Will it sell? Unfortunately, this is where most authors stop. They don't support their books through the *growth* period (with promotional support).

Traditional editors give writers anywhere from 12 to 18 months to complete a book, then another nine to publish it. (Some authors, like Nora Roberts and James Patterson, write several books a year, using a 60 to 90 day intensive time period. Most authors choose the 60 to 90 day schedule. However, Charles Dickens wrote the classic *A Christmas Carol* in two weeks, and I wrote *Autism ABC* (29 awards) in the same amount of time. Barbara Cartland is known to be the fastest novel writer, as it took her only five days to write each of her 623 best-sellers. Yikes! Faulkner wrote *As I Lay Dying* in six weeks, whereas Stephen King's first draft of *The Stand*, took 16 months. Many authors take *years* to write their books (*Tuck Everlasting*, by Natalie Babbitt, is a 140 page juvenile classic, which took 10 years to write. Frank McCourt took 30 years to write *Angela's Ashes*).

With self-publishing, PODs, and ebooks, you can take as little time, or as long as is needed, to write your book, with no prodding involved. It all boils down to how much research is involved, how long the storyline takes, and how fast you can write.

ACTIVITY: Pick a starting date, count off 222 days and mark it on your calendar (or however long you anticipate your time-frame to be). Perhaps your starting date will be at the conclusion of reading this book. See how close you can make it to your projected date. Make a commitment, follow through, and get it done.

Having said that, however, know that you can take as many years as needed to write your book. Don't feel pushed. Taking the *long* way isn't the same as taking the *wrong* way. Suit yourself.

WRITE OFTEN:

> *It is by sitting down*
> *to write every morning*
> *that one becomes a writer:*
> *Those who do not do this*
> *remain amateurs.*
> —Gerald Brenan

Just because you don't know what to write, doesn't mean you shouldn't start, suggests Mike Dooley. Practice as often as you can. Determine to write something for five days a week, early or late, whatever suits your fancy. I suggest that you write *before* your chores, and *before* reading your emails or snail mail, so you won't get sidetracked. Daily life has a habit of getting in the way. Be willing to put your day-to-day real life obstacles on the backburner for a while, to express yourself. There are either 25 or 30 lines to a page, and ten words to a line, making it a 250 or 300 word page. Nowadays, computers can quickly add up the words for your convenience.

Commit and never look back. Muster the courage to stay the course, however long it takes. Stretch yourself and scoff at the odds. Write as often as you can, whenever, and wherever you can, to make your book dream come true. Don't hold back. Go for it all the way!

> *Going the* long way
> *is not the same as*
> *going the* wrong way.
> —Neale Donald Walsch

Consider the words of Brendon Burchard, "Having an idea for a book isn't creativity; it's just a thought. Writing the book and putting pen to paper for page after page is creative expression. Real creativity ends up as *something*."

SUBJECTS OF INTEREST:

What subjects appeal to you? Experts all say to write what you *know*. (Carolyn See's father, George Laws, wrote 73 porno novels, starting when he was 69. He died, or he'd still be writing them.) Write your autobiography, or your memoirs, or a novel based on your personal experiences. Write what you know.

And I add: write what you *care* about. What are your interests? Where is your *passion*? What *moves* you? (I knew *nothing* about the subjects of autism or diabetes until I researched for those two ABC books. I was just upset about the bullying of children with special needs, and that both worldwide epidemics seemed to have escaped public notice. It was worth the time and effort, as so many people have expressed their thanks (via letters, cards, emails, phone calls, and in person.) In addition, both little books have garnered numerous awards.

> *If you do not express your own original ideas,*
> *if you do not listen to your own being,*
> *you will have betrayed yourself.*
> —Rollo May

Of course, if not having anything to say is your problem, then all the writing classes in the world won't help you become a writer. So, you must write about things you know. Notice those things that are of interest to you. In that regard, let me help you:

ACTIVITY: Your homework, should you choose to do it, is to: *List five of your childhood accomplishments.* Pick one to write about. Your accomplishment can be big or small, but it meant something to you at the time. You might never have shared it with anyone before, because it was meaningful to you, and possibly no one else. Remember, you're not in school anymore, so you can write anything and in any way you want.

Way back, when I was a seven-year-old third grader, I loved to play baseball. The big boys (5th, 6th, and 7th graders), always played 500 in front of my house. (It was a non-contact game, in which the batter would hit the ball, and the players would get so may points for catching the ball: 100 points for catching a fly ball, 50 points for a one bounce, 25 points for a two bouncer, 10 points for grounders.) I would sit on the curb, watching, aching to take part, and periodically asked if I could play. They always refused, since I was just a little girl. Finally, the guys got tired of running after some of the grounders, and let me chase after them. So I would stand behind six or eight kids, and run after the rolling balls that no one wanted to bother with. One day, I actually made 500 points. Then all the guys rushed toward me, begging to take my place at bat. I refused, walking through the angry gauntlet. As I picked up the bat, they all moved up as close as possible. I kept telling them to back up, because I was worried about hitting them, when I swung the bat around. They reluctantly took a couple of steps backward. Satisfied that I had a bigger space in which to swing, I threw the ball up, and when it came down, I socked that sucker clear into the next block! The way all their heads followed the arc of the ball, and their whistles, and wild responses as they chased after it, was very satisfying to me. And I got to play forever after. It was the first major achievement of a goal that I was really proud of, but I never told anyone about it. It was personal.

CHARACTERS

CAST OF CHARACTERS:

It begins with a character, usually,
and once he stands up on his feet
and begins to move,
all I can do is trot along behind him
with a paper and pencil
trying to keep up long enough
to put down what he says and does.
—William Faulkner

Don't worry about the plot, experts tell us. Worry about the characters. (Students always complain and *argue* about this unexpected turn of events.) But think about it: If readers are to become invested in your story, they must be invested in your characters. There must be someone they can root for, or why should they care? No one is perfect, and our motivations aren't always pure. We don't always speak well or make good choices, so neither should our characters. And since bad things happen to good people, bad things happen to good characters, as well. None of us behave well all the time, nor do we always make smart decisions. Sorry to say. And such actions have consequences. To one extent or another, every story involves a lead character's attempt to cope with a problem. Focus on your characters. Let your character's motivations and goals drive your story.

TIP: First, writers describe their major characters. Next, they select, describe, and sometimes map the location involved. Then they decide what the plot is going to entail, and generally make a timeline of the action.

> *I always begin with a character,*
> *or characters,*
> *and then try to think up as much action*
> *for them as possible.*
> —John Irving

Today we're going to consider the characters in your stories. To summarize Janet Evanovich, it's critical to have memorable characters: Bring your characters to life, and make them believable and worth caring about. Give them personalities that set them apart from other characters. It doesn't matter if the reader loves or hates your characters. What matters is the way they *feel* about them. (I was once asked on camera how I *felt* about one of the villains in my book, *The Bogeyman*, and I completely froze, and couldn't answer the question.) Know your characters!

> *Everyone is a moon*
> *and has a dark side*
> *which he never shows to anybody.*
> —Mark Twain

A character should not be one-sided, but multi-dimensional, with quirks and flaws, dreams, motivations, and values. Very few are always virtuous and pure of motive. Even those people called "good guys" have their dark sides and secrets. Characters can be unpredictable, but they must be believable. Kenneth Atchity suggests that you get rid of any character that isn't memorable.

> *A hero is an ordinary individual*
> *who finds the strength*
> *to persevere and endure*
> *in spite of overwhelming obstacles.*
> —Christopher Reeve

I recently watched a movie in which every single character was what society would consider a "bad guy" in one way or another. All but one were on the wrong side of the law. All had rough edges, and were intolerant, ill-tempered, or radiated simmering resentment at times. Although guns were blazing, and action ran rampant throughout every scene, the characters weren't always crawling in the mud. Sometimes they were funny. Sometimes they were loving and supportive, and often made intelligent points. All their scams and takeovers were money-oriented. Yet, the motivations, feelings, and attitudes differed greatly among the characters. It was an interesting look at character development. Your dialog needs to be distinctive, and in keeping with the character who says it.

> I have always been more interested
> in creating a character
> that contains something crippled.
> I think nearly all of us
> have some kind of defect.
> —Tennessee Williams

How does your character view the world? Does he or she act or react? What is his or her attitude or pattern of behavior? Does it differ from the mainstream? Determine what each character cares most about, because then you will know what's at stake.

> First, find out what your hero wants,
> then just follow him!
> —Ray Bradbury

The main character must want or need something; a specific goal of some sort. Then let your characters find something, or hold on to something, or defend something. The choices that a character makes in his or her efforts to overcome obstacles defines the character. Make your characters plausible, sympathetic, and *original*. Try to find something positive and likeable, about each character (few people are villains to the core). Identify with your characters. To make your character vulnerable, just keep him or her a little unsure of some choices. How does your character change in the climax?

When I used to teach creative writing,
I would tell the students
to make their characters
want something right away.
—Kurt Vonnegut

Scotty was a pasty-white, sumo-sized third grader, nicknamed the Michelin Man, and also Stay-Puft (the Marshmallow Man), after he sat on a sink in the Boy's Room and broke it off the wall. He was totally uninterested in learning to read. He vowed and declared that he had no *need* to read, because his goal in life was to be a TV wrestler. And Scotty had the strength and size to succeed at it. Knowing nothing about wrestling myself, I researched the subject, and found that the only wrestling school in the country was in Northern California. So I contacted the school, asking about the requirements, and had them send me their application package. I gave the material to Scotty, explaining that the first requirement for entrance to the wrestling school was a high school diploma. So, he had to learn to read, in order to complete his education, and achieve his ultimate goal. He also needed to be able to read his contracts, I emphasized. Then I bought a little children's paperback book about wrestling, as further motivation for him to learn to read. It had photographs of all of his favorite wrestlers on the left-hand pages, with some biographical information about them, on the facing right-hand pages. I told Scotty that he could have the book, when he could read it aloud to me. He was totally stoked, and learned by leaps and bounds.

KNOW YOUR CHARACTERS:

*You can never know enough
about your characters.*
—Somerset Maugham

Successful characters don't just happen. You need to give them a lot of thought. You need to know:

- Physical characteristics: age, facial features, hair, scars, tattoos, piercings, manner of speaking (use different speech patterns—which was hard for me, in the inner city);

- Emotional and/or social flaws;

- Background or history: family situation, rich or poor, married or divorced or single, childhood, major life events, disorders (anorexia: starve themselves/orthorexia: obsession with eating healthy), addictions, drug of choice;

- Interests: hobbies, favorite movies, books, or sports, favorite food or drinks, tastes in clothing, furniture, or décor;

- Friends: male and/or female, distinctive characteristics, old or new ties;

- Pets: unusual animals, or coloring, or names.

The Matthew Schudder series, by Lawrence Block, is extremely popular. Yet the major character is so flawed, that the author said he, himself, would never hire him as a private eye. Background story: As a NYPD detective, Scudder accidently shoots a little girl, can't handle the guilt and torment, quits the force, abandons his family, and takes up drinking in earnest. Within each book, Scudder is taking whatever private detective job that comes his way, as he is consuming more and more alcohol, to the point that he finally begins attending AA meetings, as he intermittently donates money to any nearby church, that he happens to pass by. It turns out that his girlfriend is a high-class hooker, and his best friend is a career criminal. Even with all his flaws, readers like him, and are rooting for him.

TIP: Don't make the major character too different from yourself (height/weight/right or left handed/ vision, etc.), as your awareness may be off, otherwise. (I can't see the top of the refrigerator, nor can I reach the top bookshelves, because I'm much shorter than my husband, who can. And my perception is off at night.) Stick with what you know. For this reason, I always thought that Lawrence Block must be either a practicing or reformed alcoholic (or at least knew someone close who was either), as the descriptions of his Mathew Scudder character are so believable.

TIP: Don't spend too much time describing your characters looks or clothes. Leave something to the readers' imagination.

In the same third grade class, Destiny was saving money for a breast-reduction operation. When I pointed out that, since her figure was straight up and down, it didn't seem to be something that she need concern herself with at this point of her life, she said that she wanted to be prepared—as she didn't ever want to be bigger than her mother, who was the perfect size.

The dialog and actions should be unique to each character. Make the minor supporting characters—the bit players, the ditch diggers, the spear carriers—interesting and unforgettable, via a distinguishing physical characteristic, an identifying dialect or favorite words, or a neurosis of some sort (think: Uncle Scrooge, the Lone Ranger, R2D2, Dumbo). Experts advise to take a quick snapshot, and move on.

CHARACTER NAMES:

I call everyone 'Darling'
because I can't remember their names.
—Zsa Zsa Gabor

Names are critical, and can make a real difference in how characters are remembered. (Scarlett O'Hara, in *Gone With the Wind*, was originally named Pansy.) "Would the most famous love story in the world be as poignant if it was called Romeo and Gertrude?" asks Julie Kagawa, in her teen novella ebook, *Summer's Crossing*, from "The Iron Fey" series. Unusual, original, and interesting names are memorable, such as Shrek,

Rumpelstiltskin, Professor Dumbledore, and Darth Vader.

The James Bond series, by Ian Fleming, all have off-the-wall names (Pussy Galore, Honey Ryder), as well as totally improbable physical attributes and unusual mannerisms. True, they are vivid and memorable, but utterly unrealistic (a bleeding tear duct?). All of which jerk the reader out of the action, realizing, *oh, yeah, this is fiction.* So keep that in mind when choosing names for your characters.

According to the James Bond series, the name—James Bond—is an honorary *title* bestowed on the top spy in Britain. And because such men don't last very long in that position, the top spy is addressed by the same name, to keep things simple. Which is why the character is played by so many different movie actors, and gets away with it. How creative and *fun* is that? What a great idea!

My first book, *Into the Hornet's Nest*, was nonfiction (well, all eleven of them actually), and I used my students' given names, just to keep them straight in my mind. I knew that the book came out long after the children had moved on through graduation, and I had moved on to another school across town, and their parents wouldn't or couldn't read my book, and neither would the individuals involved. So I felt safe from a lawsuit, in that regard. However, I *did* worry about the teachers and administrators involved, even though I had slightly changed their names. The composite school was changed to Walt Disney Elementary School, because that name is considered to be in the public domain, and there are schools in various states, named after Walt Disney, so they couldn't single me out. (I actually wanted to name the school Looney Tunes, but knew that wouldn't fly). And Silverado Park was changed to Goldenrod Park. A few teachers could figure it out, whereas the general public wouldn't bother.

To counteract the name problem in my nonfiction book, *The Bogeyman: Stalking and its Aftermath*—and because I wanted the book to be taken seriously—I wrote a note in the beginning pages of the book, which simply states: Please understand that editorial discretion has allowed me to omit certain names, out of sheer politeness.

Because I didn't want to be sued by the Long Beach Police Department, I omitted the names of those officers who weren't helpful, and included only the names of those few officers who were *supportive*. I then sent a copy of the book, along with a copy of an "atta boy" letter to each individual. In addition, I sent copies of each letter of commendation, along with a book, to the Chief of Police. I urged him to place said letters in their individual personnel files. I sent all of the packets in large Priority Mail envelopes, at the same time, to the LBPD (as I knew that this would cause a stir). As such, I clearly *named* those who should get commendations when up for promotional review, and knew that it would be easy to figure out which officers *refused* to help (hoping that they, too, would hear about it). So, besides thanking those involved, I wouldn't get sued.

TIP: Use names for your characters that give a strong visual image.

Although a character's name often suggests an ethnic (Hernando, Luigi) or family background (Junior, the IV), a nickname will suggest certain traits (Straight Gut, Slick, Motor Mouth, Hot Stuff), appearance (Bones, Red, Shortstack), or something unusual about the character (Hopalong Cassidy, Calamity Jane, the seven dwarfs). If you have a Casper Milquetoast character (a generic, vanilla person who has a quiet, weak, timid, unassertive, bland or wimpy nature), then you would use an unassuming, common name, such as Bob Jones, Mary Smith, or just an average Joe.

TIP: Consider that some given names appear to exude a character's status or wealth (Think: Thurston Howell the Third In *Gilligan's Island*).

> A friend once explained that her given name was Roselind. As such, it created an awkward wedge between her and strangers. It was incorrectly pronounced and never remembered. It was too formal and off-putting for others, who thought she came from a monied or high-bred family. It neither suited her personality nor her background. When she changed her name to Rosie (a happy, more appropriate name, that matched her friendly nature), she was easily accepted and remembered. And she appeared to become more relaxed and self-confident.

Note again that inner city school populations have given names that are much more unusual than most other schools. As such, readers often questioned what they thought of as "odd" or "unusual" names in my book, *Into the Hornet's Nest*, and I couldn't tell them that those were the *real* names of the students involved. One year in particular, my student roll sheet looked like the names on a Burlesque marquee: Lovette, Sparkle, Dazle, Melodee, Treasure, Velvet, Tiara, Mahogany, Cocoa, Cinnamon, Caramel, Ambrosia, Destiny, Liberty, and so forth. Later names included Candy, Kitten, and Precious, as well as Canada, China, Africa, and Egypt, with Emerald, Ruby, Diamond, and Pearl, alongside Star thrown into the mix.

The boys' names were equally distinctive: Prince, Beethoven, Chili, Zero, Hallelujah, Yono, Lolo, and so on. One Samoan was unhappy to be named Sandy, because, in his culture, given names sometimes pertained to the geography of their conception or births. As such, he didn't think his name was "manly" enough. I wonder if he still feels his name isn't bold or powerful, given the strength of hurricane Sandy (2012) that caused so much damage. I understand that Storm is considered to be a hot name for 2013.

> *Me, I'm still waitin' for Hurricane Ed.*
> *Old Ed wouldn't hurt ya, would he?*
> *Sounds kinda friendly.*
> *"Hell, no, we ain't evacuatin'.*
> *Ed's comin'!*
> —George Carlin

Other unusual names have included Tiger, Kingman, Valiant, and Legend. I couldn't figure out if Roach was named for either marijuana or a cockroach, nor could I decide if Viceroy was named after some cheap cigarettes, or a royal official who runs a colony, city, or state for a monarch. Can you imagine what his nickname is? (You guessed it: *Vice*. Talk about programming!).

I charged into the office of my new school, to inform the principal that Ali Baba was missing. Mr. Biggs snapped his desk drawer shut with enough force to make a sound like a pistol shot. Clearly, he did not like to be inconvenienced by intrusions. "I don't have time for such foolish nonsense!" he shouted. "Ali Baba, indeed!" he snorted, fanning his hand in the air to motion me out. I had to *convince* him that I *did* have an Ali Baba registered in my class, and that, although he had been present earlier in the morning, he had yet to return from recess. I was wounded that Mr. Biggs seemed to have such a low opinion of teachers' dedication to duty, and nursed a bundle of injured feelings all day. I am not, and have never been, a practical joker.

Vendetta's mother told me that she had so named her daughter, because that

145

was the most *beautiful* word she had ever heard. I refrained from telling her what it meant.

Cassandra's mother also didn't know what that name implied. Greek: She who *ensnares* or *enflames* men. Or, in a mythological sense: Knowing the future, but cursed with the fate of not being believed.

Another mythical name was that of Pandora, whose mother obviously didn't know the story: Out of curiosity, Pandora—who was considered to have a *deceitful, feminine* nature—opened a chest (or jar, or urn, depending on the version), which released all the evils of mankind (plagues, famines, diseases, etc.), leaving Hope trapped inside, when she quickly closed the lid.

Nicknames stick to people,
and the most ridiculous
are the most adhesive.
—Thomas C. Haliburton

Some names have added descriptives, which once attained, are rarely erased: Runaway Randy, Rodney the Ripper, or simply, The Mouth. A separate three of my students were known collectively as The Terrible

Trio (a triple threat of major proportions). All were in my *third* grade class, but were known throughout the large, inner city school, and surrounding neighborhood, and businesses, as well.

During the turmoil of the first day of school, the hall door noisily flew open, to reveal my first *white* student. For maybe about fifteen seconds, everybody in the room froze like players in a macabre tableau. I immediately focused on the newcomer's eyes, as the banjo music from the movie *Deliverance* eerily twanged through my mind, growing louder and louder, as he moved ever closer to me. He stomped over to where I stood, swung his fist at my nose, and shouted, "I don't like school, and *you* can't make me!" Then he bolted through the outside door, slamming it for emphasis. He was a good way down the street and still going full steam, before I made it to the door to yell at him. And, by the time my hollering was through, he was long gone. Needless to say, the noise level in the room rose several decibels.

I couldn't believe that I hadn't even been given a chance to say "Hi," or "Good morning," or "Welcome to Room 14." *I couldn't believe that I still had a nose on my face.* If I had bowed my head just a fraction of an inch . . . ah well, one can't afford to dwell on the negative. None of the other students looked real happy to be there either, but, at least, no one else bailed.

The office workers did not seem surprised when I informed them that I had a runaway. And although I did not know his name, they did. Suffice it to say that Randy ran away six times that morning! The last time they dragged him back to school, he didn't have his shoes on, so they had to send him home! (He wasn't called **Runaway Randy** for nothing.)

Rodney had such a tendency to lash out with verbal abuse—and was so accustomed to calling his regular teacher "bitch," and shouting similar terms of endearment to one and all—that his foul language had almost lost its shock value. The students had learned to tune him out. However, when he clashed with another third grade teacher on recess duty, she was having none of his nonsense, and asked several men to assist in removing him from the playground. As Rodney was being carted off, kicking and bucking, he finally crossed over the threshold into truly inappropriate behavior, when he screamed at the rather buxom teacher, "Mrs. Hernandez! Mrs. Hernandez! Next time I see you, *I'm gonna rip your tits off!*" That instantly got everyone's attention, and imagination as well. He was immediately dubbed **Rodney the Ripper**, and the name stuck like flypaper, much to the teacher's chagrin.

Descriptive names and nicknames have staying power. Some thirty years after the above incident, I scanned the titles in the New Releases section of a Barnes & Noble bookstore, and my eyes came upon a new book, entitled *Ripper*, and I immediately thought of Rodney the Ripper, and wondered whatever became of him. (Looking the book up on the Internet, I found eight with the same title).

During the fifties, when tricked out cars and car clubs were all the rage in high schools, one teen placed all of his old baseball and bowling trophies in the front of his car (a '55 lowered Chevy, with high-gloss black paint and a cherry-red interior). He knelt in front of it, and had a photograph taken of the display. It looked like his car had won numerous awards, and he used this to impress the girls. When the guys figured it out, they called him **The Great Pretender** thereafter (from the popular song, recorded by The Platters, in 1955). The nickname still stands, all these decades later.

TIP: Make sure your characters' names fit the time period of your story. You can't have a villain or "bad boy" image as Radar, Diesel, or Axle, before such were invented, whereas Ajax, was a hero in the Trojan War. Choose a name that is age appropriate. An older adult character would not have a name that is popular now. Authors suggest that you search through the Social Security Name Popularity List for a particular age group.

TIP: Each characters first and last names should begin with a *different* letter of the alphabet, so it's faster to read, and easier for the reader to identify them. Avoid such confusion (Darin, Durbin, Denton/Sherry, Sharon, Shirley/Trey, Tran, True).

TIP: Also avoid rhyming names. My family has Sherry, Terry, Mary, Barry, Larry, Cherry, Kerry, Gary, and Jerry. It is extremely confusing. Attending a family picnic or reunion is fraught with problems. When someone calls out a name, everyone turns and answers! It is a needless complication.

TIP: Avoid names that are similar in sound and length, such as Samantha and Savannah. It's confusing.

TIP: Never use the same name for two different characters, even if spelled differently, unless the plot revolves around it in some way. It's hard to keep the two straight in the reader's head, providing a needless and unnecessary confusion.

> In the same way that B.B. King named all of his guitars Lucille, one father named all five of his sons Frank. *"Why?"* everyone asked. If it was good enough for one, it was good enough for all, was his pat answer. As a result, all the boys were called by their middle names.

TIP: Use first and last names with the same letter sparingly (Brad Broadstreet, Mary Miller Malone). A little alliteration goes a long way.

TIP: Character names shouldn't be long (such as Uma Thurman's baby daughter: Rosalind Arusha Arkadina Altalune Florence Thurman-Busson). All her life, that child will have trouble filling out forms. As a writer, remember, you'll be typing that loooong name, hundreds of times (although now you can easily change names with the stroke of a computer key). Make it easy on yourself, as well as the reader.

TIP: Avoid those names in which the pronunciation is unsure, or takes too long to say (Xlopdy, Fyothor, Gyeznyuiy, Zyxnrid), as the reader spends too much time falling over the name, wondering which pronunciation is correct. Jawbreaker names focus the readers on the name instead of the character. Understand that needlessly unusual spellings (Chaon=Shawn) or hard to pronounce names (Ngaiire= nigh-ree) are irritating to readers. Choose interesting or uncommon names, but make sure they are easy to read. Halfway through one book, I finally gave up, as the names were just too time-consuming. It wasn't an enjoyable experience.

TIP: Research ethnic names, and the correct spelling, or you'll hear about it from readers.

> Earlene Fowler writes her Benni Harper series about a fictional city of San Celina, CA. San Celina is considered to be improper Spanish—incorrect gender agreement between the subject and the article—which she originally meant as a joke. But it is now a decision that she regrets, due to the large number of letters she receives on the subject.

SIDEBAR: A handful of countries, like Germany, Denmark, and Iceland, have official rules regarding what a baby can be named. Such laws are meant to protect children from embarrassment. (Which might make sense when you remember how our nation was shocked when, in 1971, it was reported that Jefferson Airplane lead singer, Grace Slick, named her daughter "god." Later, it was reported that the father, bandmate Paul Kantner, was kidding the nurse, who immediately called a newspaper columnist. Even later, Grace Slick said that *she* was the one who spontaneously joked to the nurse, who she regarded as annoyingly sanctimonious. Whereas, two months *prior* to the birth, a *Rolling Stone* article indicated that Grace Slick had already chosen the name. She was quoted as saying that she would name her child "god." She further explained, "No last name, no capital G," because she wished the child to be humble. "And he can change his name when he feels like it." Sounds like a publicity stunt, to me, as the baby girl's official name became: China Wing Kantner.)

But the following law doesn't fit the "embarrassment" reasoning: Icelandic guidelines do not include any names that begin with the letter C, because it is not part of the Iceland's 32-letter alphabet.

And a few countries, such as Iceland, have everyone addressed by their *first* name (even the country's president), and are listed as such in the phone directories. Adding to the confusion, surnames are based on a parent's *given* name.

If a child has a name that is not on the accepted list of names, his or her official documents (passport, bank, etc.) are identified as boy or girl. A person who wants to change a first or middle name, must go before a special committee, who has the last word on the subject. Bureaucracy prevails.

You would think that it would be a basic human right to name your child whatever you want, or that the child would be able to change his or her name later in life, but that is not always the case.

TIP: Don't introduce too many characters at once, as it's hard to keep track of who's who. When readers have to keep flipping back a few pages to remember ("Who is this, again?"), it throws them off stride, and takes them out of the story. As I have done.

TIP: Let me get on my soapbox here: Female characters shouldn't have male names, unless it has something to do with the storyline! Some novels have all male names throughout, for both sexes, and it's irritating. Or vise versa, since both Shirley and Dana are mostly girls' names, now. On the flip side, however, *The Mentalist* TV series has the leading male character's *last* name as Jane, by which he is called. A recent novel had Shelley as a man's given name, which was distracting.

TIP: Be aware that some names are overused in novels. And while you're at it, give some thought to name associations.

Too many stories have Jack as the hero's name. (I have a grandnephew named Jack, and another named Jackson. I always wondered if they were bullied as Jackass, or Jackoff, Jack O' Lantern, or Jack-in-the-box, or if they were ever teased about all of the fairytales and fables that used Jack as the main character—many of whom were somewhat dimwitted. Also, back in the 17th century, the name 'Jack' was a *generic* term for 'man'; denoting nothing unique or outstanding, just a regular guy, one of the crowd. And, of course, there's the old saw: "Jack of all trades, master of none" that now has a negative vibe attached to it. And then there's Captain Jack Sparrow, depicted as a cad and a scalawag (in the *Pirates of the Caribbean* movie series), although his portrayal by Johnny Depp is outrageously delightful.

A successful jazz and blues singer/pianist (a former chemist and high-school teacher) was named Charles Brown. Can you imagine the ribbing he received because of his name?

I also have a grandnephew named Charlie, and I was concerned about the name associations: Charlie Tuna (not good enough), Good Time Charlie (think: Charlie Sheen), and Charley horse, not to mention that the word Charlie is a substitute for cocaine. And let us not forget poor Charlie Brown, who only *endures*. My sister-in-law was concerned, because, if her grandchild later became a businessman, she thought he would need a more professional name (like Charles). To show my bias, however, my main concern with the name, was that my stalker of over a 51-year period was named Charles. And over the decades, he left presents—seemingly tons of Charlie perfume—on my porch, as a reminder that he was always around. I didn't want yet another constant reminder of him, in my very own family! It just seemed an accidentally insensitive choice, to me.

Too many books—by different authors—use Alex for the main female character. It's confusing, especially when reading one book right after the other, as the plots get mixed together.

Many years ago, a new teacher was assigned to our elementary school, late in the term. The faculty and staff were just getting to know her, when, one day, she excitedly announced that she was now engaged to Alex, and proudly showed off her ring. Plans were immediately made for an engagement party, the following week, and she was asked if Alex might be able to come for a meet-and-greet, and she said that they would compare their schedules. After school, during that special celebration, she opened all the gifts, as everyone oohed and ahhed over them, and a fine time was had by all. Just as the party was coming to a close, her beloved arrived, and was happily introduced to everyone. Alex (short for Alexandria) was a woman. Shocked looks and raised eyebrows abounded.

TIP: Avoid selecting a name for your character that is known to the vast majority of readers, especially if it has a negative connotation.

A recent novel had the name Dexter as a main character, whereas the Dexter all TV viewers know about—through commercials or print publicity, whether or not one watches the show—is the serial killer on Dexter. The series has been running for seven seasons, so it is hard to miss the name. Few parents nowadays name their boys Adolf, because of the stigma involved. And Katrina is no longer used, for obvious reasons. Even a slight taint—such as Monica—will instantly take the reader out of your story.

TIP: You might want to make sure that you use no first names for your characters that are in your own family. It may cause some dissention in the ranks.

> I have a granddaughter and a grand niece, both with the abbreviated name Alex (for Alexandria), and a grandnephew named Alexander (who could be called Alex, or Al, but prefers to be called Xander). After having written numerous nonfiction books, my brother recently wrote his first novel, with the heroine as Alex, even though I suggested that he not do so. Now, other family members are clamoring to get *their* names in his future novels. (The family is way too large to do so, causing needless hurt feelings.) Avoid such unnecessary problems.

TIP: Introduce your characters by their entire names, and then pick one of those names (or street name) to call them by, throughout the book. It is too confusing otherwise, when you have a ton of characters that are being called by their first, last, and nicknames, willy-nilly. Make it easier on the reader.

TIP: Scan through old yearbooks, telephone books, books of baby names, newspaper obits, a *Who's Who*, or check out the Internet, to choose names of your characters. Experts say to stay away from fad names, although I don't know why this would present a problem, other than dating your book (Silk, Cappuccino, Blue, Cashmere, Thor).

TIP: Whatever names you choose, keep the spelling consistent: Sherry/Sherrie/Shari/Cheri or Sky, Skye, Skyy, Skyler, or Cindy/Cyndee/Sindi, or China/Chynna. (The mother of one of my third grade students always spelled her name differently, on each note she wrote.)

TIP: Don't use the same name of a character in your book, in a later book for a different character. It's too confusing if fans read them back-to-back.

CHARACTER DESCRIPTIONS:

A good character description usually consists of a few well-chosen details, and goes beyond wardrobe and mannerisms. Stephen King says: "I find wardrobe inventory particularly irritating; if I want to read descriptions of clothes, I can always get a J. Crew catalogue." I whole-heartedly agree. When authors are talking about specific men's clothing (hat, coats, and shoes), I have no idea what they're talking about, and it is frustrating, and takes me out of the story. Yet again.

SPOT QUIZ: Can you name six or more things you can wear on your feet, that begin with the letter S? (Answers below.)

King further states: "If you read: 'a high-school outcast with a bad complexion and a fashion-victim wardrobe' you can fill in the rest, can't you? You don't need a pimple by pimple, outfit by outfit rundown. Description begins in the writer's imagination, and should finish in the readers." I totally agree.

The main character either wants something or needs something, a person or obstacles stand in the way, and choices and efforts are presented that ultimately prevail. Supporting characters are there to help move the main character's story along.

TIP: A character shouldn't be included unless he or she is helpful to the storyline, in some regard. Otherwise, the reader is left wondering, *What happened to so-and-so?*

First impressions are important. Three weeks before the new school year started, in the midst of a devastating three-digit heat wave, I began to move my educational materials from my fourth school to my new assignment—the dreaded Walt Disney Elementary School—situated on the west side of town. It took one huge truckload, three carloads, and several family members to move my teaching supplies, files, and over 4,000 personal children's books. (My vast collection of children's song records had warped and melted in the process.) Because we were extremely hot and exhausted, everything was dumped in a large pile in the middle of my classroom, to be sorted the next day at a more leisurely pace. When I returned to organize my materials and put them away, my new principal, Mr. Biggs, and I, happened to cross paths in the hall. His first words of welcome—delivered without the trace of a smile—were, *"Don't you have a garage?!"* His words did not radiate warmth. Clearly, he went to the Andrei Gromyko charm school. To put it kindly, Mr. Biggs lacked a certain social grace.

On the other hand, the caretaker, Mr. Mayo, made it a point to talk with me, and talk, and talk, and talk. He was an older, grizzled man, of morose nature: a grump with a galloping case of the glooms. He waxed enthusiastic, however, about how he got *out* of doing work—the only thing in life that made him happy—giving several examples as he warmed up to his topic. I suspected (and rightly so!), that one way he got out of work was by doing so much talking. He confided that when he encountered new graffiti spray-painted on the school walls, he just wrote "Nigger" across the whole mess, and then called downtown for the Graffiti Squad—which would only clean up the crude graphics that had sexual or racial slurs—to come out to clean up the walls for him. I hated to spoil whatever sense of camaraderie we'd established, but I couldn't wonder what he would tell me, once we *really* got to know each other. (I'm not known for suffering slackers lightly, nor do I have any patience for those who have made careers of running in place.) Mr. Mayo's nonstop habit represented sloth and delay, for which he was being paid by the hour. With my tax dollars. Wonderful.

TIP: Perceptions are different, according to one's height, vision acuity, and handedness. You might want to have your main character mimic you, as close as possible, as what you observe will be different.

She was only about five feet tall and even in her clunky heels Puller was about a mile higher that she was. He could see her dark roots among all the blond strands.

—David Baldacci, *The Forgotten*

QUIZ ANSWERS: shoes, socks, slippers, stockings, slip-ons, sandals, sneakers, skis, skates, snowshoes, stilts. I wonder why they all start with the letter s.

PET NAMES:

Continuing on with the name topic: Recognize that pets are characters, too, with special names and specific personalities.

At one point in our lives, we had five cats: B.T.—short for Bob Tail—Mama Kitty, Caboose (whose rear rend never seemed to catch up to her front), Turpy (named after the cross-eyed silent screen movie star Ben Turpin), and Licorice (all black). Now, we only have our 40+ years-old desert tortoise, named Dash (she can really move!). In addition, a neighborhood cat, named Garfunkel (whose littermate is named Simon), adopted us, and hangs out at our house on a daily basis. Dash and Garfunkel can often be found sitting next to each other in our backyard: an unlikely friendship between species.

Suspect (2013), by *New York Times* best-selling crime writer, Robert Crais, has a dog, Maggie, as a major character. The German Shepherd survived three tours in Iraq and Afghanistan, before her handler was killed, and she was severely wounded. She was sent back to California to heal, and then to Los Angeles, to be retrained. The scenes from the dog's point of view are fascinating. Although I am a cat person at heart, I learned a lot about dogs while reading this book. Remarkable!

ACTIVITY: (1) List the ten most important people in your life (alive, dead, or just gone). Were they positive, supportive, and encouraging? As a writer, the importance of people is inside you. It matters to you. Whom do you love? Or fell out of love? Who are your role models?

(2) Next, list at least five of the other kind of people you know: the *cockroaches* or *potato bugs* of your life. Who lied to you? Who betrayed you? Who criticizes or laughs at you? Who drives you bonkers? List the ones that give you chills or the willies (those strange, indecent, obnoxious, or just plain weird individuals). You might have met them only once, for a short period of time, but they left a strong, negative impression.

When I was six years old, an elderly man
tried to kidnap me from a department
store. He kept following me around, talking
to me, and making me feel uncomfortable.
He said that he wanted to buy a set of china
for his wife, and didn't know what pattern
to choose, and asked me to choose it for
her. The Housewares section was way
in the back of the store, in an unlighted
area where no one was, with one open
outside door to an alley. Even though I
was only in the second grade, I knew that
a grown man wouldn't need a child to
help him in that regard. At some subtle
level, I felt threatened in a way I didn't
understand, and I didn't know how to
deal with him, without being disrespectful.
But I knew in my bones that I would be in
deep trouble, if I got anywhere near that
open the door. The situation didn't feel
right—dark and unpleasant—and I felt
small and vulnerable. So I just pointed to
the first pattern I saw, saying, "I choose
that one!" and turned around and ran
into the crowd, that was upfront, choosing
valentines. I ran inside the clerks' counter,
and hid, as he came looking for me. I felt
vaguely ashamed at being so frightened,
and not knowing why. Remembering that

experience always gives me the creeps. I wasn't sure what might have happened, or why it was danger that I had sensed. I had no words for my experience, nor did I know what to complain about, and therefore, told no one. Even though I was raised to respect adults, and follow their directions, my intuition told me to get away from that man, as fast as possible. And I did. Teachers and parents didn't talk about predators ("dangerous strangers") in those days.

(3) Then you are going to write two or three sentences describing your important persons and your villains. Short and sweet.

I wrote my first list, and had nine family members, and then lumped four role models together—Eleanor Roosevelt, Susan B. Anthony, Elisabeth Kubler-Ross, and Valerie Plame Wilson—for the tenth. So, if you want to write more, feel free. Also, some of my characters on the first list, were also on my second list, but their descriptions were different. You may also find this to be true.

NOTE: The people on your lists don't have to be in bodily form now (a grandmother who was psychic, and a great-grandmother who spent her fortune searching for her mother who was lost during the great Oklahoma territory land rush of 1889, a great-grandfather who squandered the family fortune, and ran off with a carny, or even someone you have never met (a mother who gave you up for adoption, or a father you don't remember, who abandoned you at an early age).

Again, as a writer, the importance of people is *inside* you. Most fiction writers will write a short character sketch of a page or more for *each* of the major characters. So a sentence or two is a lot less than you would be writing for your own manuscript.

Know that every writer uses the people in his or her life as characters. They will be picked clean like chickens. These fifteen (or so) people that you have written about are *your* characters. No one else has exactly the same characters as you. You can dress them up in any costumes, place them in any setting, and in any period of time—history, now, or in the future—and they are essentially the same. They still work.

LANGUAGE

DIALOGUE:

Do you believe in free speech?
Then speak freely.
Do you love the truth?
Then tell it.
Do you believe in an open society?
Then act in the open.
—Adam Michnick

To which I would add: And write freely.

It is said that good dialog is both an art and a craft. You get better at it, as you go along. Keep practicing. Express yourself. And express yourself creatively.

Sir Winston Churchill, when confronted during WWII with members of his Cabinet who wanted to cut the budget for the

169

arts, replied that he would not. "If we are not fighting for the freedom of expression, what are we fighting for?"

Dialog is simply your characters expressing themselves, or communicating information, in an easy and realistic manner. Understand that the best nonfiction reads like a novel. So keep in mind that every subject covered below is for both fiction and nonfiction writing.

> *Talk, whether ugly or beautiful,*
> *is an index of character.*
> —Stephen King

Dialogue is easier and faster to read than description or narrative. There is no more important component of fiction than dialogue. Dialogue is crucial in defining your characters, making them easy to recognize, and identify with. It shows what happens between the characters. Dialogue advances the plot, and contributes to the atmosphere of the encounter. Dialogue will indicate if your character is smart or dumb, honest or dishonest, amusing, cranky, or lifeless. The key to writing good dialogue is a good eye and honesty.

TIP: Instead of ignoring normal crowd background noise, attune your ears to random snippets of conversation. Put yourself on the backburner, and just *listen* to the conversations floating around you.

Listen to those at the grocery store, bank, movies, restaurants, waiting rooms, and on television. Focus on the speech patterns, tone, and voice.

> *When a thing has been said,*
> *and said well,*
> *have no scruple.*
> *Take it and copy it.*
> —Anatole France

That's exactly what Mark Knopfler of Dire Straits did, when he overheard deliverymen in a New York department store complaining about their jobs while watching MTV. He wrote the song in the store, sitting at a kitchen display table. He jotted down the lyrics as he heard them, and "Money for Nothing" won a Grammy in 1986. (Sting added the refrain: "I want my MTV.")

TIP: Write down specific words, phrases, and sentences. Keep a small memo tablet in your purse or pocket at all times, and copy some of the dialogue. A few writers simply carry a 3x5 card in their pockets, whereas others carry small memo notebooks. Jack Kerouac carried a larger notebook with him, wherever he went.

There is only one trait that marks the writer.
He is always watching.
It's a kind of a trick of mind
and he is born with it.
—Morley Callaghan

TIP: Keep your dialogue natural in length. Most people do not deliver long speeches in their day-to-day conversations. Keep your phrases or sentences short. Few people deliver lectures at the drop of a hat, unless they have no people-skills, or are autistic, or are professors who are used to pontificating.

The misfortune in conversation is this:
People go on without knowing
how to get off.
—Samuel Johnson

An older man was known to hog every conversation, wherein no one could get a word in edgewise. Whenever he came walking toward a group, the neighbors fled like a flock of chickens, as they didn't want to be stuck for an hour at a time.

TIP: If dialogue runs longer than three sentences, break it up with an interjection, or a thought, or an action. Two or three sentences are better than one extremely looong sentence. Unless your character is telling a story, it is rare to have one give a monologue, monopolizing the conversation.

> When editing a manuscript, I often came upon sentences that looked like paragraphs:

> Pace knew all about Warren Dortch Jr., who was vying for another seat, a contested congressional seat against one-time Hollywood cameraman and current Congressman Dyer, who was backed by Kanaan of Kanaan Do, a local furniture magnate who wanted access to groves of pines that littered the landscape producing precious little in the way of wealth except to trailer park owners and campers who hung laundry on towering trees, thus saving on clotheslines, a manufacturing sideline in which Kanaan Do had also invested.

TIP: When conversations run long, remind readers who is speaking with a short comment or detail.

TIP: When writing dialog, make certain that the characters responses make sense. Otherwise, the reader is left with a *Say, what?* reaction.

> "How the hell did you get in here, and what the hell are you doing here?"

> "Right on both accounts," said Candy.

TIP: Make your characters' voices distinctive, via their choice of words, repetition, and rhythm. Make their grammar, and figures of speech, appropriate to who they are and where they come from (think: Pepe Le Pew accent or Foghorn Leghorn dialect).

Robert Masello advises: "If you wrote about a farmhand and had him talking like a college professor, or a cultivated diplomat sounding like a stevedore, you'd be shaking your reader's belief . . . in the character." He strongly suggests that you throw away your thesaurus. Use only the words in your speaking vocabulary, not words that you recognize:

PERFECTLY GOOD WORDS THAT
SOUND PERFECTLY AWFUL

You can't take college classes
If you're not MATRICULATED
It's such a proper thing to do
Why does it sound X-rated?

MUCILAGE is helpful
A special kind of glue
Why does it sound like entrails
Or disgusting nasal goo?

When telling of the aqueduct
Narration could have stated
"The channel branched or split in two"
But they said it BIFURCATED

For a fine upstanding person
Quite decent and well-bred
It hardly seems an honor
To be named TITULAR HEAD

A recent dinner party
Guests in a festive mood
But all were MASTICATING
Couldn't they simply chew their food?

It's not my plan to OBFUSCATE
To muddle or confuse
But these unsavory sounding words
I do not choose to use!

—Audrey Sosoka

EVERYDAY LANGUAGE:

Usage is the only test.
I prefer a phrase that is easy
and unaffected
to a phrase that is grammatical.
—Somerset Maugham

Let's all agree that the English language is the hardest to learn. It has plenty of rules, but doesn't always follow them. But those of us who know the rules, have a difficult time listening to those who are grammatically challenged (newscasters, street reporters, and such). Two little books share my pain:

Woe is I, by Patricia T. O'Conner, and *Between You and I: a little book of Bad English*, by James Cochrane. I console myself by saying that the errors I'm hearing are the result of family tradition, or those learning a second or third language.

TIP: Write dialog the way people talk, in their normal, everyday language, not the way the grammar rules dictate.

Three tenth grade boys liked the shoes I was wearing. One excitedly proclaimed, "Them shoes is *vicious!*" Another boy expressed the same sentiment in a different way: "Her kicks is *sick!*" The last shouted them to be, "*Wicked!*" I smiled and thanked them for the compliments, hoping that the student teacher would later discuss grammar issues, as well as the time and place to use slang language.

I can't allow what we learned
in English composition
to disrupt the sound and rhythm
of the narrative.
—Elmore Leonard

Dialogue should be *natural*. The key to writing good dialogue is honesty. Express the truth of how people act and talk. So, even though your English teachers said that you can't start a sentence with the words

And or *But*, you can, because that's the way people talk. Your bottom line should be: Does it sound right, and does is communicate meaning?

John Steinbeck's editor said, "John, this isn't a word," and John replied, "It is now." New words are constantly being coined (from science, technology, business, finance, and pop culture), which are yearly added to English language dictionaries, once they come into widespread usage.

At the outset, you may want to browse through some of the grammar rules that you have forgotten, or never bothered to learn in English class. A quick romp through of *The Elements of Style*, by Strunk and E.B. White should do the trick. (My copy is so old—Second Edition, 1972—the pages have all yellowed, and the highlighting has faded, several times over.) Or simply call your local library, and ask for the Reference desk, and a librarian will quickly look up the answer for you. (Whenever I am not satisfied by answers on the web, or I come across conflicting information, I often call the reference librarian for a chat about same.)

Or you might want to check out "Ezine@rticles" on the web at newsletter@ezinearticles.com. But remember: no matter what it says in the *Chicago Manual of Style*, *you* are the final authority. You know how people talk; they don't always follow grammatical rules (consider poetry and popular song lyrics).

Reports tell us that E.B. White also had this same problem, when he was a young man. When he first landed a reporter's job, one of his beginning assignments was to cover a disastrous fire. He wrote about the event that took place in the makeshift morgue, as the young husband discovered his wife's body, and exclaimed, "It's her!" When the article was published, the by-the-book editor had changed the last line, to "It is she!" E.B. White promptly quit the paper. (Although the above is a great example, I feel compelled to say that I've never read an article written about me that didn't include glaring misquotes, and/or factual blunders, so, from my experience, reporters also make changes and mistakes.)

TIP: Use a reasonable balance of dialogue and narrative. (During the writing of *The Cockroach Invasion*, I actually counted how many responses per character, for my children's series.)

I personally think we developed language
because of our deep inner need
to complain.
—Jane Wagner/Lily Tomlin

PROFANITY:

In certain trying circumstances,
urgent circumstances, desperate circumstances,
profanity furnishes a relief
denied even to prayer.
—Mark Twain

Dorothy Parker obviously agreed. In response to a letter from her editor, asking for more stories during her *honeymoon*, she famously said, "Tell him I was too fucking busy—or vice versa."

Profanity is known as cussing, coarse language, foul speech, strong language, dirty words, bad words, bad language, adult language, and vulgar language. Whether you call it potty mouths, toilet mouths, or foul mouths, swearing and cursing are modes of speech, existing in all languages. Statistics reveal that roughly 80 to 90 words spoken each day by individuals are swear words. (I find this statistic highly suspect. It is a rare occasion when I will utter a cuss word, and only in the privacy of my home—and usually when I drop something. So someone else must be swearing triple time. And I know there are a lot of people like me, out there. The closest I get to showing my anger in public, is to say, "Good Grief", or I may yell, "Rats! Rats! Double Rats!" (My elementary students said that I talked just like Charlie Brown.) It is even hard for me to *type* impolite and offensive words. I need emotional courage to do so.) In fact, I mention this topic in my book, *Recess Is Over!*, which was written for student teachers and new teachers.

A 2010 poll indicated that Canadians swear more than Americans or Britons. Who knew? *Who cares?* But it's a fact that in the inner city schools, you hear more swear words than on television!

The story, *Tough Eddie*, by Elizabeth Winthrop, is about a brave little kindergarten boy who also secretly played with his very own dollhouse. The second graders all had the same reaction to the tale, but expressed it differently, as they yelled in unison:

"Faggot!"

"Pervert!"

"Nerd!"

"Pussy!"

"Queer!"

"Fruit!"

Later on in the year, the class had the same response for Charlotte Zolotow's *William's Doll*. These children definitely made their gender choice early on, and weren't deviating from it one whit. Of course, now that action figures for boys are all the rage, I'm unsure if the response would be the same.

One Monday, a third grade boy was in trouble for using foul language. He regretted using such words, saying: "I apologize. I apologize. I'm a good boy. I'm not a cusser." His teacher sweetly said, "I know you aren't," and that was the end of it. On Friday, however, the boy didn't receive a star for a half-hour of work, and loudly expressed his displeasure: "This is *bullshit!*"

The class was well into their math activities, when we heard a girl delivering some high-decibel curses of a quite imaginative sort, coming from the third grade room across the hall. Everyone instantly recognized Vendetta's voice, so all listened as intently as possible, to identify her chosen victim. Vendetta was known throughout the school, as **The Mouth**, because she was always and forever telling someone off, being the acknowledged master of word assault. Everyone had seen her tantrums many times before, so each of us had a vivid mental image of what was taking place in her math class.

Vendetta talked so fast, and with such dramatic emphasis, that no one could ever get a word in edgewise. Her pattern was to swagger over, hands on hips, and stand as close as physically possible to her victim, invading his/her personal space, while giving "the evil eye" look. Her classic stance was getting in someone's face, ranting and raving, while wagging her finger at the helpless individual—punctuating her diatribe with various statuesque poses. She really got into it, and was a sight to behold.

Everyone listened to her nonstop monologue with gleeful attention, as Vendetta hurtled obscenities with abandon. She knew enough cuss words to avoid repeating herself for the next five minutes. She made it plain that she had had it with everything about the school: *"This school sucks! This hellhole of a school sucks the bone!"* She told off her math teacher in no uncertain terms, concluding with: "And you is a *tight-assed honky bitch*, Ms. Rothman!" Then she ran out, and slammed the door with the crackle of a sonic boom. Everyone exaggeratedly rolled their eyes and softly giggled in relief, happy in their hearts that they were not her victim this time. They contemplated the enormity of her punishment, and decided it was too grave to even consider.

We later heard that Vendetta ran over to the office and told off the counselor, whirled around and told off the secretaries, ran into the principal's office, and told him off, and then ran home. The whole office staff had been rooted to the spot during her meltdown performance—it was all so unexpected—and couldn't manage to move until she was long gone. The next day, Vendetta sent a note to the principal, via her little brother, informing him that she had suspended herself for her rude behavior. Now that's what I call taking charge of a situation.

A national hullabaloo came about when a nun banned curse words on her school playground, and then *recited* all of the offensive language to which she had zero-tolerance, in a required after-school meeting. All 5th through 8th graders met in the auditorium to hear all of the worst words and phrases to which the principal held a zero-tolerance. Egads! It became the hottest story on the Internet. The parental response was measured in extremes, between shock and applause.

Bear the elementary playground profanity in mind, when considering the following: In August, 2012, the *Valedictorian* of a public Oklahoma high school, was denied her diploma, because she used the word HELL during her graduation address. She was told that she would get her diploma when she wrote a letter of apology to the school. She said that such a letter would be *meaningless*, because she felt she had nothing to apologize for, and she didn't want to lie about it. She had been asked what she wanted to do in her life, and she responded, "Hell, I don't know. I change my mind all the time." Hers was a slip of the tongue, whereas I was in the grandstand watching a Catholic high school graduation, while everyone in the audience was waiting with bated breath, for "the word" that the Valedictorian was rumored to have planned to include in his speech. He did. Nothing happened to him.

My advice concerning offensive words is to consider your reading audience.

LITERARY LICENSE:

*A novelist has a specific poetic license
which also applies to his own life.*
—Jerzy Kosinski

Literary License is also known as artistic license, dramatic license, narrative license, historical license, and poetic license, which all denote a distortion of fact, grammar and language, or the rewording of a previously written text.

In my first book, I had intentionally taken what I called literary license, and have lived to regret it. Literary license, to me, meant the ability to apply *small* distortions (in a book, painting, song, or movie), but is intended to be interpreted as the same thing. I put the emphasis on the word *small*. Not so. Apparently, literary license can also mean either the addition or omission of details, or even significant changes, or gross distortions of historical fact. Yikes!

One of the preschool teachers was married to the then Chief of Police. Their combined salaries must have been awesome, as she drove a bright red Porsche to school everyday, which she parked on the street close to her bungalow. All the teachers told her that that was tantamount to waving a flag in front of the proverbial bull, and that she was just asking for trouble. She felt that her close ties to the police department, and the close proximity of same, would be a threat to any would-be car thieves. Besides, she countered, she had a very *expensive* alarm system installed, so if it went off, she would simply call the police, forthwith, and everything would be taken care of with a minimum of fuss and bother. *What a dreamer,* we all thought. Of course, she was looking at the system logically, and logic plays no part in crimes of convenience.

One afternoon, two brain-fried lowlifes— whose bodies harbored enough chemicals to stock a good-sized lab— were antsy from the need of a fix, and looking for an easy way to make a quick buck. As they slowly rolled down the hill in an old clunker, their eyes lit on the glittering Porsche and stuck. Being prime opportunists, they were suddenly of one mind—seeing this as a momentous occasion—and were instantly calculating just how many jolts they could get off it, once the car was successfully fenced.

So, without any advanced planning, the driver squeaked to a sloppy stop cattycornered to the sparkling red jewel—carelessly leaving a several foot clearance between the two vehicles—while the passenger jumped out and jimmied the door handle. Of course, the alarm began blasting away once he got the door opened. And a siren, probably adequate to announce the end of the world, began a great whooping noise that alternated between high notes and low notes. There also seemed to include some sort of klaxons clanging in between. Unconcerned, he then slid over the seat, slumped under the steering wheel, and tried to hotwire the car. It was not an easy thing to do, given the state of his brain.

At the same instant the car alarm began bleating and shrieking and pointing an auditory finger, the school bell rang for the kindergartners to go home. They came charging out several doors, and, attracted by the tintinnabulation, surged toward the noise. They all ran up to the nine-foot-high chain-link fence, which many expertly scaled. There they clung, at various heights for optimum viewing, while observing—and loudly commenting on—the car theft in progress.

How exciting! They loved drama, real or imagined.

The driver, incensed by the incessant racket, motion, and confusion, decided that all of this caterwauling was enough, and waggled his hands at the kids in helpless dismay. In an effort to take charge of the situation, he finally hopped out of his car and lurched about, while wildly brandishing an ancient handgun, waving it back and forth at the students. They, in turn, upon seeing his weapon, bolted, stampeding back across the playground—instinctively knowing that the safest target is a moving target—screaming and crying and running helter-skelter for cover.

"A gun! A gun!"

"That man gots a gun!"

"He gonna shoot us all!"

"Run for your lives!"

Mass pandemonium. The lookout, not thrilled with losing such total control, constantly jerked the pistol back and forth, yelling in a frazzled voice—climbing until it neared falsetto—"You all fuckin' wi' me? Fuckin' wi' me 'cuz you don' think I shoot yo' sorry ass? I don' haf ta take this shit!"

During this turmoil, a squad car slowly coasted down the hill. The officers therein—their shift over, and only a couple of blocks from the station, where they could turn in their car and go home— were not amused at the scene they surveyed. They quietly parked alongside the battered old car, effectively cutting off any attempt at a hasty departure, and quickly handcuffed the lookout, since he was only focused on all the playground activity.

The three of them silently stood by, watching the feet of the other robber, as they pumped spasmodically in the air, while he unsuccessfully tried another tactic with the wires. They watched his hapless performance with amazement. *How long could this go on?* At length, the larger officer finally clamped a viselike hand on his leg. "Let's go!" he commanded, in an economy of words. There was an instant's stillness, but the outcome was never in doubt.

The playground erupted into: "The PO-lice is here, the PO-lice is here!" as everyone happily watched the event play itself out. They all cheered as the would-be criminals were taken away. Then the children hot-footed it to the preschool bungalow, in an effort to be the first to tell of the car rescue, which, of course, was news to the teacher. Yes, she had heard all the noise, but just thought that the school bell was on the fritz once more.

We never saw that red Porsche again.

NOTE: The only thing I changed was one little word. I had changed the word *black* to *red*, much to the dismay of those who had actually observed the incident. I thought it would make a better picture in reader's mind (glittering red instead of basic black). Boy, was I wrong. The switching of the color caused me all kinds of grief, which cast doubt upon the whole rest of the book. Whenever I was giving a speech about *Into the Hornet's Nest*, readers who were there at the time the event took place, became quite irate about that one little word, questioning what they termed was an error, saying that I obviously didn't know what I was writing about, or I would have known the correct color. Tempers flared. That one little word change cast doubt upon all the rest of my stories.

Heretofore, I thought I was on solid ground, considering the fact that in L. Frank Baum's *The Wizard of Oz* book, Dorothy's shoes were *silver*, whereas Walt Disney changed them to red in the movie version, to showcase them in Technicolor. And in Sir Arthur C. Clark's sci/fi novel, *2001: A Space Odyssey*, the alien monoliths were clear crystal, whereas in the Stanley Kubrick film they were gleaming black (for background contrast).

Even being in such heady company, I determined to *never* to do that again. I now follow Joe Friday's advice, "Just the facts, ma'am, just the facts."

SUGARCOATING:

*If you intend to write
as truthfully as you can,
your days
as a member of polite society
are numbered.*
—Stephen King

Even so, my advice to you is: Don't sugarcoat anything—words or subject matter—just to appear more pleasant or appealing to your readers. If you substitute "Oh, sugar!" for "Oh, shit!" because of self-censorship—thinking the word police are going to get you, or your audience might think less of you—then you are not expressing the truth of how people act and talk.

GRAMMAR
POLICE
To Correct and To Serve
—T-shirt

For instance, I do not use the swear words that my young students used in my own working vocabulary, but I record them as delivered. (At one elementary school in which I taught third grade, the counselor always said she *loved* to read my notes when I sent a pupil to her office, because I always wrote the *specific* offensive words that were used, whereas everyone else just wrote that profanity or vulgarity was used. Which left her no place to hang her hat.) Many times, if you don't write such words verbatim, you will lose the punch and the seriousness of the situation. Be brave, and tell it like it is.

It has oft been said that profanity is the sign of an immature mind, trying to express itself forcefully. And that vulgarity is a crutch for the conversationally challenged, or that such strong words are said by weak people. True. It is mostly the voice of the ignorant and the verbally challenged. But, it is also what children learn at home; the way in which their families communicate.

Ricardo's frustration level was even lower than usual. After his pencil lead broke for the third time, his control snapped. "Jesus

Christ!" he shrieked, as he stomped down the aisle to the pencil sharpener.

"Hold it!" I yelled from across the room. "Wait just a minute!" as I launched into an obligatory discussion about the proper words for seven-year-olds to use in a classroom.

He looked at me with round, disbelieving eyes, and in all seriousness, explained: "Ms. Meinberg, I don't think you understood me. All I said was 'Jesus Christ.'" Indeed.

"Ms. Meinberg! He called me the 'A' word! The 'A' word!" Francisco shrieked, as he started ripping off his jacket in preparation for battle. "He called me an American! I'm a Mex-ican!"

Experts tell us that dialog shouldn't all sound the same, but that's often hard to do. And yet, when I wrote about those inner city children with a black dialect, or a Southern dialect, I was accused of being racist.

Granted, it takes emotional courage to be honest. Heartfelt go-for-broke truth-telling can be risky, scary, difficult, frightening, and hard to do. *Driving with Dead People: A Memoir*, by Monica Holloway (now that's a great title!), was hard to write, as it depicted a childhood of sexual abuse perpetrated by her father; whereas my book, *The Bogeyman: Stalking and its Aftermath*, recorded my experiences with stalking and spousal abuse. Both books involve violence, despair, and denial. And both were difficult to recall.

But the emphasis on awareness, and getting the word out, was stronger than our embarrassment and worries about how readers would react or respond to the message. You need nerves of steel, and an uncommon sense of resilience, to write about your ordeals, and get your message to those in need. Know that it is well worth the time, effort, and energy involved. Ten years after the book was published, people are still writing to me, and calling me, for help and guidance. You have no idea as to how many people you will help, through sharing your experiences.

GOSSIP:

*The greatest advantage of being a writer is
that you can spy on people.
You're there, listening to every word,
but part of you is observing.
Everything is useful to a writer, you see—
every scrap, even the longest and most boring
of luncheon parties.*
—Graham Greene

Wherever you are, listen to people talking. Pay attention the dialog. Play with it, memorize it, jot it down, and store it away. You can hit paydirt with some eavesdropping. It is often said that there is no greater source of information in this world—easily surpassing the Library of Congress, encyclopedias, and the Internet combined, than plain, old-fashioned gossip. Henry James got ideas from attending 300 parties, while eating custard.

Any time I hear the words, "You're not going to believe this!" or "You didn't hear it from me . . . " my ears perk up, and my interest is focused. Unfortunately, when visitors start to relay something juicy, my husband always stops it cold, saying he doesn't want to hear it. I, of course, am dying to know whatever it is, but he successfully squashes it. He is obviously a better person than I.

Gossip is known to be a kind of interpersonal barter, where many trade nuggets of information. Gossip is the unofficial version of events, which is often quite different from the publicized account. *Shhhhh!* We learn a lot about people from other people, swapping stories, opinions, jokes, and observations, often before the media has the full story. Again, writers listen intently to the conversations around them.

The women in the beauty salon were having a fine time, complaining about their husbands. Each story was worse than the last, leaving the group with the understanding that men sure had it easier than women. Finally, in a burst of exasperation, one woman yelled, "In my next life, I'm coming back as a *man!*" Turning to another gal, she asked, "What do you think?" The unexpected answer was: "I don't think I could be that *BIG* of an asshole." Everyone fell out.

In order to make it back to school on time for Open House exercises, I had to make a stop at a fast-food place for dinner. I was waiting for my order at the local Taco Bell window, where a handful of teenagers were working the night shift. They were all excitedly talking over each other, which turned my attention to their conversation.

"You remember Bill, don' cha?"

"Sure!"

"Yeah!"

"What's he done *now?*"

"Well, you know he's been dating his

teacher, right?" Everyone nodded in vigorous agreement.

Upon hearing this news, I shamelessly and inconspicuously inclined my head through the window. (I am the victim of professional curiosity, so I was fairly *hanging* on every word.) I scolded myself without mercy, as I panted for further details.

"Well, they checked into this motel . . . "A babble of voices greeted this new information. (This eaves-dropping showed some promise. *Give me a name! A name!* I silently pleaded.) Pant, pant.

"But Billy kept bumping into members of his family there . . . " Hmmmm, now *that* sounded vaguely familiar. The talk continued as I racked my brain. Where had I heard *that* before?

Their conversation was rudely interrupted, as I dissolved into hysterical laughter, realizing that I was not over-hearing fresh gossip, as everyone was discussing the previous week's T.V. episode of *Soap.*

I was eating lunch at a fancy restaurant with a friend, when my attention suddenly focused on a long table nearby. Eight women were intently focused on the speaker, when she said, "And he had a little *lizard*," and everyone laughed heartily. The noise volume in the restaurant suddenly shifted into high gear, and I lost the rest of the conversation. I have *no* idea what they were talking about, but it sure piqued my interest.

A closed mouth gathers no feet.
—Sam Horn

I was scheduled to give a presentation to a school district in Colorado. I flew into the Salt Lake City International Airport, in Utah, through a heavy driving rain storm, where I was met by two principals, who would drive me to their destination. As total strangers, killing several hours, we talked to while away the time. Late in the conversations, grasping for subject matter, one man said, "Oh, I hear that you received your doctorate at BYU." When I answered in the affirmative, he said that he had also graduated from BYU, and started quizzing me as to who I knew on campus, name by name. No, no, and no, I responded (after all, it had been awhile). Then he started asking about various professors. Only a few names were familiar to me. Then, seemingly as an afterthought, he asked about one in particular, which I knew well, as he was a professor of a required class for my doctoral group.

Even though we students were all long-time educators and administrators, we raced to sit in the back row in his classroom. The room was small and closed in, with little air conditioning, and our instructor could sweat, BIG TIME! In addition, he had terrible body odor. Every time he'd raise his arms, the front rows would be practically wiped out.

Deodorant versus antiperspirant became *the* topic of discussion at night, regardless of what we were supposed to be studying. What we learned from that class had little to do with the subject at hand: Deodorant keeps you from smelling bad when you perspire, whereas antiperspirant attempts to keep you from perspiring at all. We covered the pros and cons, facts and fables, urban legends and internet myths, commercial versus natural deodorant, dry-cleaning problems, and whatnot. "At least the class wasn't a total loss!" I said, finishing with a flourish.

An uncomfortable silence inserted itself, before he responded: "He's my brother-in-law."

Good grief! Here I was in a car with two total strangers, in a different state, and out of millions of people in California, Colorado, and Utah, I have to tell my tale to *him*. What are the odds? Boy was my face red. *I determined to never gossip again!* Later, after I twisted in the wind for a while, he admitted that his whole family felt the same way about the professor. But the damage was done.

Only a fool
tests the depth of the water
with both feet.
—African Proverb

Let the above anecdotes remind you, as Sam Horn says, to "Put your mind in gear before you put your mouth in motion." My advice is: Listen, don't tell; write about it.

HE SAID/SHE SAID:

Lawrence Block advises, "If your characters are good, and if the dialog you hand them is natural, you should leave it alone as much as possible. Put them onstage and let them talk to one another. And stay the hell out of their way."

TIP: When long passages are involved, or lots of characters are together, you need a few he said/ she saids to lesson the confusion. Make it clear who is saying what to whom. Readability is key.

TIP: Use the name to establish who is talking, and then stick with *he* and *she*.

TIP: Don't be concerned that there are too many *saids* in your book. Dean Koontz makes it an absolute rule never to use any verb but *said* in dialogue. Other authors concur.

TIP: Other authors use he said/she said mostly, with occasional alternate verbs. Use words like drawl, murmur, and whisper, to indicate *how* a line is spoken. We are cautioned that the words state, aver, avow, affirm, and declare are used by newspaper reporters, and are generally not used in novels.

SCENES

As a nonfiction writer, I only have to remember the settings, whereas if you are a fiction writer, you need to see it clearly in your imagination.

SETTING:

You will have a setting for the whole book (country/ state/city/urban, small town, rural, national park, and so forth), as well as settings for each specific scene (room/house/specific building/outdoors, and so on).

In nonfiction books, the setting is already determined. In fiction books, you get to choose the setting. Understand that your setting is more than just a specific space, it is the total environment and culture. Provide the setting and atmosphere as close to the beginning of your book, as possible, providing a sense of place. It is said that the locale is much more important to the reader's sense of actually being *in* the story than any physical description of the characters.

> The burg is a close-knit, blue-collar, residential chunk of South Trenton that runs on gossip, good Catholic guilt, and pot roast at six o'clock.

> —Janet Evanovich, *Notorious Nineteen*

The following example shows the elementary school's high energy state, within the urban neighborhood, where poverty, drugs, violence, and death are common. The fact that it is filled with a large in-your-face ethnic mix is shown, not told, throughout the book, and didn't need to included here. This paragraph deals only with the general atmosphere.

> When an incident takes place in an inner city school, it happens with an intensity that makes it a thousand times worse. Nothing just simply occurs; it bursts, explodes, detonates, blisters, rages, and erupts. It's like continually tap-dancing on land mines, or perpetually playing with a Jack-in-the-box—you know *something* is going to shoot out at you—you just never know what, where, when, or how. It is totally unpredictable, and stranger than fiction; a place where the balance point seems to be constantly moving and

shifting, so one always feels a little off-center, as if the rug is continually being yanked out from under your feet.

SCENE:

Home is where your story begins.
—Attributed to Annie Danielson

Scenes are little stories that communicate information or make a point: an incident, an experience, a conversation. In each scene, something must happen (big or small), and some kind of action must be involved (subtle or wild and wooly). Your scenes must keep your reader engaged.

A good scene has dialogue, description, and detail. Add reflective elements, to help the reader see connections, as to why you are telling this story.

No matter how old you are, and the older the better (back in my day we had nine planets), you have had many significant experiences in your life, in which you have learned something, from situations that were eye-opening, sobering, shocking, or entertaining. You are telling such stories as you remember them. Rachel Friedman Ballon explains: "A scene is a unit of drama, just as a brick is a unit of a building. You lay out each scene as you would bricks on a building." Every scene must be connected. A vignette can be considered a scene. A scene is an incident or a happening—big or small—that you either experienced or observed, or something that you heard, and you are sharing that story. Each scene has a beginning and an ending.

A sense of place and atmosphere is central to good writing, but it mustn't take the place of the story. When it comes to scene-setting, experts say that a meal is as good as a feast. Just a few details are sufficient. Your job is to write what you see—like a photograph—and then get on with the story.

> The first week of school this year, my kids rushed in with the exclamation, "Did you know that if you get shot right in the head your brains goosh out?!"
>
> —Frank Marrero

Mark the place of connection: a specific place for the scene's action. Where are your characters? What type of building are they in (laundromat, school, funeral home, police station, doughnut shop, bar)? Engage as many senses as possible (sounds, smells, touch, feelings). But remember, it's not about the setting, anyway, it's about the characters and their story.

> As an adjunct professor at BYU one summer, I was teaching off-campus with a number of student teachers, in their last required all-day, four-week class,

before certification. It was a show-and-tell experience, in which I presented tons of exciting projects to use in their own classrooms, to spice up otherwise dull subjects. Everyone eagerly participated in whatever lesson I presented, with much laughter and gusto involved. All became close to each other, except for one older gentleman, who kept a reserved, dignified distance. He was obviously retired, and teaching was to be his second career. Besides having gray hair, he always wore a three-piece suit, with a long-sleeved white shirt and formal-colored tie, while everyone else was dressed in colorful, casual summer outfits. So he not only looked, but acted differently than his classmates. I was concerned that he hadn't jelled with the group, as easily or quickly as others had. I suspected that he came from a supervisory position, in some other field, and was unused to such familiarity and frivolity.

So one fine, extremely hot day, I happened to overhear a clerk mention that it was the gentleman's birthday. I decided to do something about it, in an effort to solidify his position in our class family. Later that afternoon, I explained to the class, that we were going on a walking field trip, and everyone enthusiastically followed me outside. They enjoyed the breezy walk (it was cooler outside than inside), and were quite surprised, as I led them to an ice cream parlor, several blocks hence. I explained that we were there in celebration of his birthday.

Everyone happily clapped and congratulated him, in one way or another, and we all spontaneously sang "Happy Birthday," as other customers joined in the festivities. The class was delighted when I said that each person was to choose his or her own ice cream, as my treat, so we could all party together, on his special day. It was interesting to see all of the different flavor choices that were made, as we sat at the little tables, relaxing, eating and interacting, with much laughter and hilarity involved. As we were close to the end of our school day, the man stood up in front of us, and began to thank us, but started crying instead. You can imagine how stunned we all were to hear this older man haltingly say that he had *never* had a birthday party in his life, and it meant so much to him. You just never know how your actions will impact others.

RESEARCH:

Research is formalized curiosity.
It is poking and prying
with a purpose.
—Zora Neale Hurston

Understand that the *illusion* of reality is a requirement for the enjoyment of fiction. You know you don't like to see mistakes in movies or T.V. commercials, as it takes you out of the experience, spoiling the story or scene. An upside down reel on a fishing pole drives my husband to distraction. I become upset when characters do not swallow while supposedly drinking coffee or sodas, in sit-coms and commercials, or when actors pick up supposedly heavy boxes, when it's apparent that there is nothing inside but air. I am especially incensed upon seeing all *new* clothes and shoes on inner city kids—and compounding the problem, with *different* brightly-colored outfits in every scene. Nor do I like to see *any* kids in high-dollar, spotless clothes, with no wrinkles or missing buttons, and perfectly-fitted, color-coordinated outfits, playing with all brand new toys. It is such a total disconnect from reality. *Unbelievable!*

One movie had the victim and her body guard suddenly on the run, without having the time to pack, hiding from her pursuers. Yet, day after day, she wore a different outfit. Women know how long it takes to find the right stores, for the perfect fit, and matching clothes, with 'just right' accessories, as well as shoes and a purse. (She had no cash, and couldn't use her credit cards, because the bad guys could easily track her.) *Riiiight.*

How many times have you seen this in the movies or on TV? After a night of drinking, carousing, and wild sex, the heroine arises from entangled limbs and trashed bed sheets, with perfect makeup and not a hair out of place. *Say what?* (Inexperienced young men may be unpleasantly surprised at their first morning after encounter, to find makeup smeared all over the woman's face, and her hair looking like a fright-wig. They will not have been prepared for the *reality* of the situation.)

It's something akin to the inexperienced couple who had their first sexual encounter on the beach, close to the Normandy invasion when it first began. The ground was shaking, skyrockets were bursting in the air, with a whole background of sound effects. That first sexual experience was costly, as it ruined such encounters forever after, as it would never, ever, be the same. The earth never moved for them anymore, nor were there sound effects or pyrotechnics involved. The thrill was gone.

And then there are those movie chase-scenes through the jungle, across rivers, sliding down mountains, and exploring caves, in which the heroine is wearing a white outfit, and her pants are *still* white, at the end of the romp. *Get real!*

And spelunking, again, where the guy is dressed appropriately, completely covered, and the gal wears shorts and a thin sweater, which she takes off, leaving her in a skimpy blouse. True, temperatures inside caves vary somewhat, but cold air remains in underground chambers in the summer, as well. To my way of thinking, with only limited personal experience, it's too cold down in the bottom of caves to be shedding one's clothes.

Consider the numerous, horrendous, and bloody fight scenes in both movies and television, wherein the next day scene, there are usually two tasteful cuts on the character's face (one on the forehead, and one on the cheek), or perhaps a butterfly Band-Aid on a nose. In following scenes, there are no lumps, bumps, and bruising in evidence, and no twingeing, wincing, or grimacing, to show that healing is in progress. Every now and then, a gauzed thumb or arm sling may appear. *Give me a break!*

Lee Child's latest book, *A Wanted Man* (2012), in the Jack Reacher 17-book series, has Jack having been in a horrible fight, before the story starts. The tale continually tells of the bad condition of our hero's face, alongside an off-center broken nose. He is often depicted throughout the novel as monster-looking, scaring people, left, right, and center. I can't wait to see how a movie might handle this unusual turn of events. As it stands now, Tom Cruise is in the film adaption of *One Shot* (2012), based on the 9th Reacher book. Fans consider this the worst casting possible, for the main character is much taller (6 foot, 5 inches), much heavier (250 pounds), with "hands as big as frozen turkeys," and buzz-cut *blond* hair; a rugged looking, former military investigator, who has gone off the grid;

not a pretty-boy, by any means. We'll all just have to suspend our judgment, as we watch the film adaption.

One T.V. movie had an older teenage girl—who was supposed to be working on her family's failing ranch—who had long, perfectly polished fingernails, with fashionable bleached stripes in her bottle-blond hair. Financially—and time-wise—it just didn't compute! She neither looked nor acted the part of an impoverished, hardworking, ranch-hand (making viewers wonder whether the actress was sleeping with the producer or the director). Inconceivable!

Another T.V. show had a sharecropper woman (who had been daily working in the fields alongside her husband), who suddenly decided to be a homemaker only, and in one day, transformed the beat-up old dusty shack into a cozy, colorful home, with a stew cheerfully bubbling on the stove. (Time-wise, it didn't compute, not to mention financially. And where did all the extra furniture and decorative items come from? And how did she manage to clean them, lift them, and move them around, with time left over to bathe, with no running water, and iron her clothes, and dress herself, while cooking a dinner, all at the same time? A credibility gap, for sure. It made me tired just looking at all she had to do, off screen.) Viewers and readers notice such stretching of imaginations. Improbable in the extreme!

In addition, it is vitally important to get your geographical and historical facts straight (landmarks, hospitals, freeways), as well as timing, dates, and simple details, or you will blow your credibility. As Robert Masello observed about locale: "Chicago better not have palm trees, San Francisco better not be flat, and Miami shouldn't be arid." You must be knowledgeable about the setting.

Trust me: Four big guys can't fit into a little sports car. (I have a big sports car—a 370Z— in which only two people can fit. Sports cars are known as *selfish cars*, since few can ride in them at once.) Doubly doubtful!

Earlene Fowler takes six weeks each year, to go to San Luis Obispo, the city (San Celina) that her fictional mystery series is built upon, to walk the streets, to see what her characters will be doing there. Another friend actually vacationed in

Brazil for eight months, to immerse herself in the geography, culture, and scene location, since her leading character's mother (in her mystery novel) was "born" there.

TIP: Cultural differences also mean differences in communication. Know that you will also need to study the country's etiquette, so you don't unintentionally offend residents by violating their cultural norms.

In some countries (Bulgaria, Macedonia, Albania, Sri Lanka, parts of Greece, Yugoslavia, Turkey, Iran, and Bengal, as well as the Maoris in New Zealand, and the Dyaks of Borneo) the shaking of the head from side to side means yes.

TIP: Be careful not to step on anyone's religious toes, as you're sure to hear about it.

No doubt you've heard the story about the priest having sex in a confessional (without regard for the wall that separates the priest from the supplicant, or the fact that anyone passing by might overhear). Ridiculous!

A friend, who is a serious Catholic, objects to various religious mistakes in TV soaps, shows, and movies. Her latest complaint was that of a character who returned to the show as a priest, and a woman asked, "Oh, did you learn that in the monastery?" My friend was quick to point out that monks go to monasteries, and priests go to seminaries. She would jump at the chance to be the Catholic fact-checker person for such shows.

Both printed and spoken mistakes are distracting, annoying, and time-consuming, which begs the question: *Why didn't anyone notice that?*

TIP: Get your facts straight before publishing. Even if you *think* you know, check it out, to be sure.

One highly successful author, who is a master of crime fiction, lives in the Los Angeles area. He wrote in one mystery, about a frantic race down the 405 freeway, from Hollywood to Disneyland, in 25 minutes. It is not possible to drive that far in *dense traffic*, and then idle in line for *a parking space*, in that period of time, day *or* night. (A simple tour would have dispelled him of that notion.) Not only that, but he referred to the City of Long Beach as being in Orange County on five different pages. Long Beach happens to be in Los Angeles County. (A simple check on a map, or the Internet, or with a local librarian, would have quickly cleared that misconception.)

DICTIONARY: An assumption is to suppose that something is true without checking or confirming it; something that is believed to be true without proof.

Never assume.
You'll make an ASS
out of yoU and ME.
—Attributed to a 1973
episode of *The Odd Couple*
(but I recall a professor demonstrating it
on the blackboard in the 60s)

EXAMPLE: Don't be lazy. Don't assume anything. Do your own fact-checking. One author's article was discussing power plants, and wrote that a new plant in the east looked like the breasts of California's San Onofre Nuclear Power Plant. Wrong. (He should have checked out photographs of the two plants before making such a statement.)

EXAMPLE: One high school author-to-be had five of his characters simply walking about, wandering around L.A. neighborhoods, in search of a police station. I told him that the *City* of Los Angeles is almost 500 square miles, and is the largest city in California, and the second largest in the nation. It is larger than the combined areas of the states of

Rhode Island and Delaware, so one can't simply stroll here and there, willy-nilly, in search of a police substation, or anything else, for that matter. In addition, one would need to consider some of the gang-infested areas that should be avoided at all costs. (L.A. County is even larger, at 4,752 square miles.) This student could have Googled maps or checked out Wikipedia.

Again, the same student wrote: " . . . in a decrepit, abandoned warehouse on the outskirts of Malibu . . . " I had to explain that Malibu is an *affluent* beach-front; a 21-mile strip along the Pacific coastline. It is famously called the "Riviera of America," and as such, has no decrepit or abandoned *anything.* His story involved several dilapidated wharfs, piers, and ships, and I had him look at photos of the *one* pristine Malibu pier, with no boats or ships anywhere to be seen. I suggested areas that could be considered as perfect geographical settings for his story, which he totally ignored. In his next draft, he wrote: " . . . in a decrepit abandoned warehouse on the outskirts of Beverly Hills . . . " I had to explain that the City of Beverly Hills is only *five* square miles—which is completely surrounded by Los Angeles. It boasts the *affluent* Rodeo Drive, which is the most famous street in the world, even though it is only *three* blocks long. (He needed to look at some maps, and do some of his own geographical research, before I would read his next draft.)

Peter Benchley, wrote in *Jaws*, what he had always heard about sharks: that they were aggressive loners. While most readers and film viewers were scared silly, some young scientists became fascinated with sharks. Inspired, they set out to actually research them. One became good friends with Benchley, and later became a marine biologist, majoring in sharks. He always shared the newest information about sharks with him. Benchley said that if he were to write *Jaws* today, it would be a completely different story.

TIP: Note that research can add to your story, just don't let it dominate. You're writing a novel, not a research paper. Readers often are given information they could have done without. As Stephen King says, "[T]here's a difference between lecturing about what you know and using it to enrich the story." He continues with, "[R]esearch belongs as far in the background and the back story as you can get it."

*All I'm armed with
is research.*
—Mike Wallace

DESCRIPTION:

Be aware that nothing distracts from the flow of the story more than a long description. Too much detail stops the momentum cold. Let the reader imagine the setting and scene.

Avoid over-description, like James Lee Burke. (I love his books. He has pages and pages of *beautiful,* vivid landscape description and atmosphere—of New Orleans in particular, and Louisiana in general—but it drives me crazy. "Get on with the story!" I complain). Or consider those long, graphic descriptions in medical mysteries, which take place in the coroner's morgue. *"Who needs it?"* I ask anyone who's listening, as I skip over those gross and gory scenes. Or those detailed steamy sex scenes in novels that go on and on for pages. "I'm too old for that!" I grump.

Oftentimes, authors are so enamored with their powerful descriptions, they lose sight of the priority to keep the ball rolling, and the flow of their story skids to a standstill. Good description employs fresh images and simple vocabulary. (When I come across words that I've never seen or heard before, they are usually used regionally, only in a small area of the country, or are terms used in obscure businesses. It jolts me right out of the story, and the focus is then upon the specific word, causing me to check my dictionaries (to no avail), the Internet, and two local library reference sections. It is usually a waste of my time, effort, and energy, as the word can't be found, as it is long out of current usage. When I return to the story, it has lost its momentum and appeal.)

TIP: Never forget: The story is the thing. Experts suggest that you leave out those paragraphs that *you* skip when reading novels.

Keep your characters physical descriptions at a minimum. A little goes a long way. Readers can imagine what each character looks like from the way they talk and act. That's why many say that the movie version characters don't match those in their heads.

ACTIVITY: Write 2 descriptions:

- Where would you like to be right now (Hooters, Paris, Disneyland, the mountains, river rafting)?

- Where would you really, really, NOT like to be (spelunking, the desert, the Artic, in sewers, river rafting)?

GENRES

I believe we all have an obligation to pass our knowledge on to following generations. Write something that matters. Put your personal stamp on history, and make an impact on society. Leave a legacy through your letters, stories, books, and poems. Understand that your small, personal issues are just as important as big ideas and world events. Touch your readers, and affect their lives.

The little things
and little moments
aren't little.
—Jon Kabat-Zinn

The two main categories separating the two different genres are fiction and nonfiction. And, of course, there are preschool age, children, teens, and young adult books that are written in many of the below listed categories. Some subgenres are listed below:

FICTION:

I have often heard that the novel is dead.
But I see novels produced,
I don't know how many a week, in France.
I have the impression
it's carrying along quite well.
—Nathalie Sarraute

I, too, have both read and heard that the novel is dead, and that reading is dying. I don't believe it. I recently attended the annual (2013) Long Beach Festival of Authors, with 780 women in attendance. The Literary Women's group has supported this festival for 23 years, with no publicity involved. Some of us discussed this issue amongst ourselves, and determined that we all read for fun, for escapism, and entertainment, as well as for knowledge. They don't believe it, either.

Imagination is the key word regarding fiction.

Fiction general categories:

- BOTS
- drama
- erotica
- fable
- fairytales
- fantasy
- folklore

- graphic novels & comics
- historical fiction
- horror
- humor
- legend
- mystery/cozy/noir
- mythology
- novel
- poetry
- police/private detective/spy
- realistic fiction
- romance/chick lit
- science fiction
- short story
- spy
- suspense/thriller
- tall tales
- war & military

BOTS are considered to be a hybrid form of writing and moviemaking, which simply means: *based on a true story*. It is adapted from real events (many of which are ripped from the daily headlines). Thousands of novels, programs, and films, are considered to be BOTS. They may present *some* facts, but are mostly fiction, so it is a blending of the two. Of course, the dialog has to be made up, and the sequencing is often in error, and important scenes may be deleted, or blown out of proportion. So, even though the era, the costumes, and the characters might be correct, the storyline may contain many errors, or myths, and the geographical setting and background scenes may be in question. So BOTS *must* be considered fiction, as experts repeat that one can't be considered half pregnant or half dead.

NONFICTION:

Writing nonfiction is said to be producing well-researched material that is reorganized, updated, or repackaged in some fashion. Take to heart the words of Steven J. Snelling: "Rule number one—don't attempt to change the facts. Rule number two—always remember Rule number one."

Nonfiction is also called creative nonfiction, and narrative nonfiction, as well as the literature of reality. It may read like fiction, but the stories are factual. According to Lee Gutkind, "The pledge that writers make to readers—that can not, should not, must not, be violated—is the anchor of creative nonfiction: *You can't make this stuff up!*"

Nonfiction General Categories:

- aging/retirement
- animals/pets

- anthology
- architecture
- autobiography
- biography
- body/mind/spirit
- business/career/sales/leadership
- computers
- cooking/food
- cosmology
- crafts & hobbies
- culture/social change
- current events
- death & dying/grieving
- design
- drama
- ecology/environment/nature
- economics/finance/investment
- education/academic/teaching
- essay
- family & relationships
- fine art
- fitness
- gay/lesbian/bisexual/transsexual
- gift/speciality
- green living/sustainability
- health & healing/medicine/nutrition
- history
- holidays
- home & garden
- humanitarian

- humor
- inspirational
- Internet
- journalism/investigative reporting
- language
- media
- memoir/personal journey
- multicultural/indigenous
- music
- nature
- parenting/family
- performing arts/music/dance/film/theater
- personal growth/self-help
- philosophy/classical studies
- photography
- poetry
- political science
- popular culture
- psychology/mental health
- recreation
- reference
- religion
- relationships
- science
- self-help
- sexuality
- social science
- special needs
- spirituality
- sports

- technology
- traditions
- transportation
- travel
- true crime
- war/military/spy
- wellness/prevention
- women's studies/issues
- writing/publishing

MEMOIRS are your personal memories of your life, including childhood stories about you, that you were too young to remember.

---

*God gave us memory
that we might have
roses in December.*
—James M. Barrie

Regard your life as a serious of short stories, and then knit them together for a book. If you are yearning to share your memories, your motivation will carry you through. My husband's favorite saying is: "Don't let the bastards get you down!" Write about it. (Which I did, in both *Into the Hornet's Nest, my* first book, and *The Bogeyman,* my third book.) It was cathartic.

*The greatest gift
is a portion of thyself.*
—Ralph Waldo Emerson

Know, without a doubt, that there are readers who want to read your work, and your experiences will last forever. Carolyn Myss says, "Never underestimate how important you are to someone else."

Writing is a form of therapy.
—Graham Greene

Expressing your feelings in the face of cultural and social pressures may seem risky and daunting. Do it anyway. Yes, it takes courage: you may feel rejected, ostracized, and shunned by family, friends, and co-workers alike. Do it anyway. Do not censor yourself, even if you feel that you are committing hari kari. In the words of Dan Millman, "The lessons of experience are always positive, even if the experience is not."

We do not remember days,
we remember moments.
—Cesare Pavese

Much writing of memoirs is the breaking of silence: a stepping out on an emotional ledge: a whistleblower, of sorts.

Good memories are our second chance
at happiness.
—Queen Elizabeth II

STRUCTURE

*Successful novels have a definite structure
and all the chapters lead to the end
or to resolution of the plot.*
—Rachel Friedman Ballon

You have chosen your main characters, subject or issue, and location. Now it's time to develop the proper structure.

IDEAS:

*Life is a tragedy for those who feel,
but a comedy for those who think,
and a musical for those who sing.*
—Horace Walpole, Jean De La
Bruyere, and Anonymous

Your ideas and material are what you most care about. It is said that if you are lucky enough to have survived your childhood, then you have plenty of stories to tell. As Gordon Livingston reminds us: "Childhood is a series of disillusionments in which we progress from innocent belief to a harsher reality. One by one, we leave behind our conceptions of Santa Claus, the Easter Bunny, the tooth fairy, the perfection of our parents, and our own mortality."

Instead of wallowing in misery, rage, or self-pity, turn your experience of childhood trauma into a way to help others, by writing about it! Turn your anger, devastation, sense of betrayal, and frustration of early adulthood, into the strength to carry on. Consider the following memoir written by Frank McCourt.

> The happy childhood is hardly worth your while. Worse than an ordinary miserable childhood is the miserable Irish childhood, and worse yet is the miserable Irish Catholic childhood. People everywhere brag and whimper about the woes of their early years, but nothing can compare with the Irish version: the poverty; the shiftless loquacious father; the pious defeated mother moaning by the fire; pompous priests, bulling schoolmasters; the English and all the terrible things they did to us for 800 long years.
>
> —Frank McCourt, *Angela's Ashes*

If you have become an expert in what *not* to do

(alcohol, drugs, sex, gambling), write about it, and help others. If you have dealt with disease, disability, or dysfunctions, accidents, adoption, and such, write about it. Recognize that living a good life is the best revenge (especially if you've had a nasty divorce). Write about it. Turn any failure and disaster into success, by writing about it.

When I think of all the crap
I learned in high school,
it's a wonder I can think at all.
—Simon & Garfunkel, "Kodachrome"

One of the great benefits of reaching retirement is that we've been through many experiences. We have learned and unlearned and relearned a lot. We have perspective.

The human mind is kind of like . . .
a piñata.
When it breaks open,
there's a lot of surprises inside.
—Jane Wagner

She encourages us to "get the piñata experience." (Of course, she's talking about literally losing one's mind, but I like to think of it as celebrating the *opening* of one's mind.) One of the great things about being a writer is that everything we do, overhear, and observe, is material. Be thankful for all of your experiences, good or bad, large or small, beautiful or ugly. Becoming a writer is a life-long effort. Your whole life has been about gathering material. *Express yourself!* Don't let your experiences die along with you. Don't let your song die, without being heard.

Ideas are elusive, slippery things.
Best to keep a pad of paper and pencil
at your bedside,
so you can stab them in the night
before they get away.
—Earl Nightingale

Know that you have a story to tell that cannot be told by anyone else. And your characters are yours and yours alone. You can find a way to tell your particular story, with your motivations, inspiration, and confidence. Ultimately, the manuscript you create out of the stuff of your life, out of the darkness and into the light, is the one work of art that really matters.

Ideas are like pizza dough,
made to be tossed around.
—Anna Quindlen

Relish your ideas. Toss them around like rice at a wedding. Throughout your lifetime, along the way, you have seen many individuals who have changed the religions in which they were raised, or have moved from the city, state, or country in which they were brought up (consider the Amish, Mennonites,

Gypsies, Native Americans, and ex-pats). Some individuals saw no need for further formal education, and dropped out, while others attended traditional universities. Still others changed the careers in which they were groomed to enter. A few have even chosen to live entirely off the grid. All are those courageous people who thought for themselves, and refused to walk in someone else's shoes. Freedom is the issue here. Write about it.

POINT OF VIEW:

Perspective is key.
Perspective is everything.
—Neal Donald Walsch

At the outset, you must determine who is going to tell the story: (1) first-person—it's just the "I" talking—or the "eye" of your camera, which is easier to read and write); (2) third-person (he or she); or (3) omniscient—the all-knowing narrator, in which both the author and the reader knows what is going on in the heads of many different characters. Pick one.

Then decide your characters' points of view, and express that in your writing. A point of view different from your own might well be worth entertaining. After all, as it has been said before, if everyone thinks the same way, only one of us is needed. Dr. Wayne M. Dyer suggests that we respond with questions, refusing to judge: "I never thought of it that way; tell me more." Or, "That's an interesting point of view; when did you first learn about this?"

When presenting the homework assignment to my over 55 age students, I was trying to describe the villains in their lives. "You know, the potato bugs in your life." "*Eeeyu!*" was the overwhelming response, as they grimaced, and talked over one another. They all had a story. One woman, however, took another view, entirely. She found potato bugs to be *fascinating*. We all shuddered and groaned. But she adamantly stood her ground, to the point that I went directly home, and researched them. At length. I still find them to be icky ("Satan's fetus," as one country calls them), but it was refreshing seeing them from her viewpoint.

In the midst of winter, a friend had a visitor from another country. The foreigner asked me—in all seriousness—"Do you belong to the religion that *kills* trees?" I was astounded. Talk about a different perspective during the Christmas season!

PLOT:

A story to me means a plot
where there is some surprise.
Because that is how life is—
full of surprises.
—Isaac Bashevis Singer

We are born (the beginning), we live (that's the middle), then we die (the end). A plot also has the same three basic parts. The plot is the main story of your book. It grows through the characters. The plot is concerned with the relationship between the characters. As such, experts tell us not to worry about the plot, but to worry about the characters. Just remember: It doesn't matter how great your plot is, if readers don't care about the characters.

Plots thrive on events, plots thrive on tragedy, plots thrive on conflict. Plots do not deal with the routine, normal everyday activities, and the boredom thereof. (That's why TV action police shows work: they don't focus on all the waiting, and the endless paperwork involved, which actually constitutes the bulk of their days.)

Plots hold readers' attention simply by their wanting to know what happens next. Plots are repetitive and useful. They are made to be used again and again. And yet again. Plots are as old as the hills, the only difference being the characters, the setting, and your point of view. As Sir Winston Churchill once remarked,

"You create your own universe as you go along," in much the same way as you write a book.

Plots are like wooden hangers in a closet.
You don't refuse to hang up your shirt
because the hangers have already been used
a couple of times.
—Carolyn See

It is essential that your plot has a goal. Your plot needs ups and downs, mountains and valleys, ebbs and flows, to hold the attention of your reader. There might be surprises, and changes of direction, as events unfold, or unexpected situations. There must be complications or conflict or a crisis involved, that leads to a change in the character(s), or the situation.

SUBPLOTS:

A subplot gives another dimension to your story. It is a less prominent plot; a side story to your main plot. Subplots often involve supporting characters, either with or without the main character's involvement.

The main plotline is often called the "A" story. The "B" story is the secondary subplot, and the "C" story is the tertiary subplot. Most stories can handle up to three subplots, but more than that is often distracting, and dilutes the focus of the reader.

Each subplot must relate to the "A" story in some way, generally through relationships (family, romance, or problems at work). Such scenes can occur anywhere in the storyline, although they usually have at least one scene in the beginning, the middle, and the end. They are all about contrast and complications, and can make the story more interesting.

In suspense novels,
even subplots about relationships
have to have conflict.
—Jeffery Deaver

SUBTEXT:

While the sheet
is what you see and feel,
without the feather (subtext)
the pillow would be a lifeless shell.
—Stanislavski

"All good writing contains sub-text," says Rachel Friedman Ballon. "Sub-text is the unspoken feelings and thoughts that hide beneath the words; that which is unsaid." There is more going on in a scene than is being said. People act differently from what they're feeling or saying. It's the emotions under the surface.

An odd event happened the first night I met his family. As I prattled on (as is my wont), relating several recent experiences, his sister finally asked, "Who is this *Chuck* you keep talking about?" while the rest of the family members nodded in agreement, also showing their confusion. It turned out that the family had always called him by his given name, *Charles*, or a diminutive of his middle name, *Fredrick*, and had no idea that he had told me his name was Chuck. Abruptly, the room fell silent as everyone turned to stare at him, while he showed no emotion whatsoever. Meaningful glances were exchanged during this awkward moment, making me feel vaguely uneasy. I wished I understood what the heck was going on. Clearly there were underlying subtexts here that I didn't understand. Mentally giving him the benefit of the doubt, however, I decided that Chuck was just embarrassed about trying to make a fresh start of some sort—a new beginning—and that a new name represented a way of overcoming some difficulty in his recent past: a tragic lost love, or a long-term friendship gone sour, I romanticized. Little did I know.

OUTLINES:

*If you don't know
where you are going,
you might wind up
someplace else.*
—Yogi Berra

I must confess that I do not use outlines; never have, never will. So I am not the best person to speak on this topic. From junior high onward, I always wrote my papers first, and made the formal outline from my finished assignments. I continue to make lists instead, adding arrows here and there, and changing the numbering as needed, while scribbling notes in the margins.

*I write synopses
after the book is completed.
I can't write it beforehand,
because I don't know
what the book's about.*
—Jackie Collins

James V. Smith, Jr. doesn't bother with outlines either, as he has formulated his own Ten-Scene Tool device. A friend taped her outline across the length of her hall walls. Her timetable entailed the plot points (the beginning, the middle, the crisis point, and the end), showing a definite direction to follow. In the same manner, Janet Evanovich uses a huge dry-erase board that hangs on her wall, for storyboarding. Others use 3x5 cards to shuffle around for easy changes.

Timelines are not carved in stone, as you will generate details and subplots along the way. As J.K. Rowling explained, "I always have a basic plot outline, but I like to leave some things to be decided, while I write." According to Lee Gutkind, outlines are "a guide, not a straightjacket." Flexibility is the watchword.

> *I usually make detailed outlines:*
> *how many chapters it will be*
> *and so forth.*
> —John Barth

I would hazard a guess, however, that most writers use outlines of one kind or another. Some authors are known to have detailed outlines that run from five to 50 pages, that pinpoint details and direction. Jesse Kellerman has outlines that run 60 to 90 pages, and take from four to six weeks to write. Good gravy! (That's almost a third of the way through a book!) Still, others do not. They create their own systems. And some simply wing it.

> *We will either find a way,*
> *or make one!*
> —Hannibal

Design your own blueprint. Design your own map. Design your own itinerary.

> *You have brains in your head,*
> *you have feet in your shoes,*
> *you can steer yourself*
> *any direction you choose.*
> —Dr. Suess

BEGINNING:

> *To begin is the most important part*
> *of any quest,*
> *and by far the most courageous.*
> —Plato

Confucius is reported to have said: "Pay attention to beginnings." Your Opener is important. Readers want to dive right into the story or information. Note that books that begin with a long foreword, then a long introduction, followed by a long prologue, are annoying. Too often, the foreword and the introduction give away the treasures to behold, so it's like you're reading the same book *twice*. (I have the same issue with teachers and librarians that take primary students on a Picture Walk, to show all the illustrations in a children's book, first. *"What do you think will happen next?"* discussions, alongside that of the pictures, give away the whole storyline, so there is no reason to actually read the print, since the reader already knows what's going to happen. I also have the same problem with book cover flaps that give away too much information. I consider them to be Spoiler Alerts.)

People who are excited about the book, want to get to the meat of it, without further ado. (When I was in the second grade, one librarian showed our class how to handle a brand new book, by carefully folding each page back, *before* reading the story. (Nevermind the fact that none of us ever owned our own books.) Even then, I knew she wasn't a reader, because someone who loves books can't wait to start reading them! All that folding of pages was taking time away from the story!) In the same way, readers skip over the dedications, acknowledgments, and credits. If I like the book, I may peruse those pages later, after reading the story and the author's bio. But then, again, I might not.

> *I'll tell you a secret—*
> nobody *knows how to start a novel.*
> *There are no rules,*
> *because each novel is a case unto itself.*
> —Lawrence Block

Open BIG. Grab your audience immediately. Get their attention. The first sentence, and the first paragraph, are crucial. As Betsy Lerner (an editor and author) says, "In just a few introductory sentences, we know whether we are traveling by Concorde or ocean liner, whether we need seat belts or life preservers. And more important, whether we want to go along for the ride."

Hook the reader right away, with something exciting, edge-of-your-seat stuff, or humor, an unusual idea, an interesting fact, or a question. Or open with some kind of action or fast-paced dialogue. You might even start with a personal vignette. You only have *three seconds* to sell the book (potential buyers quickly check out the author, front cover, back cover, flaps, and first paragraph)! As a reader, if the first sentence or paragraph doesn't speak to me, then I'm off to consider the next book.

Never open a book with weather.
—Elmore Leonard

So, that leaves out 'It was a dark and stormy night' beginnings. In his book, *Elmore Leonard's 10 Rules of Writing* (which was originally published as a *short* article in the *New York Times*), he recommends: "If it's only to create atmosphere, and not a character's reaction to the weather, you don't want to go on too long. The reader is apt to leap ahead looking for people." However, he does admit that, "There are exceptions."

Will Schwalbe, in *The End of Your Life Book Club*, suggests: "Some novelists start with opening lines that foretell the major action of the book, some begin with hints; others with words that simply set a scene or describe a character, showing the reader a world before a deluge—with no hint as to what is to come. What never needs to be written is: 'Little did she know her life was about to change forever.'"

Authors often struggle with the opening paragraph, spending weeks at a time, fooling around with it. Many have written the whole manuscript, and then go back to the first paragraph, and agitate over it.

The beginning of your plot introduces the main character(s), as well as the core conflict, the setting, and the tone. Rachel Friedman Ballon suggests that you ask yourself three opening questions: (1) Why is this day different from any other day? (2) What happens at the onset that is going to set off the entire action of my story? And: Will my readers know what the story is about?

> When I was a little girl, I used to dress Barbie up without any underpants. On the outside, she'd look like a perfect lady. Tasteful plastic heels, tailored suit. But underneath, she was naked. I'm a bail enforcement agent now—also known as a fugitive apprehension agent, also known as a bounty hunter. I bring 'em back dead or alive. At least I try. And being a bail enforcement agent is sort of

like being bare-bottom Barbie. It's about having a secret. And it's about wearing a lot of bravado on the outside when you're really operating without underpants. Okay, maybe it's not like that for all enforcement agents, but I frequently feel like my privates are alfresco. Figuratively speaking, of course.

—Janet Evanovich, *High Five*

Well begun
is half done.
—Aristotle

MIDDLE:

According to Anna Quindlen, "Life's not so much about beginnings and endings as it is about going on and on and on. It is about muddling through the middle." Others agree.

The middle of things are not always welcome (in the middle of the night, the middle child, middle school, middle age, middle class, the Middle East). The middle represents neither a bright beginning nor a victorious end, but merely the plodding through; like being stuck in the boring middle between the wedding and the divorce. The middle is the journey itself.

Some writers know the beginning and the ending

of their book, but have trouble with the middle. The middle of the story often suffers most. "Saggy middles can occur when the conflict isn't as intense or powerful as in the beginning or the end," writes Janet Evonovich, who says she hates the middles. She always knows the beginning and end of her stories, but has trouble filling in the middles. Other writers begin writing the most exciting parts, somewhere in the middle, and then fill in the before and after. A good story moves forward when things go from bad to worse, because the readers want to know how it will all turn out. You can always add some subplots early in the middle phase, as an aside, or red herring, or filler, behind the private face of that really have nothing to do with the main plot.

Some writers begin their manuscript at the beginning, and plow straight through in a linear fashion. Others start at the end, so they know where they're headed. A few, such as Lee Gutkind, begin anywhere in which they feel the most excited and involved.

ENDING:

> *A shotgun introduced on page one*
> *must go off*
> *before the end of the story.*
> —Anton Chekhov

The climax includes a catastrophe or tragedy, in which it appears that all is lost. A proper ending ties up loose ends, and includes an epiphany of sorts, some kind of fulfillment, that is moving and emotionally satisfying. We see an almost daily reminder, by looking at the sky, that endings can be beautiful, although not all days and stories end on a positive note.

Your climax is critical. Authors know that with a good beginning, readers will read your book, and with a great ending—going out with a bang—they will buy your *next* book. If you leave too many loose ends, or have a limping, wimpy last chapter, or if the bad guy hasn't gotten his due, your name may be quickly forgotten. Your story must *satisfy* the reader.

A number of authors, such as John McPhee and James V. Smith, Jr., prefer to write the closing scene first, or at least sketch it out; they begin the writing process with the end, which gives them direction and a destination.

If I didn't know the ending of a story,
I wouldn't begin.
I always write my last line,
my last paragraph, and my last page first.
—Katherine Ann Porter

Then there are those writers, however, who do not worry about endings, until the story gets close to its conclusion. As Stephen King says, "Why be such a control freak? Sooner or later every story comes out somewhere." Well, he may never have a problem coming up with a credible ending, but others have. It is said that Hemingway rewrote the ending to *A Farewell to Arms* 39 times, before he was satisfied. Yikes!

Those mysteries that have withheld information, and have an unknown character suddenly pop up in the last chapter as the who-done-it, leave readers cold with fury. Not fair. And those novels in which the author can't figure out a proper ending, who have the devil or his henchmen make an appearance in the last chapter, leave readers fuming.

> I recently saw a TV mystery, in which the killer turned out to be a member of the board of the business involved. She never had a line in the whole show, until the very end. She was only quickly viewed in a scene showing the collective board members. All the board members were sitting around a long table, when she was accused, and openly admitted it. *Say, what?!* This was a very unsatisfying ending, reminding me of some of the old Perry Mason shows, in which someone out of left field, fesses up, standing in a courtroom audience, declaring his guilt. Not believable.

Have some idea early on, as to a possible ending. You can always change it. Make your ending believable to the genre. Novels or mysteries sometimes have a snapper of a surprise ending, or a totally unexpected turn of events, leaving readers bug-eyed with astonishment. But you don't have to have a surprise ending to satisfy the reader.

If you have a series in mind, the adventure in each book must end, but the main characters, and their relationships, continue on in the following books. Other characters will be introduced in the next book, to deal with that particular adventure. It is just like you, when you move from house to house, or from job to job, you have a whole new set of individuals that will fit into your life, in one way or another. Your secondary characters can come and go, throughout your series.

In the climax, the main character must experience a change of some kind. Does your character achieve his or her goal? What is the resulting emotional reaction? The resolution brings your story to a close, clarifying all points, and tying up loose ends. The villain will have received his or her punishment in some way, hopefully, and there is nothing left to say.

> Great is the art of beginning,
> but greater the art of ending.
> —Henry Wadsworth Longfellow

TIP: You can start your ending, several chapters beforehand. To step up the pace, start shortening the sentences, and add action-packed dialogue and verbs. Then begin to slow down close to the conclusion.

Never leave your readers with a "so what?" attitude. (I had been highly praising the books by a well-known author, throughout my lectures. His new novel came out, and the students asked me what I thought of it. I gave a so-so hand gesture, and a lukewarm answer, something along the lines of, "Out of all his books, I liked it the least." Such unsatisfying word-of-mouth critiques can kill your readership.

The last paragraph
in which you tell
what the story is about
is almost always best left out.
—Irwin Shaw

CLIFFHANGERS:

A cliffhanger is nothing more
than an unresolved ending.
—Janet Evanovich

Terry L. Neal's eighth book, but his first novel, *The Search for Zarahemla*, is thinly based on his own life—a *real* Indiana Jones!—but few loose ends have been tied up by the end. In fact, the ending is abrupt, and unexpected. He says that that is the way life is, especially *his* life. He says that not all endings are neat and tidy. This is called a Cliffhanger. He plans to write two sequels, for a trilogy. (Stay tuned.)

When I was young, and was able to go to the Saturday afternoon movies, the theaters ran one or two cartoons, and then a cowboy adventure serial. There was always a cliffhanger ending, so as to ensure the viewers return the following week, to see how the hero survived, and what happened next.

And then, the final scene of the 1979-80 season episode (March 21) of the old TV series *Dallas*—which is now a new series—presented the first real television cliffhanger, causing the entire nation to wonder all summer long, "Who shot J.R.?" T-shirts were worn with the same catchphrase, strangers talked about it for months, and impromptu votes were taken. The question was not resolved until November 21, 1980, in the "Who Done It" episode. Cliffhangers are meant to evoke an emotional response, and this one surely did.

I opened the door on the second knock. Didn't want to seem overly anxious! I stepped back and our eyes met, and he showed no sign of the nervousness I felt.

"Howdy," I said.

He looked amused at that, but not amused enough to smile. He stepped forward into the foyer, closed the door, and locked it. His breathing was slow and deep, his eyes were dark, his expression serious as he studied me.

"Nice dress," he said. "Take it off."

—Janet Evanovich, *High Five*

The heroine had been juggling two hunky guys— Morelli and Ranger—throughout the series, and in this fifth book, the ending didn't give a clue as to which guy came through the door. Readers reactions ranged from confusion, to astonishment, to anger, to total outrage. *"Who was at the door?"* all wanted to know. Me, included. There was even a vote as to the favorite. Readers had to wait a whole year to find out which guy it was. And the following book, *Hot Six*, began with the above end page. *How clever is that?*

Cliffhangers can also be used at the end of chapters to encourage further reading. But they should be used sparingly. If used too often, they can become irritating to the reader. After all, the book is already being read, and the reader needs no further prodding to continue. Most cliffhangers are used at the end of a book, to encourage readers to buy the next book in a series.

TRANSITIONS:

*Transition is what makes a book
painless to read,
and keeps the reader
effortlessly turning pages.*
—Janet Evanovich

She continues on to say that good transitions should seamlessly take you from one scene to the next, or from one structural element (such as dialogue or action) to the next (such as description).

Transitions should occur during a shift in location, time, event, or point of view. Some easy transitions can include: *This morning, yesterday, last month, later, soon after, then,* and so forth. Days of the week, months of the year, and seasons, show a moving time frame. Weather shifts also show the passing of time, as well as a change in locations.

ACTIVITY: Every successful person has a turning point, a change—that big break, or a moment in time, when one faces in a new direction. Your homework is to write about a *turning point* in your life. Such as:

> During my youth, I wanted to be a teacher. So every morning, before I went to school in the lower grades, I dressed my dolls, and placed them on my bed (which I pretended was their school),

and surrounded them with little books that I had made for them. Then (as their mother), I pretended to go to work and teach (like my mother).

From junior high on, I would critique my teachers, during their daily lessons. I knew what they could have said to interest the sports-minded, or the popular kids, or the nerds, or the "bad boys," or even those who had no interest in school, whatsoever. I wished I could have explained it, so those students would interact in class discussions, and get excited about the subject, and more out of the lessons. As such, I felt well-prepared to be a teacher.

Unfortunately, both of my parents, and several aunts and uncles, as well as three adults on our block were teachers, and they were all so strict and formal and serious-acting. I thought I was "too different" from them, as I liked to laugh, and dance, and be creative, which I felt didn't go hand-in-hand with the role of an educator, judging from my role-models. So, because I thought all teachers acted in the same manner, I put my passion on hold.

As a senior in high school (1957), I had my life all planned out: I was to sign a dancing contract shortly after graduation, as I had been dancing on the stage for 15 years, since I was two-years-old. An older girlfriend was already on the dancing circuit, and I was to follow in her footsteps, on tour.

That Christmas, our parents threw a party, that neither my brother, nor I, knew anything about. As we were leaving for our separate activities that night, guests began arriving early. We were absolutely dumbfounded, as our parents had never hosted a party before (or since). *They didn't even go to parties!* They only rarely interacted with neighbors. We watched in total amazement, as many bottles of liquor were being carried through the door.

Now we had been raised with a teetotal mindset (no drinking, no smoking, no gambling, no swearing, no carousing, no drugs, no nonsense, and such). Total abstinence. Our lives were reminiscent of the later 1982 *Goody Two Shoes* song, by Adam Ant, with the lyric refrain: "Don't drink, don't smoke, what do you do?", to which I would always shout in response, "Not much!"

So my brother and I decided to stick around for a bit. We were absolutely fascinated to watch the teachers, strangers from two different districts, and two different grade levels—elementary and middle school—happily carrying on together: talking and laughing and dancing, and obviously having a good time. A smaller group was huddled around the piano in the dining room, singing Christmas carols at the top of their lungs, when for some reason, our mother wanted it moved to the living room. So the piano player kept banging away on the keys, as several burly men picked up the piano, and the crowd of carolers moved as one, into the next room, while neither the music nor song skipped a beat. I was thunderstruck! Talk about a radically changed belief system.

As we left our window-watching perches, I had reached my turning-point. My whole life changed in an instant. Teachers could have fun! They could laugh and joke, and sing! Teachers could have *fun!* They could act silly, shout, be creative—and even *drink and smoke!* Egads! Teachers could actually have FUN! (Not that I would ever act silly or drink or smoke, but it was the *idea* that I couldn't if I wanted to; it was a matter of freedom of choice, and too many implied rules.)

I immediately scrapped my dancing plans, and went on to college, and earned several degrees. And then taught for *fifty* years! (I retired for a whole 14 months, couldn't take it any more, and returned to teaching.) I find it remarkable, that by observing that one unexpected party, my life was profoundly altered. It staggers the imagination.

MECHANICS

Consider the words of Natalie Goldberg: "I was a GOODY TWO-SHOES all through school. I wanted my teachers to like me. I learned commas, colons, semi-colons. I wrote compositions with clear sentences that were dull and boring. Nowhere was there an original thought or genuine feeling."

GOOD ADVICE:

Experts routinely offer their own rules for writing. For instance, Elmore Leonard agrees with Stephen King, saying that we should only use the word *said* to carry the dialog, and others concur. Several point out that only two or three exclamation points should be used per 100,000 words. Other authors even go so far as to tell us what words not to use (such as *however, in addition*, and *et cetera*). I, however, fail to heed such wise offerings! I *add* words instead of deleting them, I use other words than *said*, and I routinely use clichés and colloquialisms in both speaking and writing. In addition, my whole life is an exclamation point, so it is hard to limit them from my writing. Etc.

Make sure that your manuscript is reader-friendly. To paraphrase someone else (the poet John Lyngate, and later attributed to Abraham Lincoln): You can't please all of your readers all of the time; you can't even please some of your readers all of the time; but you really ought to try to at least please some of your readers some of the time.

WORDS:

In the beginning was the Word . . .
—The Gospel of John 1:1

Words are powerful and have meaning. "Words count. Words can inflict pain or inspire greatness," says Brendon Burchard. They can be used for healing and joy and encouragement, or as weapons, via repeated verbal abuse. The phrase 'Sticks and stones may break my bones, but words can never harm me,' was found in print as early as 1872. It was used to teach children to have a thicker skin when being teased with name-calling; to allow negative words to go in one ear and out the other; to flow off their minds like water off a duck's back. It was meant to toughen them up, and not take things so personally. But to say that such comments are "just a bunch of words" is to deny the power of those words to affect a person. Ill-spoken, reckless words, whether delivered through spur-of-the-moment thoughtlessness or malice aforethought, can cut like a knife, and leave lasting scars. Hateful words are not easily forgotten or forgiven.

"What becomes powerful is realizing that over time, our words come to reflect who we are, and they either hurt or help the world," Brendon Burchard continues. Spiritual leaders and philosophers together suggest: Choose your words carefully. Consider whether your words are thoughtful, truthful, and necessary.

> When in the fifth grade, on a family road trip across the states, we were driving in the middle of nowhere, through a seemingly endless Arizona desert. Although the weather was clear, the car radio mentioned a chance of flash floods, and I excitedly said that I would *love* to see one, since I couldn't picture it in my mind. Mother became quite upset that I would say such a thing, and admonished me for doing so, ending with: *"Be careful what you wish for!"*
>
> The sentence was barely out of her mouth, when, on cue, a powerful flash flood swept across the highway, washing the pickup truck in front of us off the road, landing it nose-down in a ditch.

An enormous amount of water coursed around it with such force, that the doors couldn't be opened.

All traffic was stopped, unable to cross the dangerous fast-moving water, and we had a front row seat to the powerful destruction that a flash flood can wreak. I was further shocked to see that the driver of the pickup was a young woman—gender issues were stuck in 1949—and that she had a small baby with her. Both were crying, so we didn't know if they were injured, or just freaking out about the unexpected situation, but we were unable to help.

Since cell phones were nonexistent at that time, someone had to turn around, and drive all the way back to the closest town, to get the sheriff. He and a helper finally arrived, with a heavier truck, ropes, and chains. We watched the ropes being used, as the sheriff battled through the water to rescue the baby first, and then went back to pull the woman to safety. Both were hauled out through the cab window. It was a long and arduous process. At length, the heavier truck pulled the pickup back onto the highway, and shortly thereafter, the flash flood had finally lost its punch. At that point, traffic was able to continue on, as if nothing had happened. Mother acted as if the whole experience was my fault, and I realized just how *powerful* our spoken words are.

A powerful agent is the right word.
Whenever we come upon one of those
intensely right words . . .
the resulting effect is physical,
as well as spiritual,
and electrically prompt.
—Mark Twain

VOCABULARY:

The most important thing
is to read as much as you can.
It will give you an understanding
of what makes good writing,
and it will enlarge your vocabulary.
—J.K. Rowling

Writers are readers first and foremost. Many of us are compulsive about it, like Thomas Jefferson ("I can't live without books"). I read a book a day, when I am not in writing mode, and I generally have between two and six books going at a time. The more you read, the more facility you develop with words—and that's what makes you a writer. Words are your tools of the trade.

It is often said that as you increase your vocabulary, you expand your mind. "The more words you know, the more precise your thoughts, and the more explicit your ideas," says Joyce L. Vedral. The English language totals somewhere around 750,000 words, the largest number in any language. Your personal working vocabulary is a tad smaller, anywhere from 2,000 to 10,000 words. We greatly limit ourselves.

"You know more words than a dictionary!" a child once complained to me. Unfortunately, it wasn't always so.

> When I was a five-year-old first grader, my Father decided that it was high time for me to have a bank account. (I didn't have a job, and I never had any money given to me for any reason, but that apparently was a minor point that didn't concern him, as his motivation was pure: financial responsibility, and all that.) We walked into the bank together, and Father asked for the proper forms, which he filled out. Then he thrust a card at me, asking for my signature. I had no idea what he was talking about, never having heard the word before. I froze,

thinking it was something that I ought to know. (I had always been told that I was soooo smart, and didn't want to show my ignorance by asking.) My mind was desperate for a clue, as his voice was getting louder and more demanding. He kept repeating *signature*, but never the words, *name*, *print*, or *write*. As all eyes were on me, I left in disgrace. It was years before I heard the word *signature* again.

For your born writer,
nothing is so healing,
as the realization
that he has come upon
the right word.
—Catherine Drinker Bowen

Focus on precise words, synonyms, and comprehension.

When a new student asked another second grader what *dead meat* meant, he was told, "You know man, like when yore *cooked*. Like yore bottom gonna git warmed like in the microwave! Like yore ass'll be fryin' like bacon!"

Exasperated with the new boy's lack of city knowledge, one third grade girl—in an effort to make a put-down statement—suggested, "Oh, go ride your concubine!" This, of course, showed what she knew about country life, as there is a vast difference between a combine and a concubine.

Know your audience. Word choice is critical in writing. Avoid ordinary, tired, and boring words, for creative words that plant specific images in your reader's head.

The difference between the right word
and the almost right word
is the difference between lightning
and the lightning bug.
—Mark Twain

Julia Cameron says, "Picking words is like picking apples: this one looks delicious; that one leaves a sour taste." String your words together like beads, choosing one over the other. Leave out the overused or boring ones.

I recognize that I am a prude, and I do try to combat that trait whenever possible. But, after all these years, I still have trouble talking about specific body parts, and maintain that there are certain things that should remain unsaid, while one is eating.

One night, my husband and I went to

dinner at a local restaurant. As the sixteen-year-old hostess was seating us, she loudly exclaimed, "You guys smell just like baby butts!"

Say what?! "I beg your pardon?" I strangled in reply, as diners turned to gawk.

"You guys smell just like baby butts," she happily reiterated, as my husband and I exchanged shocked looks and raised eyebrows.

Hmmmm. "You mean like talcum . . .?" I tentatively asked, treading lightly, although fearing the worst.

She quickly interjected, "No, no! It's not a *bad* thing. You know, like after a baby's bath, you sprinkle baby powder."

Ahhh, it finally became clear: Baby powder she understood, talcum powder she didn't. It all boiled down to a simple generation gap. Just another linguistic mix-up.

*A great many people think
that polysyllables
are a sign of intelligence.*
—Barbara Walters

Avoid using larger words, when smaller ones will do. Don't make the mistake of trying to dress up your vocabulary. Use words in your own *working* vocabulary, not ones that you only recognize. You don't want readers to come to a screeching stop, and have to refer to a dictionary, or the Internet, or call the library reference desk, just to understand what you are saying.

> *[Hemingway] has never been known*
> *to use a word*
> *that might send a reader*
> *to the dictionary.*
> —William Faulkner

Unfortunately, I brought my glasses case to class, but my prescription glasses weren't in it. I can't see anything without my glasses. So, during my lecture to the older 50+ crowd, I asked the students to read several paragraphs aloud—Round Robin style—of a short story I had written, to illustrate the point I was trying to make. Listening to their stumbling over several words therein (tantamount, klaxons, tintinnabulation, falsetto, spasmodically, hapless), I realized that I still needed to tone down my vocabulary, in the same manner as that of Ernest Hemingway's response to the above quote: "Poor

Faulkner. Does he really think big emotions come from big words? He thinks I don't know the ten-dollar words. I know them all right. But there are older and simpler and better words, and those are the ones I use."

As Dan Poynter advises, "Steer away from jargon (words that are unique to a certain audience), coinages (words that aren't in the dictionary), and buzzwords (words that move in and out of vogue)."

One day, the second graders asked about my favorite color. I said that I preferred orange, whereas my husband liked red; so I had an orange V.W. and he had a red V.W. I looked upon a sea of blank faces. "What's a V.W.?" they wanted to know.

"Oh, it's a Bug!" I explained, thinking that everyone had seen the Walt Disney movie, *Herbie, the Love Bug*. Silence again.

"What's a Bug?" they chorused.

"A VeeDub." Nothing.

"A Volkswagen!" Nada. Zip. Zilch.

Not until I took them outside and showed them, did they get the picture. The word *car* would have sufficed.

Words form the thread on which
we string our experiences.
—Aldous Huxley

Focus on brevity. Keeping my writing short is hard for me. It's difficult to edit out the junk.

Never use two words
when one word will do.
—Thomas Jefferson

Experts say that the best vocabulary to use is *the first word that comes to mind*, if it is colorful and appropriate. Only use big words when being precise, and long sentences when making a point. Your readers must be your main concern. Do not confuse them, or divert them from the story.

Words are all we have.
—Samuel Beckett

CRUTCH WORDS:

Crutch words are those words that you lean on, which is too much of a good thing. Do not overuse your favorite words or phrases. It's annoying. One high school student's pet word was crimson, so the word was often used in his writing, but never scarlet, ruby, vermilion, cardinal, or just plain old red. Every night, a TV weather gal always says, "as well." (I wait for it, and sometimes can count up to six within one short segment!) Check to see that you are not using the same words over and over again, such as: basically, well (which is my personal bugaboo), very, such, then, as it were, like, cool, just, actually, seriously, honestly, awesome, and whatever. Curtail such repeat endings as: "so to speak", "and everything," "Mark my words," or "you know?" A college student was forever saying, "Everything is relative," seemingly dozens of times, during each class session. Much eye-rolling followed this remark.

TIP: Circle your word repetitions during your revisions, and substitute synonyms, when appropriate.

SENTENCES:

"You can't really succeed with a novel anyway; they're too big. It's like city planning. You can't plan a perfect city because there's too much going on that you can't take into account. You can, however, write a perfect sentence now and then. I have," said Gore Vidal. And we can certainly try our best, when we remember the following:

- Simple sentences stand alone. They are less

than 25 words, although a dozen words are best.

- Complex sentences have one independent clause, and at least one dependent clause.

- Compound sentences could be two separate sentences standing alone, connected by *and* or *but.*

- Convoluted sentences have two or more ideas involved.

There's a great power in words,
if you don't hitch
too many of them together.
—Josh Billings

Avoid writing elaborate or complicated sentences. You don't want readers stopping in mid-sentence, to say to themselves, *What the heck does that mean?* Now and again, I will come across a sentence that I have to read several times, to try to understand it. Forget the dumbing down of America theory, and use the basic vocabulary from the old Dick and Jane primers (the lower the grade level, the better). As a teacher, this offended me when I first heard it, but it is clear that the best-selling authors use shorter words (averaging 4.5 letters) and shorter sentences (15 words or less) making them easier to read. And they rarely use more than 30 words at a time. What a shocker!

Focus on comprehension. Check out the sentence below. It looks like a paragraph. I suggested that the writer break it into at least three shorter sentences.

> Pace knew all about Warren Dortch Jr., who was vying for another seat, a contested congressional seat against one-time Hollywood cameraman and current Congressman Dyer, who was backed by Kanaan of Kanaan Do, a local furniture magnate who wanted access to groves of pines that littered the landscape producing precious little in the way of wealth except to trailer park owners and campers who hung laundry on towering trees, thus saving on clotheslines, a manufacturing sideline in which Kanaan Do had also invested.

Be brief. Write in short, simple sentences, conveying a fact, an act, or an image. The shorter the sentence, the easier the comprehension. James V. Smith, Jr. shows, in *The Writer's Little Helper*, that an average of a dozen words is best, as less than 24-word sentences are the easiest to understand. Comprehension declines with the length of the sentence. So, if you write a 50-word sentence, your readers will understand only half of it, whereas only a quarter of your readers will comprehend a 75-word sentence (the above example has 82 words). So pay attention to your word count.

Denny Hatch says it another way: "Tests have shown that a sentence of eight words is very easy to read; of 11 words, easy; of 14 words, fairly easy; of 17 words, standard; of 21 words, fairly difficult; of 25 words, difficult; of 29 or more words, very difficult; so this sentence with 54 words, counting numbers, is ranked impossible."

Word-carpentry is like
any other kind of carpentry:
you must join your sentences smoothly.
—Anatole France

TIP: Vary your sentence lengths. Long sentences should be surrounded by shorter sentences.

Words have weight, sound and appearance;
it is only by considering these
that you can write a sentence that is
good to look at
and good to listen to.
—Somerset Maugham

PARAGRAPHS:

> Use short words,
> short sentences,
> short paragraphs.
> —Andrew Byrne

The first sentence in your paragraph should either suggest the topic, or help the transition from the preceeding paragraph. Each paragraph should connect with the previous and following paragraphs. Always remember: If a reader doesn't understand the paragraph, don't blame the reader. Rework it. Be specific. Make sure your paragraphs are easily understood. What a reader assumes is not always the case.

> One male teacher's voice could be heard reverberating through the halls: "You are not to *touch* another child's privates! Didn't I already tell you *that?*" It seemed to the youngster, at least, that the answer was *no*. He had been told not to *kick* . . . About a week later, that same boy was at it again, as the teacher was heard to shout, "You do not stick kids in their privates with *umbrellas!*"

GRAMMAR:

*I don't know any but the simplest rules
of English grammar,
and I seldom consciously apply them.
Nevertheless,
I instinctively write correctly and,
I like to think, in an interesting fashion.
I know when something sounds right
and when it doesn't,
and I can tell the difference without hesitation,
even when writing at breakneck speed.
How do I do this?
I haven't the faintest idea.*
—Isaac Asimov

A fan wrote to Janet Evanovich, asking: "Do you need excellent grammar and a superb vocabulary to be a writer?" And she answered, "It ain't necessary, but it don't hurt." You can always hire an editor.

Accuracy in academic language counts. However, trying to obey *all* of the grammar rules can sometimes lead to tongue twisters and grammatical gymnastics, resulting in some bending or breaking of the rules in poetry and song lyrics.

*This is the kind of English
up with which I will not put.*
—Sir Winston Churchill

Think of Pink Floyd's wildly popular song, *Another Brick in the Wall, Part II*, in which the lyrics say, "We don't need no education, We don't need no thought control." (Original album released in 1973. All lyrics by Roger Waters.) Both sentences are grammatically incorrect. They are double negatives, which really means, yes they do. But listeners know that this is an accepted way of speaking, and the meaning is exactly as portrayed: They don't need an education or thought control. And clearly, they don't need no rules of grammar, either.

The Rolling Stones' #1 hit song *Satisfaction* (by Mick Jagger and Keith Richards, 1965) has the lyrics saying, "I can't get no satisfaction," which is also a double negative, meaning, "I can get satisfaction," but the accepted understanding is the opposite.

And let's not forget Elvis Presley's triple negative in the song *Hard Knocks* (lyrics by Joy Byers, 1993): "Nobody never gave nothing to me but hard knocks."

There are always poor examples on television interviews, newscasters, and commercials:

- "She don't need nothing."
- "I ain't got no . . ."
- "I seen . . ."
- "I had went to . . ."
- "I had tooken it . . ."
- "I do got this."
- "Me and him . . ."
- "Our cats, we lost 'em up."
- "These is mines."
- "I dood a lot mores."
- "I thunked it myself."
- "Wha's wrong you face?"
- "I don' gots none."
- "He be grubbin'!"

Upon hearing such grammatical errors, it's always good to remember:

For last year's words
belong to last year's language,
And next year's words
await another voice.
—T.S. Eliot

TENSES:

Nostalgia is like a grammar lesson:
You find the present tense
And the past perfect!
—George Eliot

Keep your tenses straight. Things can happen in the present, in the past, or in the future. The tenses you use show what time you are talking about.

ASIDE: The text on a T-shirt tells the classic joke, especially for grammarians:

The past,
the present,
and the future
walked into a bar.
It was tense.
—T-shirt

SPELLING:

Ducking for apples—
Change one letter
and it's the story of my life.
—Dorothy Parker

Proper standard spelling is a must. Poor spelling is often regarded as an indicator of a less than adequate education, a poor reader, low intelligence, illiteracy, or a lower class standing.

My spelling is Wobbly.
It's good spelling but it Wobbles,
and the letters get in the wrong places.
—A.A. Milne, *Winnie-the-Pooh*

A propos of nothing, one second grader happily announced to the class, "I know how to spell 'soap powder': A-L-L."

When speaking of a child that didn't have good common sense, another girl tapped her finger to her head, while explaining, "She ain't too B-R-I-T!"

One third grader tattled: "He said the F word! The F word! You know: F-O-R-K!"

If you can spell "Nietzsche"
without Google,
you deserve a cookie.
—Lauren Leto

TIP: Surely you have a dictionary close by, or you can call the library reference desk, if need be. One or two accidental misspelled words or typos (in your whole manuscript) are understandable. But it takes readers immediately out of the story. Know that editors will consider you a rank amateur if you have spelling, punctuation, or grammar mistakes in your manuscript. Take a tip from a sweatshirt message: **Always run spell check. It's impotent.**

Many years ago, I was asked to edit an elderly woman's manuscript, which was about three inches thick. I did. It took me forever. Not only was the story *boring*, but she had 20 to 30 errors on each page. She couldn't even keep the same spelling for her characters. It was a disaster, what with my red marks and arrows everywhere, alongside marginal notations. I'm sure she was shocked. Needless to say, I never received a Thank You. Although, years later, I heard that she began taking a writing class, so maybe all my work wasn't in vain, after all.

As I walked around the shards of wine bottles onto the school grounds, I stared at the scabrous surroundings with some astonishment. I could tell that the students had mastered their phonics lesson that week, as all the new chalk-scrawled graffiti said PHUCK. I couldn't suppress the silly ear-to-ear grin on my face, taking that as a good sign. (Teachers must take solace in small victories.)

PUNCTUATION:

All morning
I worked on the proof
of one of my poems,
and I took out a comma;
in the afternoon I put it back.
—Oscar Wilde

SPOT QUIZ: There are 14 punctuation marks in English grammar. Can you name them all? (Answers below.)

Punctuation is not just a trifling matter.

My father was born in a sod house, in the Oklahoma territory, before statehood. As such, he had little schooling at first. Individuals who were sixteen years old were allowed to teach, so as a child, his education was hit and miss. When the family moved closer to a town, he arrived at a new school, and was asked to read aloud. He was prideful of his ability to read words at a rapid rate. Which he did. Thereafter, the wide-eyed and openmouthed students erupted into hysterical laughter. He was stunned and highly embarrassed, not knowing the cause of the hilarity. It turned out that he had never learned about punctuation, and never knew to stop at a period. He just plowed through word after word, with no meaning or expression involved. Many years later, surprisingly—during the Depression—he graduated from college with a teaching credential. He became an educator throughout his life, teaching mostly English (grammar and punctuation skills).

If your book is to be published, it must be written in English, with proper punctuation, no grammatical errors, and correct spelling. You need to check for mistakes before you send in your manuscript. And, once your final edit is published, you'll need to proofread it again.

The cover of my *Into the Hornet's Nest* had an 'S on the front cover, and an S' on the spine and the interior title page. The apostrophes actually worked either way, but one must be consistent.

Most people tend to ignore the letter S with an apostrophe. When the children's book, *In Our Mothers' House*, by Patricia Polacco, was first published (2009), few paid attention to the title. The cover illustration showed two happy women with three happy children, that obviously were multicultural. It could have been seen as simply a book about adoption. But a closer look at where the apostrophe was placed, brought a whole new meaning to some readers. It wasn't a story just about adoption, but a nontraditional loving family, with two mothers. Hence, the s'. As such, some people have tried to have the book banned. So much for the basic right of the freedom to read.

Any time you are reading a book, and you come across an error, it is distracting, and you immediately lose the flow of the story, and focus on the mistake. Was it the author's mistake, the editor's mistake, or the printers?

I *love* all of Robert B. Parker's books, but he had a problem with question marks. In too many instances, they were omitted. Finally, I had reached my tolerance limit, and wrote him a letter. I was concerned, and asked if he had had a negative experience with a question mark at an early age. He answered on the backside of a printed form that he had crossed out with a large X (which gave the message that he received too many letters to respond to, as he was busy writing his next book). In longhand, he wrote a lengthy letter. At the end of each statement, he placed a question mark, except for the last sentence, that *needed* a question mark, which he left blank. I received it on the day in which I presented a lecture at a school district conference, and read it aloud. His letter received howls of laughter. It was the perfect lead in to my presentation.

See how the meaning changes, depending on the punctuation used in the following sentences:

- A woman without her man is nothing.
  A woman: without her, man is nothing.

- He didn't mean to kill her.
  He didn't mean to kill her?

- Let's eat, Mommy.
  Let's eat Mommy.

Commas save lives.
—T-shirt

- Spotted manatee found off South Carolina beach.
  Spotted: manatee found off South Carolina beach.

- Coast Guard: Body found near burned Gulf
oil rig
Coast Guard Body found near burned Gulf
oil rig

SIDEBAR: Did you know that National Punctuation Day is September 24th of each year? It is "A celebration of the lowly comma, correctly used quotation marks, and other proper uses of periods, semicolons, and the ever-mysterious ellipsis." Check it out on the Internet.

QUIZ ANSWERS: period, comma, colon, semicolon, dash, hyphen, apostrophe, question mark, exclamation point, quotation marks, brackets, parenthesis, ellipses, and the uncommonly used, braces.

NOTE: "The way you live your day is a sentence in the story of your life. Each day you make the choice whether the sentence ends with a period, question mark, or exclamation point," Steve Maraboli explains. I have always lived my life as an exclamation point! Won't you join me?

SPACES:

Even spaces are important to meaning, as Eric Norwood shows, in an article published in the *Living Well Journal*, "A Page Without Punctuation is a Life Without Spaces" (3/16/12): "So much meaning is missed without proper punctuation. And so it is with life. We miss so much of life's everyday meaning without those gifted spaces and brief interludes."

- He was outstanding in his field.
  He was out standing in his field.

- The suitcase is expected to go to court.
  The suit case is expected to go to court.

The space between . . .
is the space that lies between
the observer and the observed;
it is the space of the creative act
that brings a poem or painting to life.
—F. David Peat

PACE:

Pace is the speed at which your story unfolds. (Some are so slow, and the buildup is so gradual, that it drives me crazy. But that plodding, gloomy, pace is my friend's favorite.) Vary the pace to keep your writing fresh. According to Janet Evanovich, if you want to get your readers turning pages quickly, you have to gradually step up the pace. First, by shortening your sentences. Next, by using action-packed dialogue and action verbs. Then you have to start slowing down as the resolution materializes.

Strunk & White, in *The Elements of Style*, caution against too many simple sentences in a row, so you might want to throw in a compound sentence now and then, or change the length of your sentences. You are advised to vary the pace, to keep the writing fresh.

ACTION/VERBS:

God is a verb.
—Buckminster Fuller

Nouns are words that name what is (person, place, or things), and verbs are words that act and tell what's happening. Gordon Livingston says that "We are a verbal species"—actions speak louder than words. It takes more than dreams, wishes, and good intentions to live in this world; it takes action. It doesn't matter who you are, or how smart you are, or how talented you are, only action brings your potential to life. We only grow stronger, and get better, by our own efforts. Check out the sharp action verbs.

TIP: Try not to have any extraneous elements in chase scenes. Keep your sentences short and filled with action verbs.

TIP: When something is wrong with a sentence, more often than not, it can be improved by changing a word or two.

ADVERBS:

Adverbs usually end in ly. They are words that are used

to describe a verb, or other verbs, participles, and adjectives, and are usually placed near it. Adverbs use the passive voice, as in: He closed the door. He closed the door *firmly*. He slammed the door.

Adverbs are considered to be tiresome and unnecessary, by many authors. Elmore Leonard says to go "Easy on the adverbs." Stephen King is often quoted as saying, "The adverb is not your friend." He has also written, "I believe the road to hell is paved with adverbs." Mark Twain appears to have hated adverbs: "I am dead to adverbs; they cannot excite me. To misplace an adverb is a thing which I am able to do with frozen indifference; it can never give me a pang," and so on, and on, calling adverbs "a plague."

For the life of me, I can't understand how adverbs can cause so much ire. How can people get so riled up over an adverb grammar issue? I find adverbs to be quite useful in both my speech and writing. At least, I'm not alone:

> *I'm glad you like adverbs. I adore them;*
> *they are the only qualifications*
> *I really much respect.*
> —Henry James

SHOW OR TELL:

Most writing experts emphasize showing. But there is a place for both.

Showing brings your descriptions and characters to life. Let the reader discover what you're trying to say, through the action and dialog.

Don't tell me the moon is shining;
show me the glint of light
on broken glass.
—Anton Chekhov

Instead of saying the third grade boy was sad, show it:

> I was concerned about Hallelujah—one of my best pupils. He was upset, but not especially at me, which was a refreshing change. Several times during the hour, he came up to me, to whisper his grief about his pet bird that died that morning. Thinking to console him, I rummaged through my stacks of books, and finally found *The Tenth Best Thing About Barney*, by Judith Viorst. The book is about a little boy whose cat had died. I thought it might help Hallelujah to see how another youngster had handled a similar loss.
>
> Later that afternoon, after I had presented a lesson about continents, and everyone was engrossed in the map follow-up assignment, Hallelujah came up to me and slammed the book down on my

desk. "Well, I read it, and I didn't like it!" he announced.

"But why?" I asked, thoroughly shaken, while mentally flogging myself for my good intentions.

"Because it was sad, and it's too much like what happened to me," he explained. "You know, he continued softly, "everyone has been so *nice* to me today. And everyone has tried so hard to cheer me up. But you know, Ms. Meinberg, I just *can't* be happy today, no matter what. *It's just too soon!*"

I marveled at the wisdom of this child. I don't like to recall how many years it took me to discover that time, does indeed, heal all wounds.

Instead of saying the father was mad, show it:

Dad burst through the back door, slammed his keys on the table, and yelled, "Who the hell tracked mud in my brand new car?"

But know that there is also value in simply telling. Consider Charles Dickens first line in *A Tale of Two Cities*. He tells us in the very first sentence, "It was the best of times, it was the worst of times."

MANUSCRIPT DIRECTIONS:

Know that each publishing house has its own way of doing things. But they all pretty much agree on the following items. There are plenty of dos and don'ts when it comes to your manuscript presentation:

- Use 20-lb paper;

- Don't use notebook paper, shiny paper, colored paper, or scented paper;

- Don't use stickers, logos, or drawings on the pages;

- Don't send any folded, ripped, or dog-eared pages;

- Don't use staples, paperclips, or brass fasteners;

- Don't use binders;

- Use an easy-to-read font, like Geneva (no fancy, crazy, or cursive script);

- Use 12 or 14 pt.;

- Don't justify your right margins (unless you're using POD publishing);

- Double-space;

- Print one side only;

- Reasonable margins (such as: Left Margin 1.5 inches, Right Margin 1.7 inches, Bottom Margin 1.3 inches, Top Margin 1.9 inches);

- Include your name and page # in upper right hand corner (or left) of each page (0.5 inches from top);

- Include the title (or abbreviation) all CAPS on upper left hand corner (or right) of each page (0.5 inches from top);

- Chapter Heading: Drop down a third of the page for each new chapter (all CAPS);

- Write the end, end, *30*, or #, or 000.

- Back up your work. (I lost the entire 6th chapter of *The Bogeyman*, when my computer fried. Smoke billowed, as the smell permeated the rooms.)

ACTIVITY: What is the biggest risk you have ever taken? How did it work out for you? Keep in mind what James Patterson wrote in *Merry Christmas, Alex Cross:*

"[S]ometimes even the best choices have adverse consequences."

LEGAL

There are legal issues that you must be aware of, before your manuscript goes to print. This usually consists of checking for libelous statements, or falsified facts regarding people, businesses, or events. Both fiction and nonfiction work must consider defamation and invasion of privacy matters.

HONESTY:

Honesty is the first chapter
in the book of wisdom.
—Thomas Jefferson

As it has been said many times before, honesty is the best policy. If your story is fiction, say so. Otherwise, your name will be dragged through the mud, and people might say that you lie like a rug, or they wouldn't believe you even if you had a halo above your head; or as Judge Marilyn Milian once shouted at a defendant in her *People's*

Court, "I wouldn't believe you if your tongue was notarized!" And if you are caught being dishonest in print, you may have to pay restitution, or might even land in jail.

If you tell the truth,
you don't have to remember anything.
—Mark Twain

The Third Eye, by Lobsang Rampa (1950), was a global bestseller. Reporters became suspicious, and tracked down the author, who was a small town English postman, by the name of Cyril Henry Hoskins (1910-1981). As the son of a plumber, he had never been to Tibet, nor did he know the language. Reporters called him a charlatan and a con artist, even as he continued to write 18 more books, involving Tibetan religion and occult material. The author finally said that his body was occupied by the spirit of Lobsang Rampa, after he had fallen from a tree, and landed on his head. I had earlier heard that he was channeling the words of Lobsang Rampa. Either way, I was unhappy to hear the uproar about his series, as his descriptions were fascinating. And even though the Dalai Lama said the books were "highly imaginative and fictional in nature," he refrained from further input, since the series had brought so much *positive* attention to the troubles of Tibet.

There are three kinds of lies: Lies, damned lies, and statistics.
—Mark Twain

Marlo Morgan's book, *Mutant Message Down Under* (1991), swept the world, with its incredible odyssey of an American doctor in Australia—except for Australia—which hadn't heard of it (which should have been our first clue that the book was fiction). Red flags abounded, but were overlooked, as she swore left, right and center that the book was true. I liked the book so much that I bought and gifted many copies. I was concerned when readers in Australia finally got wind of the book, and the response was a shrill hue and cry, with negative remarks following. I later attended a lecture (along with about 500 other concerned readers) that Morgan presented, wherein she stated that she was now calling her book a novel, simply to protect the Aborigines from legal involvement. A tall, impeccably dressed gentleman with a strong British accent, stood by her side, and said he was an Aboriginal Chief (which should have been yet another clue that things weren't as said, since he was elaborately garbed). I felt duped. Although I wanted to believe in the books accuracy, I finally had to admit that it was a work of fiction. I was extremely embarrassed that I had given copies to others under false pretenses. Now, later editions, have the following message, which is quite the opposite from what she maintained in the first few years of its publication:

"This book is a work of fiction inspired by my experience in Australia. It could have taken place in Africa or South America or anywhere where the true meaning of civilization is still alive. It is for the reader to receive his or her own message from my story." —M.M.

More recently, James Frey's wildly popular *A Million Little Pieces*, turned out to be a million little lies—a total sham—much to Oprah's dismay (she had highly touted the book, and it sold around the world). When found that they had been duped (his confession as an alcoholic, a drug addict, and a criminal was total fiction), only 1,729 book buyers asked for a refund—for a grand total of $27,348. A 2.35 million dollar fund was set up to cover a class-action lawsuit. Yowsers!

Remember back in 1971, when Clifford Irving released his fake book, *The Autobiography of Howard Hughes*? He later confessed (1/28/72), was indicted for fraud in federal court, and found to be guilty (6/16/72). He was sentenced to two-and-a-half years, but served only seventeen months. But he had to return the $765,000 advance, to his publisher, McGraw-Hill. He later complained that the movie about him, *The Hoax*, staring Richard Gere (which opened 4/6/2007), was a distortion, "a hoax about a hoax," which is funny, coming from him.

More recently, Lance Armstrong, and his publishers, Penguin and Random House, are being sued for fraud and false advertising, after he admitted to systematic doping. He has since been stripped of all his honors and awards. The plaintiffs claim that after buying and reading his books, *It's Not About the Bike*, and *Every Second Counts*, they felt "duped," and "cheated," and "betrayed," to find out that they were not true. Under the California consumer protection laws, Armstrong is accused of violating the false advertising and fraud laws by selling his books as nonfiction. Libraries are now in the process of moving his books to the fiction shelves. Stay tuned.

If your book is nonfiction, be prepared to prove it, if need be. Do not expect your editor or publisher to protect you, after being snookered by other authors. If you are sued, you're on your own.

WHISTLEBLOWER:

A whistleblower is one who writes or tells the public, or someone in authority, about dishonest or illegal acts, or misconduct occurring in a government department or a private company or an organization, or a direct threat to public interest. The misconduct would be a violation of a law, rule, or regulation. Whistleblowers often face reprisals of some sort, at the hands of the accused.

My motivation was pure. I felt a moral responsibility to try to right the wrongs that I saw in my local public schools. As a result, I wrote my first book, *Into the Hornet's Nest: An Incredible Look at Life in an Inner City School* (1993). My innocent desire was that if the public was aware of the educational problems therein, we could all work together to fix them. Wrong. I was shocked and dumbfounded at the huge and lasting response. It had a divisive impact, that I couldn't have foreseen: The book clearly divided the district. The teachers thought I was the best thing since sliced bread, and the administrators thought of me as a traitor. And I was shunned, because, as one person put it, "I had held the district's dirty laundry out for everyone to see." It was *not* a pleasant experience. Decades later, after retiring from 34 years teaching, I became a professor at a university in a different county. I had three adult students (over the course of my 16 years therein) who checked *out* of my classes, because their parents had been administrators in the district, when the book had first been published. (I did not know their parents, but the taint still stood.) Even though I considered my efforts to be righteous, the repercussions persisted. Every now and then, someone from the good old days, will say, upon first meeting me, "Oh, you wrote *that* book!"

LIBEL:

To libel is to defame someone, or a product, or a business, by *knowingly* and *maliciously* writing or printing things that are untrue, or damaging, to their character, fame, or reputation. This also includes photographs. If you publish something that is false, in a letter, blog, article, or book, that harms a person or a company, either personally or professionally, even if you read the information elsewhere, you are still at risk. So you must engage in more of your own fact-checking.

Even if you have changed a person's name, or said that your book is a novel, you may not be protected. Lee Gutkind tells us: "If a person is identifiable, if you've left a birthmark on his right cheek, or a tattoo on his forearm, or he has a recognizable accent, you could be in big trouble."

Understand that a brand for a company is no different than a reputation for a person. Trademark laws and interstate or international laws may be involved. Be cautious. It is best to say nothing derogatory about anyone, or any business, or at least camouflage them. Court is expensive and time consuming. Stay out of it.

Again, there are two differences of opinion. Some say you should *never* write out of vengeance, whereas others say you should *always* write out of vengeance.

Some say to change everything that is specific to the person in question (warts, scars, tattoos, etc.), whereas others say to only thinly disguise them. (Anne Lamott suggests that you give the male character— who would be the most likely to complain—"a teeny little penis and anti-Semitic leanings" so he will be less likely to come forth, and won't say the book is written around him. Yikes!)

Most states maintain that you can't libel a dead person, but in California, Texas, and Rhode Island, you can. Avoid such litigation, at all costs. Police yourself.

COPYRIGHT:

Some new authors are worried that if they send their proposals out to unscrupulous agents or editors, that their ideas will be stolen. Common Law says that your *original* work is copyrighted the moment you put your words on paper; you just haven't registered it yet. Those words belong to you, for the duration of your life, plus *seventy* years beyond. So your heirs will also benefit from your words, if you mention it in your will.

> *All his best passages*
> *are plagiarisms.*
> —George Gregory

Copyright law states that there is no protection for

facts, ideas, or concepts. It is the manner in which you express your words, the way in which the material is written, the way in which you string your words together. It's the actual *form, the configuration,* that makes the difference.

You may have written a similar story to that of another author, but if you weren't privy to the piece in question, and had no knowledge of it, you aren't infringing. Still, this is hard for me to do, since long after I have written something, thinking it original, I sometimes find the same thing already in print—and often printed years earlier—and so I feel that I have to change my word placement, since it is so close.

TIP: You can copy ideas and facts, but you cannot copy any *three words* in a row. That's the hard part. Do not print word for word. The emphasis is always on uniqueness.

Understand that there is no copyright protection for titles, names, short phrases or expressions, either.

Plagiarize,
Let no one else's work evade your eyes,
Remember why the good Lord made your eyes,
So don't shade your eyes,
But plagiarize, plagiarize, plagiarize—
Only be sure always to call it please "research."
—Tom Lehrer, "Lobachevsky"

You are allowed to quote anything in the public domain without getting their permission. When you quote the ideas of others, it is considered to be reporting or teaching, as long as you give them credit.

> *Great literature must spring*
> *from an upheaval*
> *in the author's soul.*
> *If that upheaval is not present,*
> *then it must come from*
> *the works of another author*
> *which happens to be handy*
> *and easily adapted.*
> —Robert Benchley

RIGHT OF PRIVACY:

If you have photographs in your book that include those other than family members, it might be wise to protect yourself by getting a written release signed. Not everyone wants to have his or her picture in a book. Privacy issues are at stake, if you are unknowingly showing a stalking or abuse victim, a person under Witness Protection, or persons purposely off the grid for reasons of their own, putting them at risk. By law, teachers are not allowed to show photos of students, who may be pawns in the middle of a nasty divorce matter, and/or where kidnapping may be a concern. Privacy counts.

NEGLIGENCE:

If you are writing a book concerning health, safety, diet, or food, make sure you write a disclaimer and place it in the front pages, in case readers claim you misled them, and they decide to sue. They can claim that your book did them great damage in some way. I wrote a full page disclaimer in *The Bogeyman: Stalking and its Aftermath*, as well as *Toxic Attention: Keeping Save from Stalkers, Abusers, and Intruders*. I had enough troubles with my own stalker, and didn't want to see the inside of a courtroom any more than was necessary.

TRADEMARK:

A trademark is to be used as an adjective, not a noun (Ray-ban sunglasses, Xerox copiers, Kindle ebook readers), as it *generalizes* the brand. *Who knew?* I always thought that companies would take it as an *honor* to be the brand known for a whole category, like Kleenex for tissues. Apparently not. Writers are also directed to avoid using a trademark in the plural: "Where are your Yoplaits?" (Saying instead, "Where are your Yoplait yogurts?") It sounds awkward to me. So much for fast communication.)

Know that product manufacturers, as well as owners or managers of restaurants, hotels, theaters, casinos, and the like, can be just as angry over negative trademark infringement as a private citizen. And they can, and are, more likely to sue. (They have both the time and the money to do so, whereas you may not be so endowed.) My advice is to either say nice things about such products and establishments, or change their names in your manuscript.

Having said the above, however, I recently finished reading the latest James Patterson book (#19) in the Alex Cross series: *Merry Christmas, Alex Cross*, and I was shocked to see three major world-wide brands (McDonalds, Coke, and Macy's) included in the book. The crux of the story had a jihadist terrorist place a poison capsule in the nozzle of a Coke machine, in a McDonald's eatery, while carrying get-away clothes in a big Macy's bag. Maybe being a major world-wide author helps in this regard, and brings free publicity to the brands. If you're not famous, it's a chancy situation.

Revision

There will come a time
when you believe
everything is finished.
That will be the beginning.
—Louis L'Amour

DRAFTS:

All genres require rewriting. You can't just type The End to your manuscript, dust your hands, and think that you're finished. Noooo. Perish the thought. You must put your manuscript away for a while—days, weeks, months—and come back at it with fresh eyes. Kenneth Atchity says that the longer you've been away from it, the better your revision is going to be.

I'm not a very good writer,
but I'm an excellent rewriter.
—James Michener

Anne Lamott says that all writers write "shitty first drafts," and that she herself writes "really, really shitty first drafts." She further explains: "The first draft is the down draft—you just get it down. The second draft is the up draft—you fix it up. The third draft is the dental draft, where you check every tooth, to see if it's loose or cramped or decayed, or even, God help us, healthy." She continues by saying, you later "clean things up, edit things out, fix things, and get a grip."

> *Many people*
> *who want to be writers*
> *don't really want to be writers.*
> *They want to have been writers.*
> *They wish they had*
> *a book in print.*
> —James Michener

It takes time, effort, energy, and work, to write a manuscript, and then revise the manuscript, over and over again. Former poet laureate, Mark Strand, says that some of his poems go through forty to fifty drafts, before they are finished. Ellen M. Kozak says that she retyped a 10,000 word short story, *fourteen* times, before anyone saw it.

John Gould believes that when you write a story, you're telling yourself the story. When you rewrite, your main job is to take out everything that is *not* the story. Take a positive and practical view of the revision process: Understand that every draft you write is practice for the next draft. Each draft gets better and better.

Write your first draft with your heart.
Rewrite with your head.
—Mike Rich

Understand that rewriting applies to every genre of writing. And a rough draft is rarely shown to anyone. It is messy and full of errors. Mine have large arrows, and Xs across paragraphs, and lines drawn through phrases, and blacked out words, with scribbled notes in the margins. As a famous author once remarked, your first draft needs a safe hatchery. You need to hide your ugly-duckling growth stages.

Your first draft is a rough draft, emphasis on rough. You just get it down as quickly a possible, without regard to correct spelling, punctuation, or typos. You didn't stop to revise, or look up words, or check back to see if you were repeating yourself. You just kept going at all costs. (Think of Jack Kerouac.)

When you are finished. Take a breath and a well-deserved break. Let your finished rough draft sit for weeks (take a vacation, if possible!), before diving into your rewriting. There must be a space of time between the act of writing, and the act of revision. You must be able to see your first draft with new eyes.

Proofread carefully
to see if you any words out.
—Author Unknown

Understand that revision does not simply mean adding or deleting words, but mindfully choosing words.

Then, step back and take a long look at why you even bothered—why you spent so much time, effort, and energy on this project. Why did it seem so important to you? Will your readers find it useful? Your rough draft isn't a waste of time, if you use the practice wisely. Experience writing as a blessing, not a burden. Handle your challenges with a chuckle instead of a curse.

If you can laugh at it,
you can live with it.
—Erma Bombeck

Your job in your second or third draft is to make your writing even more clear. You need to take out all the things that are *not* the story, and stick to the interesting parts.

The wastebasket
is a writer's best friend.
—Isaac Bashevis Singer

You may be a history expert, but make sure your story is front and center. One student was so fascinated with dinosaurs (from a very early age), that he put one whole chapter about them in the middle of his sci/fi manuscript. Although it was his best descriptive work, I convinced him to save it for another book, as it had no good reason to be in his story, and it would divide the reader's focus.

As any writer will tell you, it's not the writing that gets to you, it's the constant rewriting. Revision varies from writer to writer. You can rewrite and rewrite as you are typing your manuscript, so there is little to redo when it's through, or you can wait until it's finished, to start your revision. According to Jesse Kellerman, the majority of the work is done on the second through the 30th draft. Hemingway rewrote the last page of the ending to *A Farewell to Arms*, 39 times, before he was satisfied. Yikes!

Ignore your self-doubts. Look for glaring holes or errors. A friend, to her dismay, found that she had a nine-day week. Raymond Chandler forgot an entire character—the murdered chauffeur in *The Big Sleep*. When asked about this forgotten plot point, he replied, "Oh, him. You know, I forgot all about him." Egads!

Some writers take out items; other writers put in items. (I'm a putter-inner.) This is the time to polish, and check for accuracy.

One student wrote: " . . . spinning Patti Duke-style." The spelling of Patti should

> have been Patty, and my other red-letter
> written remarks were as follows: Although
> Patty Duke was in several *Amityville* and
> *Rosemary's Baby*-type flicks, I think the
> head-spinning happened in *The Exorcist*,
> starring Linda Blair. You may want to
> check it out, to be sure.

Revising your manuscript fifty times, or as many times
as you need to, "is what separates the professional
from the slug, the sung from the unsung." (I remember
the phrase, but not the author. Sorry!) Tolstoy revised
War and Peace over five drafts—all 1,225 pages
of the original manuscript—completely by pen. If
he could do it without the aid of a typewriter, or a
computer, you can, too. All you really need is paper
and a pencil.

Richard Paul Evens (11 books) says he writes for about
two months, then edits it an average of "800 times."
Yikes! I am constantly editing—even in my sleep.
(There are times when I will dream of a specific word
that would be perfect in a particular manuscript, but
when I race to computer room to make the change,
I find, to my dismay, that the book has already been
published!) Whatever I'm doing, if I think of a perfect
word or phrase, I run to the computer, and enter it
ASAP. Otherwise, I scribble it in the margins, or copy
down my treasure on any old torn piece of paper or
Post-it note, to insert whenever I get around to it.

CUTTING:

*I always listen for
what I can leave out.*
—Miles Davis

Experts tell us that every manuscript is collapsible to some degree, through prudent deleting. Kenneth Atchity says that 90 percent of your revision is cutting. Drop kick anything that takes away from the story. Cut the humdrum and the mundane. Terry L. Neal is a history scholar, and as such, included a ton of historical information in his novel, *The Search for Zerahemla*. Realizing that not everyone shares his passion for the past, he cut 25,000 words, and placed much of the history into an appendix, even though it was a novel. And Hemingway chopped the first four chapters of *The Sun Also Rises*. The rest of us would do well to follow their good examples.

*I believe more in the scissors
than I do in the pencil.*
—Truman Capote

We are advised to take out the boring parts, and leave in the interesting parts. Or, as Elmore Leonard says, "I try to leave out the parts that people skip." (This is tough for me, as I am usually *adding* phrases or paragraphs.) If something takes away from the story, you must be ruthless, and cut, cut, cut, even if you love it. As William Faulkner famously said, you must "kill your darlings." "Omit needless words," as Strunk and White famously wrote, while Thomas Jefferson said to never use two words when one word would do. Hemingway said that he wrote one page of masterpiece to 91 pieces of shit. The trick was to put the shit in the wastebasket. (But remember, practice makes perfect: Manure fertilizes the soil, even if it stinks to start with.)

It is perfectly okay to write garbage—
as long as you edit brilliantly.
—C.J. Cherryh

REVIEW: Before you end your writing process, check to see if you've followed the suggestions by Kurt Vonnegut, Jr.: (1) Find a subject you care about; (2) Do not ramble, though; (3) Keep it simple; (4) Have the guts to cut; (5) Sound like yourself; (6) Say what you mean to say; and, (7) Pity the readers.

Rewrite until you think that the book can't be improved any further. That's the time to send it in. Know that in the days of yore, agents and editors would work with authors to refine the manuscripts they felt held promise. Not so anymore. Nowadays, editors want a completely finished, highly polished product. Keep that in mind.

Best advice on writing
I've ever received: Finish.
—Peter Mayle

PART II

THE PUBLISHING PROCESS

PUBLICATION

Now this is not the end.
It's not even the beginning
of the end.
But it is, perhaps,
the end of the beginning.
—Sir Winston Churchill

C ongratulations on the completion of your manuscript! You have turned your wishes, desires, and aspirations into solid form by focusing on your writing. Your goal solidified, day by day, by aiming at your target with intention, attention, and total focus. You now have your finished manuscript—the Brass Ring—in hand. Hallelujah! Take some time to celebrate your efforts and the attaining of your goal. This is your "Look at me, I'm Sandra Dee!" moment; your time to shine. Pat yourself on the shoulder, and do a Snoopy happy dance. Have yourself one helluva party, if only in your mind. Savor it!

> *. . . to make an end*
> *is to make a beginning.*
> —T.S. Eliot

PUBLISHING BUSINESS:

> *You fail only if you stop writing.*
> —Ray Bradbury

As you may have heard many times, writing is an *art*. And you have done that. Now it is time for Part II of the writing process: publication. You must come to the cold, hard truth that publishing is a *business*, and you need a whole new set of knowledge and skills. It is often said that to be successful as an author, you must have something to say, you must know how to write it, *and* you must be able to sell it.

> *In America*
> *only the successful writer*
> *is important,*
> *In France, all writers*
> *are important,*
> *In England*
> *no writer is important,*
> *In Australia*
> *you have to explain*
> *what a writer is.*
> —Geoffrey Cotterell

When you first decide to write a book, the challenge

is to finish it. Once you do, you learn that completing the manuscript is just the beginning of your adventure. Creating your manuscript is simply Act I. Act II is the publishing your book. And Act III is getting it publicized.

As anyone in the business will tell you, there are few Cinderella stories in publishing. For every book that hits the bestseller list, or wins the Pulitzer Prize, thousands disappear without a trace. Traditional publishers of today simply can't afford to take a risk on an unknown. So unless you are involved in something notorious, or are already a celebrity, or have made a name for yourself in some other field, you're going to have to find a different way to get your work out before the public.

When my third book, *The Bogeyman: Stalking and its Aftermath,* was published (2003), several newspaper articles were written about it. *The Los Angeles Times* had a half page article (by Jill Stewart), above the fold, with the response being immediate, and *huge*. Former students, from all over the state, were calling the newspaper, asking for my contact information ("How dare someone mess with their third grade teacher!"), as were producers with movie offers. During that period, I was teaching full-time, delivering stalking speeches on weekends, and giving interviews, while mentoring victims on a face-to-face basis, as well as having book signings at various bookstores. So I didn't have the time or inclination to deal with the offers that were pouring in (some with checks upfront). As such, I hired a lawyer, to sift through them, to find the best representation.

She suggested that I sign with the William Morris Agency, which I did. I was under contract for a year, and the scriptwriter and some of the actors were in place, when everything came to a screeching halt. The O.J. trial began, and everyone in the world knew who Marcia Clark and Christopher Darden were, due to the daily televised court proceedings, and no one knew me from Adam's ox. So I was kicked to the curb, and they were hired. It certainly made sense, from a business point of view. Oh, well. That's showbiz!

AFTERNOTE: Over nine years later (2012), the book raised interest in some producers at the Investigation Discovery channel. One called (I initially hung up on him, thinking he was a telemarketer, and didn't answer his call the second time. He called a third time, after lunch, and I recognized his voice, and proceeded to give him a lecture again, before finally realizing that he was legitimate). A film crew arrived from New York, during the summer. Three producers were involved, and later complained about having too much material, for such a short time-slot. (According to the FBI, I was the longest-stalked person in the nation, at 51 years. My stalker died in 2011.) The episode became the Premier of a new season of "Stalked: Someone's Watching," on December 12th, of 2012.

INDUSTRY CHANGES:

If you've been paying attention to the industry, the publishing world has changed. Drastically. Small, independent bookstores have gone the way of the Dodo bird, as the giant bookstores and mega stores have taken over. Like Pac-man, the larger booksellers have gobbled up their competitors, with Barnes & Noble finally taking down Borders. Now, as the last man standing, Barnes & Noble is on its wobbly last legs. It appears that half the B&N stores square footage is now selling toys and teachers' supplies, to keep themselves afloat (which is also sounding the death knell to those few teacher's stores that are left).

Publishing houses have also been going under at a fast rate, as the bigger fish have been gobbling up the smaller fish. As a result, there are less publishers that are interested in new authors (being backlogged 2 years already), and less money is involved, and there are fewer bookstores in which to display them.

A friend got an acceptance, and then that company went under. Another friend, with a newly signed contract, has seen her publisher bought out by another publisher, who wouldn't publish the book. Other authors who had been given bonus money upfront, were then told to give it back. Friends who have called to complain about something or other to their editors, find that their editors have been fired, retired, or moved on to another publishing house. Those newbies who religiously send out their manuscripts, find them returned, unread. So they are out the postage both directions, and time, and are no further along than before. The industry is clearly in turmoil.

It used to be that you had to have three successful books in paperback, and then, if things went well, and you were lucky enough, you were granted a hardback. One friend took all the money she received from her first two books to publicize her third book, so as to ensure breaking into a hardback edition. Now, if you go the self-publishing or POD route, you can get a hardback right off the bat. But it costs more. And hardbacks aren't as popular any more, especially since ebooks are now all the rage. Since I was more interested in getting the word out, and had gone the submission route with my earlier books, I opted for POD, and later, ebooks, and have never looked back. (All authors, at heart, are driven by a desire to share their stories, ideas, or information, and to connect with readers, on some level.) Also, being concerned for my reader's pocketbooks, I had earlier opted for paperbacks, anyway. Of course, now, many established authors are choosing the ebook (Kindle, Nook, Sony reader) route, for a better money return.

In any case, whether you opt for traditional publishing houses, self-published books, POD, or ebooks, or whether you use the services of an agent, publicist, or marketing services, you *still* must be your own advocate. As Dan Poynter points out, "Books do not sell themselves. People sell books."

TIP: If you want to skip the whole query letter, rejection, agent, editor, publisher process, you can assure yourself of publication 100 percent, if you opt for self-publishing, or POD, or ebooks. You can write what you want to say, in the exact way you want to say it. And, to top it all off, unlike traditional publishing (in which, as Carolyn See rather harshly put it, that your book is *dead* after four months), your book can be available on the internet forever, like a sculpture or a painting.

TRADITIONAL PUBLISHING:

> *The large publishers are becoming*
> *increasingly irrelevant,*
> *and Amazon probably views them*
> *as the walking dead.*
> *They're probably right.*
> —Mark Coker, Smashwords

As mentioned above, the major publishers are not what they once were. According to Dan Poynter, "The relevancy of major publishers today can be compared with that of the traditional music industry (all but dead), FM radio (all but dead), or the three major TV networks (still breathing, but of increasing irrelevance in a 600 channels/D.I.Y. world)." They are teetering on the edge, and going the way of buggy whips. Many are those who say that traditional publishing is already dead.

QUERY LETTERS:

Query letters are simply meant to pitch an idea for an article, story, or book. Within the letter, you must also convince the agent or publisher as to why he or she should consider your work (no whining, boasting, or threats), as well as your qualifications to write it. There is an art to writing query letters, and whole chapters and books have been written about them.

Know that you don't have to have completed your project, to send out proposals (nonfiction) or partials (fiction).

Note again, that all this time, effort, and energy, can be avoided, if you self-publish or write POD or ebooks.

AGENTS AND/OR PUBLISHERS:

*Try to submit
to an agent or publisher
and you will be dead
before you hear back.*
—Denny Hatch

For years, I've heard it said that it is harder to get an agent, than it is to get a publisher. And it is also said that a publisher will not read a proposal unless it is presented by an agent. A seemingly Catch 22. Either way, it is time-consuming in the extreme.

The procedure for contacting both agents and publishers is pretty much the same: you submit a cover letter, biographical information, an outline or chapter-by-chapter description, and either a sample chapter or around fifty pages of material. In addition, you must include a return address, postage, and packaging.

You must tailor your cover letter to *each* individual agent or publisher by name and title, so even more time is spent in researching. (No "To Whom It May Concern" letters allowed.) And even if you find the right individual, by the time your package is received, that person may have jumped ship and now works for another company, or has retired, or died.

AGENTS:

Agents are essential,
because publishers will not read
unsolicited manuscripts.
—Jackie Collins

Experts say that you should have an agent. Most traditional publishers will not open your submission, unless it is presented by an agent. Unfortunately, I must confess that I have not had good experiences in that regard, so I can't speak to subject with any authority. Just know up front, that an agent will take 15 percent from your sales. I do know, however, that you must be your own advocate, whether or not you have an agent.

Two agents who were a team, told me to stop writing *The Bogeyman: Stalking and its Aftermath*, and work on *Toxic Attention: Keeping Safe from Stalkers, Abusers, and Intruders* instead. I couldn't understand why, since *The Bogeyman* was my personal story—as the longest-stalked person in the nation—and *Toxic Attention*, was a companion self-help manual. But I did what they suggested, stopping work on the 6th chapter—when I was on a roll—to begin the new book. When I finally finished it, I had lost track of the agents, and I never heard from them again. *The Bogeyman* then won The Book of the Year Award in the Category of True Crime. I learned the hard way, to believe in myself, and pay attention to my gut.

Know at the outset that I am a true bibliophile. I love books, and always treat them with respect. Even if I hated a book, and didn't want anyone else to read it, I couldn't bring myself to destroy it. (I even shudder at the TV commercial in which a mother throws a book over her back.) At a time in my life when I was overwhelmed by my daily schedule, I decided to hire an agent for help with my book publicity. I paid her $6,000 upfront, for a six week period. She requested copies of my book, and I sent her a crate full. I was already unhappy that she found fewer radio shows for interviews, than I had found for myself. The kicker came when I saw that she had ripped the covers off my brand new books, to paste on the front of pocket file folder kits, that contained info about the book. Hadn't she ever heard of a copy machine? *My heart hurt.* She could have sent the whole book, instead of just the cover. *What was she thinking?* I immediately severed our relationship.

SUBMISSIONS:

You must be absolutely relentless about submissions, over and over again. You cannot let this sort of thing disappoint and bother you. Take the view that a *specific* editor didn't like your story on a *specific* day. Maybe he had a fight with his wife or boss. Or he's having problems with his teenager, or has a financial concern. Or it could be that he is having problems dealing with his own novel. Who knows?

Most of the time, the packages are turned around without a glance, especially if they are submitted "over the transom" or into the "slush pile"(without an agent).

Hundreds of manuscripts arrive on a daily basis, and are simply too many to deal with. Publishers do not have the time or manpower to unwrap each one, read it, consider it, review it in a typed letter, rewrap it, and return the submission. So they simply ship the packages back, unopened. I was shocked, the first time it happened to me. I didn't realize that this was a daily way of operating.

When working on my doctorate, I was absolutely stunned to hear a Canadian Superintendent of Schools say that there were *no* openings in his district, and they were absolutely swamped with teacher applicants. So the secretaries kept the folders in which the applications arrived, and dumped the contents *without review*, not bothering to say, "Thanks, but no thanks." I was amazed to hear that this was also standard behavior in many American school districts. So many teacher applications arrive at small district headquarters, that they don't have the time, money, or personnel to *respond* to the applicants. I later talked with Superintendents in several small California school districts, who said the

> very same thing. One told me that her district had to hire extra clerks to deal with the onslaught (over 4,000 applications for *one* open position). It was mind-boggling.

And it is the same with publishing houses. Too many manuscripts come through the transits every day. Enormous odds are against your manuscript even being read. For instance, the editor of a small, literary magazine buys only three or four stories per issue (four issues a year). So the market is 12 or 15 stories *per year*, to which he receives 4,000 submissions. The odds are overwhelming, so the more you submit, the better your odds.

> *I don't want to know the odds.*
> —Han Solo, in *Star Wars*

Also, take into account that it is said that fewer and fewer people are reading fiction, and those who do are getting older and older. It is predicted that within a few years, there will be no fiction market left. I find that suspect, and hard to believe, but . . . Remember: Don't listen to the naysayers.

Not only that, but the industry is continuing to go through major changes, like newspapers. As mentioned before, first, the giant bookstores were running the independents out of business, gobbling them up like Pac-Man. Next, to further lessen bookstores income, the big retail giants, discount warehouse stores, supermarkets, and airports began selling books in earnest. Then came the nation's financial downturn. Finally, when only two national book companies were left, Barnes & Noble bought out Borders. Now B&N is having trouble making ends meet (with toy purchases at Christmas keeping them afloat). And, then, of course, the Print-On-Demand technology came upon the scene. The final blow has been the success of digital media, via wireless networking: ebooks (Kindle, Nook, ereaders), internet newspapers, magazines, blogs, and so forth.

REJECTIONS:

*If you're afraid of personal attacks,
you're never going to
make a difference.*
—Gloria Allred

Rejection is a rite of passage, a fact of the writing life. Every author has had rejections, especially some of the biggest names in the business. It is nothing to be ashamed of.

*You can't lead a cavalry charge
if you think you look funny on a horse.*
—John Peers

Look at rejection as a *process*, not an event. Your manuscript may not even have been read. The editor may have stepped in dog poop, or lost his keys, or experienced a bit of road rage on the way to work. The fact that *one* person doesn't like your manuscript, doesn't mean that it's no good. Ellen M. Kozak says, "In publishing, success is often based on the luck of the draw and what the editor had for breakfast the day your materials came in." Robert Orben (a humorist) agrees: "Do you realize what would happen if Moses were alive today? He'd go up to Mount Sinai, come back with the Ten Commandments, and spend the next eight years trying to get them published."

No one suffers as much as
the rejected writer.
—Betsy Lerner

Repeated rejections have been known to fill notebooks, insulate an attic, or paper the walls of some of the better-known writers. By the time most good writers start to publish their work regularly, they've amassed many hundreds of rejection slips, in all shapes and sizes. One author, Bob Kimber, calls it Ping-Pong. "You shoot a manuscript out, they shoot it back; you whack it back out there, it comes back." Many return without even being opened.

Sticks and stones can break my bones,
But words can break my heart.
—Robert Fulghum

A student teacher was heard to say: "You are a cancer. Cancer is bad!" she hissed. Now I ask you, *how does this help?* (I had recently had an operation in which a five-pound cancer had encapsulated my kidney, and both were removed. So that comment rather startled me.)

Words are loaded pistols.
—Jean-Paul Sartre

I suggest that you read negative reviews and rejections, only once, to see if there is a kernel of truth in there somewhere, and then toss them in the circular file. Don't ignore the feedback. Just decide whether it is valid. Be open, receptive, and responsive, just don't dwell on it and get all moody over it. You don't have to make any changes that are suggested. Go with your gut. And THROW THOSE REJECTION FORMS OUT! Then move on. While you're at it, note that editors don't always agree with each other. (One critic didn't like some of the titles of my wedding anecdotes, while the very next one said she *loved* the titles.) Know that you can't please everyone. If two or more say the same thing, however, you may want to take a closer look at your story.

If at first you don't succeed,
you're about average.
—Anonymous

NOTE: There are those who suggest that you keep such dated rejections for the IRS, as proof that you are attempting to run a business or sell your books. But it has been my experience that the taxman simply doesn't care. You have four years to turn a profit, after which they cut you loose, by saying that you only have a hobby. Vow not to let such discouraging words sway you from your writing efforts. *What does the IRS know about creative writing?*

Revise only if you see merit in the suggestions. Don't follow advice unless you believe that it has merit and is *sensible*.

Make sure that such a change would actually *improve* your material. **Reject the rejections!** Do not feel discouraged, slighted, or unworthy. Don't spend any time and energy on beating yourself up. Just determine to continue playing the Ping-Pong game. Or, looked at another way: Writing is a long-distance race. Never give up. Your main task is to persist.

If a wad of rejection letters
is all it takes to get you to quit writing,
then accept the consequences,
but understand that it was you
who gave that wad its power.
—Betsy Lerner

Always remember: It's the manuscript that has been rejected. Not you. The only person whose rejection really counts is your own. Take your frustrations out by whacking a ball on a racquetball court, or a golf course. Or you could try the bumper cars at an amusement park. Continue writing, and don't look back.

Rejection along with uncertainty
are as much a part of the writer's life
as snow and cold are of an Eskimo's.
—Ted Solotaroff

ACTIVITY: Write the title Rejection Letters at the top of the page. Draw a ladder with 6 fat rungs in it. Starting from the ground up, write:

- Rung 1: My manuscript is returned unopened.

- Rung 2: I receive a rejection form letter.

- Rung 3: I receive a rejection form letter with a scrawled note.

- Rung 4: I receive a personal note, saying in effect, keep trying, you're on the right track.

- Rung 5: I receive a note saying that they don't want this story or project, but send more work.

- Rung 6: I receive an acceptance letter. Yay!

Take heart as you climb the ladder. Remember,

writing is a Long-Distance Race. Submit your writing and continue on. Don't stop and wait for an answer. Keep up your momentum. (Of course, keep in mind that you can avoid all this wasted time and negativity by going the POD or ebook route.)

And speaking of ladders: I came across this paragraph, that really made me stop and think about how different our perspectives are:

> Remember the monkey bars? That "flat ladder across the sky" at the playground? That thing always intimidated me. First, there was the ladder up. Then the reach—waaaayyyy out. And then, when I finally grabbed on and let myself out on it, hanging from the bars felt like my arms were going to pull out of their sockets. Of course, there was more to it than what I understood—I had to do all that and swing to have fun on it.
>
> —Mary Lloyd

Personally, I *loved* the monkey bars! It never occurred to me complain about the blisters, blood, pus, or occasionally falling to the ground. I thought it was FUN! I was startled to read that someone found the monkeybars to be a negative experience.

In the same manner, I was shocked to see that a teacher would dash the hopes and dreams of a budding writer:

I am returning this
otherwise good typing paper to you,
because someone has
printed gibberish all over it
and put your name at the top.
—Purportedly by an English professor
(name unknown), at Ohio University

SELF-PUBLISHING:

Bookstores will die,
old-fashioned publishers will die,
and 90% of new books
will be published by their authors.
—Dan Snow

"Self-publishing was the only form of publishing for 400 years between Gutenberg and the Victorian era. It is not only honorable, it is historic," Godfrey Harris declares. Many well-known authors have switched (such as Stephen King, John Grisham, Louis L'Amour, and numerous others) to self-publishing.

TIP: Keep writing. Understand that each piece you write makes your being published more likely.

TIP: Your odds of being published become 100

percent the minute you are willing to self-publish. Write no matter what. Share your writing.

TIP: Don't throw anything out. Keep in mind that, years later, when you become known, you can republish your first books as is, or dust off some of your old ideas, rework them, and then publish them.

Know that many first books sell few copies. The odds are against you, but so what? Quality isn't a guarantee of success, for many reasons. (One being that over 300 titles are published each day.) Dan Poynter tells us that three books out of ten will sell well, four books will break even, and three will be losers. But if your main focus is to share knowledge, or a good story, what do you care?

> *You have reached*
> *the pinnacle of success*
> *as soon as you become*
> *uninterested in*
> *money, compliments, or publicity.*
> —Thomas Wolfe

The average self-published books sells 100 books. But you will print only as many as you want, at a reduced price. Selling more than 5,000 books is a rare occurrence. However, it can be done, as Louise L. Hay clearly shows. She says she was clueless about the publishing business, and ordered 5,000 copies of her first self-published book (because the more one prints, the cheaper they are). She sold them all within two years. Her second book (POD), *You Can Heal Your Life*, has sold 40 million copies worldwide. Wow!

TIP: If you grew up dreaming of having a book published by a traditional publisher, you can always have your manuscript self-published first, and then send copies of said book to agents or publishers. They can make an offer that you can either accept or reject.

PRINT ON DEMAND:

The POD books mean that you never have to buy a ton of books and store them in your garage, or haul them around in your car anymore. Readers order a book through your print company, or Amazon (and such, online), and it is manufactured on a laser printer in minutes, and delivered swiftly and directly to their doors. POD books also bypass the whole query letters to agents and publishers, and the rejection routine, saving yourself a lot of time, hassle, and stress.

COVERS:

There are books of which the backs
and covers are by far the best parts.
—Charles Dickens

We all know that you can't judge a book by it's cover. Still, it is done all the time. Especially by me. If I don't like the artwork—or lack thereof—I figure that the editors haven't bothered spending time or money on this book, so why should I? First impressions are important. Dan Poynter says, "Money invested in your cover will pay off in sales. Do not skimp on your cover."

The first week that J.K. Rowling's new adult book *The Casual Vacancy* was released, I couldn't believe the cover. It had the title and the author, and little else, other than a small square with a checkmark in it. Obviously, that didn't present a problem to other readers, as within hours of its release, it became number one on Amazon.

I had to argue about the cover of my first book. (A rough and tumble inner city two-story bunker of a school, including graffiti and trash vs. sleek one-story architecture with beautiful landscaping). For my second book, I found a T-shirt artist, and tracked him down, and asked him to draw the pictures, and do the cover (I paid him cash upfront! And when the book was published, he looked me up and asked for more money). My third and fourth books just arrived one day, out of the blue, with the covers already in place.

> (Thank God I liked them both! I know of authors who have wept over their covers.) I had numerous discussions concerning the children's cover for *Autism ABC* (very time-consuming!). And I was offered two choices for both of my *Imperfect Weddings are Best* and *Diabetes ABC*.

After explaining what you envision for your cover, POD publishers will give you choices. You can choose from their list of artists, or you can use your own artist, or you can do it yourself. You have input on both the covers and illustrations).

Jackets, like faces, tell you what's inside the book. The front flap, I've found, often tells you too much, giving away the whole storyline, so I never read them, until *after* I've read the book. Nowadays, after 51 years of being stalked, I scan the back cover and front inside jacket for the word *stalked*, and if found, I immediately move on to another book. (I don't need to dredge it all up again.)

Keep in mind that readers take an average of *three seconds* to choose a book. Of course, if I like the author, I automatically buy the book, without checking anything else. Most readers quickly scan the front cover, the back cover, and some will read the flaps. I go directly from the covers, to the first page, and read the first paragraph. That's it!

ILLUSTRATIONS/MAPS:

Know upfront that the illustrations and maps will take the longest time to complete, and that fact is not considered when giving you a publishing end date. I call it the Waiting Game. Illustrations can add as much as six months to a year to your end product. You are usually given the choice of illustrator (by style), and as much input as needed. Make your requests known beforehand.

Maps are your responsibility, which is difficult nowadays, as nothing seems as antiquated as a paper map. Terry L. Neal had to find an expert in Mesoamerican history, who could draw maps of various Mayan archeological sites. His search found a professor in Texas, who would draw the maps for him, at Neal's expense. After they were completed, and sent to him for approval, Neal sent them on to the publishing company. When all was said and done, the maps were reversed when published.

EBOOKS:

Bookstores are a lousy place
to sell books.
—Dan Poynter

Ebooks shorten the time between author and reader," explains Dan Poynter. To print your book electronically means that there are no printed copies to mess with. Your manuscript is simply in electronic form, on the buyers' Amazon Kindle, Barnes & Noble Nook, Sony Reader, iPad, iPhone, computer, and other such devices. It is the fastest, easiest, and most economical way to get published.

Even college textbooks have gone digital. "Each week, indie authors are hitting the ebook bestseller lists in all the major ebook retailers, as well as lists maintained by the New York Times, USA Today, Wall Street Journal, Galley Cat, and Digital Book World," says Mark Coker, of Smashwords.

Although the Oxford Dictionary of English defines ebooks as "an electronic version of a printed book," they can also exist *without* any printed equivalent. Some authors now write for ebooks only, and have made themselves millionaires in the process.

The number of people
who are reading printed books
is declining.
But reading isn't.
—Steven J. Vaughan-Nichols

SIMULTANEOUS PUBLISHING:

You can also publish an ebook at the same time you publish a print book, alongside that of an iphone, Pocket PC, and such. The print version establishes your credibility in a particular field, whereas an ebook will bring you a wider audience. Your pbook and ebook should look the same.

In addition, after your manuscript is finished, you have a built-in script for audio products (CDs, DVDs, or sold as a download).

AFTER PUBLICATION:

The road to publication is long, and the festivities are short lived. Anne Lamott points out that, "Publication is not going to change your life or solve your problems. Publication will not make you more confident or more beautiful, and it will probably not make you any richer," to which I add, Hallelujah to that. In fact, the publicity will cost you, over and above the printing costs. So, you're not going to make a fortune. But that will not be a concern to you, whose motivation to write is not financial.

Ten years from now, we will all be
authors, publishers, and booksellers.
—Mark Coker

PART III

THE PROMOTION PROCESS

PUBLICITY

I t is often said that the book business is 50 percent about writing, and 50 percent about visibility and promotion. Know that every form of book (printed, large-print, audiobooks, or electronic books) must be promoted by the author, whether they are traditionally published, self-published, PODs, or ebooks). This will cost you time, effort, and money. Understand that even if your book is on store shelves, you still have to get the buyers in the doors.

Calvin Trillin once famously said, that "The shelf life of the average trade book is somewhere between milk and yogurt." To which Carolyn See added: "The life of your book is directly comparable to boysenberry yogurt." Four months is the usual shelf life. So you must work to get your promotion in place, before your book is on the shelves. But if your book is a POD,

351

it can last a lifetime on the Internet (so the copyright date has no meaning for readers).

> *The oldest books*
> *are still just out*
> *to those who*
> *have not read them.*
> —Samuel Butler

Authors long for the ideal, which is a book that achieves both critical *and* commercial success. There are thousands of talented writers, but statistics show that less than 5% can support a family on their income.

My books have garnered much critical success (over 70 awards to date), but I have yet to be a commercial success, as I end up donating my books to various libraries, individuals, and causes, and I haven't invested in the proper publicity. (I am a teacher at heart, simply wanting to get the information out. In other words, I'd rather write than publicize.) Learn from my mistakes. Support your book!

PRESS RELEASE:

Press releases are common in the public relations field. For your purposes, a press release (news release, media release, or press statement) is a written communication directed at members of the news media, for the purpose of announcing your new book. They are typically mailed, faxed, or emailed to assignment editors at newspapers, magazines, radio stations, television stations or networks. There are commercial, fee-based press distribution services, as well as free website services, such as that offered by Dan Poynter's *ParaPublishing*.

A press release represents a potential interview or review opportunity. Last week a press release went out for *Diabetes ABC*. I received ten requests in one day, two the next day, and one on the third day. One came from Australia, and two from Canada, which really surprised me. The rest came from various states. Fraser P. Seitel refers to press releases as "the granddaddy of public relations writing vehicles."

REVIEWS:

> *Most of us would rather be*
> *ruined by praise*
> *than saved by criticism.*
> —Norman Vincent Peale

"The biggest mistake people make when it comes to self-publishing is that they expect to just put out a book and have it magically sell," says David Conroy of CNET Reviews. One way to support your book is through reviews. Book reviews sell books!

A book review is a critical analysis written by a third party (either a family member, friend, or book reviewer). It is important to get your reviews posted online (Amazon, Barnes & Noble, and so forth). Encourage lots of positive reviews. Target your audience via specialized publications: category magazines, journals, organizations, newsletters, ezines, and blogs, to see if they would be interested in interviewing you, or reviewing your book. Send out review copies.

Review copies are the least expensive
and most effective promotion
you can do.
—Dan Poynter

For a fee, you can get professional reviewers on your own. Try Publisher's Weekly, Kirkus Reviews, ForeWord Reviews, Library Journal, Booklist, and The US Review of Books, for valued opinions. There are websites on the Internet where you can get your book reviewed for no charge: Amazon.com, BooksaMillion.com, B&N.com, Smashwords, and so on. And check out AcqWeb's Directory of Book Reviews on the Web. You can also list your request for a review on Publishing Poynters Marketplace newsletter ezine.

I love criticism
just so long as
its unqualified praise.
—Noel Coward

Experts tell us that a bad review is better than no review, and that criticism is a form of caring (which may be hard to accept!). We are advised to say, "Thank you for caring. I feel warm all over."

The beginner scorns criticism.
The wise soul carefully weighs it.
And the master says, "But, of course!"
—Mike Dooley

Negative reviews will be hard to take, and you will see them as worse than they really are. "I have gotten prepub reviews that said I was a treadmark on the underpants of life," Anne Lamott assures us, adding in the next breath, "Perhaps this is not exactly what they said, but by reading through the lines, I could see that this is what they were implying." Don't do that.

Never pay attention
to what critics say.
Remember, a statue has never
been set up
in honor of a critic.
—Jean Sibelius

In response to Ayn Rand's *Atlas Shrugged*, Dorothy Parker said: "This is not a novel to be tossed aside lightly. It should be thrown with great force." Yikes! Even if a reviewer writes something negative, you can use the few positive words as quotes in your letters and advertising. Don't let it throw you. Find those nuggets and use them in your marketing and promotional material. Such quotations can also be used on the cover or jacket of your book. (Know, however, that you can't add words or alter the substance, and you must credit the reviewer.)

Focus on the amount of ink,
not the character of the words.
—Dan Poynter

Exposure of any kind will bring in orders. Some reviewers, such as BlueInk Reviews, will place your review on their website for a period of time, and then it will be moved to, and remain in, their archives. Dan Poynter says, "Hope for good ink and be grateful for bad ink. Ink is ink and ink is free."

I'm not interested
in pleasing the critics.
I'll take my chances
pleasing the public.
—Walt Disney

Then again, there is the opposite approach, encouraged by Jean Cocteau, when he said, "Note just what it is that the critics don't like and cultivate it. That's the only part of your work that's individual and worth keeping." And yet another voice is heard on the matter:

I don't read my reviews,
I measure them.
—Joseph Conrad

ADVERTISING:

Do not spend money
on advertising
until you have exhausted
all the free publicity.
—Dan Poynter

Publicity is free, advertising is not. Advertising in national newspapers and magazines is expensive (a full-page ad for one issue in the *New York Times* Book Review Section is more than $40,000!) This is justified by the fact that it will reach over four million people. But you are banking on the fact that all will actually *read* that section, and pay attention to your ad. I'll pass, thank you very much.

Check out the more reasonable and affordable local weekly or bi-weekly newspapers, and monthly magazines, and periodicals. And every now and then, they offer two for one deals, or other savings at a fraction of the cost.

Joe Vitale, author of numerous books, and a leading internet marketer, says that " . . . your business cards, letterhead, flyers, sales letters, and ads—everything you produce or hire someone to produce to market

DR. SHERRY L. MEINBERG

your business—all carry your energy in them." As a result, they will attract—or repel—the readers you say you want. He continues, saying that if you unconsciously don't believe in your book, that belief will appear in your marketing materials, and people will sense it.

Your unconscious beliefs and feelings count. If you are only in the writing business for the sake of money, and have no sincere desire to help or serve others, your attitude will show up in your advertising materials. People can feel your vibe, and your sincerity, and your book's benefits. Your confidence appears in your advertising. "A good ad can increase your business," he adds.

Sandra Zimmer, a public speaking and communication coach, who runs the Self-Expression Center in Houston, says, "Advertising is important, but it's the energy you put in the ads that does the work. It's really the law of attraction at work."

Esther Hicks agrees, saying, "It doesn't matter what you put in the ad. People will sense who you are, and what you are offering, and make a decision from that feeling." It's the intentional channeling of energy you put into your marketing materials that produces results.

The thing to remember is to set your intention, and magnetize your desire with your positive thoughts.

358

Vitale continues, "The energy you send out attracts what you get later." Keep your focus and energy on your target. He suggests that you create a powerful *thought form*, or ball of energy, and send it out into the world, to make your book dreams come true.

ARTICLES:

> *If you don't read the newspaper,*
> *you are uninformed;*
> *If you do read the newspaper,*
> *you are misinformed.*
> —Mark Twain

"I never expected to be in the papers. I personally never expected to be in the papers. The height of my ambition for these books was, well frankly, to get reviewed. A lot of children's books don't even get reviewed . . . forget good review, bad review. Personally, no, I never expected to be in the papers, so it's an odd experience when it happens to you," J.K. Rowling explained in an interview.

My first newspaper article, about my first book *Into the Hornet's Nest*, was printed in the Long Beach *Press-Telegram*, by columnist Tom Hennessey. It meant so much to me that I had it enlarged and framed. It still hangs in my husband's study. Since that time, I've had many interviews, in both small and large papers and magazines. Some ten years later, Hennessey wrote another article about my third book, *The Bogeyman:*

Stalking and it's Aftermath, and referred to the first article. That was really special to me.

According to Michael Levin, "People no longer read the newspaper, so they no longer read or are influenced by book reviews in newspapers." Yowsers! That may be so for the majority of readers, in this electronic age, but there are still those of us left who continue to read both local and national newspapers and magazines.

TIP: Send the publisher or specific columnist a letter, along with a copy of your book, suggesting an article or interview. It is worth repeating, that review copies are the least expensive and most effective promotion available.

INTERVIEWS:

Get your name out there! I enjoy being interviewed in local community newspapers (both daily and bi-weekly), as well as magazines. I have been interviewed in offices, restaurants, and in my home. All were interesting and relaxed experiences. Within one four-week period there were six articles written about me or my books (with different photographs), and then later, I placed ads in two of the newspapers. All of which engendered numerous responses. Emails, cards, and phone messages were all saying, "You're everywhere!"

I used to keep track of all the radio shows on which I had been interviewed, by placing their call letters on the back of my computer room door. When they finally covered the door, I discontinued that practice. I started out by sending a cover letter with my book, to hosts that I thought might be interested. When I ran out of local shows that I knew about, I then took out an ad listing on the *Radio-TV Interview Report*, and people started calling me. I was interviewed anywhere from 15 minutes, to two hours per show. Some were straight interviews, and others were listener call-in shows, from all around the nation.

Check out the *Radio-TV Interview Report* on the Internet. Each magazine issue reaches over 4,000 producers, hosts, and program directors. Being a guest on radio and television shows provides you with instant credibility and widespread recognition. Or you might try Alex Carroll's Radio Publicity Program. Over 200 million American commuters listen to the radio on their way to and from work, every day.

Mark Victor Hansen and Jack Canfield, co-editors of the *Chicken Soup for the Soul* series, insist on averaging at least one interview a day. Most radio talk-show hosts will interview you at your home. I can just roll out of bed, and be interviewed in my jammies, if the hour is too early for me. It doesn't matter what you look like, or how you are dressed, providing a much different experience than when you are interviewed at a radio or TV station.

Understand that you don't pay a station to be interviewed, and the station doesn't pay you. You are simply getting exposure; getting your name out there to potential buyers all across the country. Two cable stations asked for a good deal of money—around $2500—for a short interview, with more money being required for a longer interview. Yikes! Both were from Florida, which meant that the interviewee would have to pay for a round-trip ticket, food, and lodging, as well as transportation to and from the station. *Were they crazy?* I thought, since I was, by then, used to stretch limos picking me up from the New York airports, and so forth. (CNN recently sent a chauffeured Mercedes town car to pick me up from home, and drive me to and from the Los Angeles building site, for a short interview.)

Years after I no longer advertised in the *Radio-TV Interview Report*, I continued to get calls, so it was well worth the initial subscription fee. I was flown to New York on three different occasions (the TV shows paid for my flight, lodging, meals, transportation, and travel expenses), but the majority of my TV interviews were local shows and cable stations. After a half-page article about my stalking plight was published in the *Los Angeles Times*, a TV crew from Japan came over to my house, and interviewed me for nine hours straight. None of them spoke English, and I didn't speak Japanese, so an interpreter was the go-between. It was exhausting!

AWARDS:

> *I don't deserve this award,*
> *but I have arthritis*
> *and I don't deserve that either.*
> —Jack Benny

Awards are the most economical way to achieve recognition and publicity. Book Awards are said to represent the highest achievement of the writer's craft. They are noted to encourage new ideas, present new ways of thinking, and pave avenues for introducing much-needed changes in our world.

When my first, and second books were published, I didn't even know there were awards for books. Then, when my third book came out (2003), it received The Book of the Year Award, in the Category of True Crime, for *The Bogeyman: Stalking and its Aftermath.* Some nine years later, it became a TV premiere episode on the Investigation Discovery Channel in 2012. I was stunned. Since that first win, I have been honored with over 70 awards, to date.

Being a winner in a book award contest gives your book a solid Seal of Excellence unequaled by other forms of media exposure. Experts suggest that the best way to find out if your book has merit is to enter it into several book award contests. Along with the honor of winning one of these coveted awards, you will receive wider recognition and bragging rights, alongside the various festival benefits offered to the winners:

- Trophies, medals, plaques, and/or framed certificates;

- Cash for grand prize winners;

- Listings on their websites;

- Listings on your personal website;

- Listings published online;

- Listings in various magazines (Example: NAPPA gold winners are published in 40 parenting magazines);

- Press releases announcing the awards are forwarded to industry and consumer publications;

- Free classified ads;

- Seals/stickers for your books;

- Images of seals for your personal website;

- Images of logos for reprinted book covers;

- Marketing materials;

- Exhibits at trade shows;

- Increased exposure via social media; and,

- Testimonials for your next printing or sales materials.

Search for local writing groups in your area, and start to schmooze. Then check out regional, state, and national listings. The Internet is full of forums in which to voice your opinion, and make yourself known as an expert: genre-sites, chat rooms, and writing groups.

Amazingly, I have been a critical success, but not a monetary success. (One woman published a page of my *Autism ABC* on her website each day!) Luckily, my motivation is to write on particular subjects is to get the word out. (She got it out, all right.) In addition, I donate numerous copies to readers who will profit from the information involved, and to charities, and other organizations. I am still a teacher, at heart.

My advice is to check out the various book programs, contests, and festivals, to see if they would work for you. Being a winner in any category will gain you publicity, interviews, and talking points.

SPEECHES:

It usually takes me
more than three weeks
to prepare a
good impromptu speech.
—Mark Twain

Presenting speeches at various club meetings (while selling books at the back table) is a good way to be recognized as an expert. Clubs will place your name, and the name of your book, in their newsletters, both before and after the event. Some will even place ads in local newspapers. So, if nothing else, your name will be publicized. The number of those who show up for your speech will depend upon the size of the membership, and whether the event is open to the public, as well as the topic involved.

My first book, *Into the Hornet's Nest*, my third book, *The Bogeyman: Stalking and its Aftermath*, and my fifth book, *Autism ABC*, brought the most crowds. My favorite presentation, however, is a show-and-tell about censorship. I discuss close to a hundred children's books (depending on the time element involved), that somehow have managed to get banned. The audiences become outraged, and quite lively in their responses, when they find out that their favorite childhood books have been banned somewhere, for the most ridiculous of reasons.

TIP: Make your handouts memorable, and fit the occasion. Whatever printed materials you offer, try to match the colored paper with your outfit (branding). Whenever I present an anticensorship speech, I hand out little round, red, I READ BANNED BOOKS lapel buttons, as they leave (which I buy from the American Society of Journalists and Authors), as well as information sheets on various national anti-censorship organizations.

You never know what to expect. I drove several hours away, to a city that I hadn't been to before. When I finally found the place where the event was to be held (it was extremely hard to find), it was getting dark, and I needed to eat dinner beforehand. I was afraid to get too far afield, worried that I would get lost again. So I asked random people where the closest restaurant could be found. I got the strangest looks and responses. I later found out that I was in what was considered to be the seedy part of town, and that people were expecting me to be either a panhandler or a prostitute. Their odd expressions showed that I neither dressed nor spoke the part of either, and they were thoroughly confused.

One speech had about sixty people in the audience, with everyone interested and totally involved. Then a thoroughly drunk couple wandered in the door, and sat down in the last row. While the audience was focused on me, I could see the couple's antics, and it was hard not to watch them, as they were so out of control. They were trying to be quiet, but talked in stage whispers. At length, the woman started to get up to leave, lost her balance, and landed in a heap on the floor. The man tried to grab her, and fell on top of her. They both started giggling, and then laughed uproariously, as they rolled around on the floor, knocking the folding chairs this way and that. At which point, I completely lost the audience . . . until the couple left the building.

One Saturday, I was scheduled to give a speech at Sherlock's Home, a mystery bookstore. Just as I was about to leave, someone from the Teacher Supplies of Long Beach called, saying they were out of my books, and the customers were getting unruly, and pleaded with me to bring them some more copies. Since the stores were both on Second Street, about a mile or so apart, I said I'd bring some down. I hastily tossed a bunch in a large paper bag, and took off. The parking at the shore is difficult, so I wasted some time finding a space. Then, as I was hurrying down the sidewalk, the paper bag tore apart, and books fell all over the place. People helped stack them in my hands, one on top of the other, as I held the top one in place with my chin. I moved on to the front door of the shop, where a crowd was trying to enter the already packed store. One woman elbowed me in the side, to move in front of me. (I'd always heard of such rudeness, but had never been on the receiving end beforehand.) Everyone was loudly clamoring to get in. When a clerk opened the door, they demanded my books, which they had ordered some time prior, and were tired of waiting. (Think peasants storming the castle.) It was gratifying, and scary, at the same time. The woman in front of me was quite vocal, arguing with the clerk, who responded that the shop was out of said books, but that the author was standing behind her, and perhaps she had brought some books with her. All talking stopped, as everyone turned to stare at me. The rude woman, without saying a word, grabbed a book, and then so did the mob. Suddenly, I was pushed through the door, *without* any books, that had all quickly vanished. Everyone had questions, and wanted me to answer them, right then and there. I said that I couldn't, as I had a speech I was to deliver down the street, but someone hauled over a stool, and everyone was insistent. The owner and the manager were beside themselves, since I had no idea how many books I had brought, so money was an issue. Since I had to leave forthwith, they decided just to tally how many *Into the Hornet's Nest* books were sold that day, and we would deal with it later. The teachers were not happy that I wouldn't give them a Q & A period, even though I had a valid excuse. I left some unhappy people behind, who thought *I* was being rude.

BOOK SIGNINGS:

When you have book signings at bookstores, remember to say something that readers won't find in your book. Answer all questions, and stay as long as you can. That makes it worthwhile for readers to make the effort to come out and meet you. After all, they can read your book, but they came to see *you* in person. (I have already read, underlined, and highlighted authors' books before I make the trek to listen to them.)

TIP: My advice is to choose particular passages to read aloud, and don't wait until the last minute. I thought that all of my examples were funny, and that I could just flip open the book to any page, and find a great example. What I didn't take into consideration was the fact that many of the students I was quoting, used foul language, which I am unaccustomed to saying. So I was reading along at a fast clip, and came to a screeching stop, when I came upon certain words that I couldn't say aloud. My apology fell on deaf ears, as some of my audience thought it was a ploy to have them buy my book. Boy, was my face red!

TIP: Place Post-it notes and several pens on the back table, next to your books. Have each person who is buying a book—and wants it autographed— to PRINT his or her name, so you can easily copy it correctly. It will save you time, and you won't ruin any books with misspellings.

I have experienced many book signings in various Barnes & Noble bookstores, independent bookstores, teachers' supply stores, clubs, schools, libraries, and conferences. They were all different, and memorable, in one way or another. At one such event, I sold only three copies, at another, the Borders managers told me that they had never had such a heavy turnout, as my line snaked back and forth and out the front door. One little bookstore had me sitting outside on the sidewalk, as pedestrians and their dogs passed by. At another, I sat next to Steve Allen, and we chatted and laughed throughout the whole conference. You just never know what to expect. (For instance: I received an email from Apostrophe Books—where I had a book signing several weeks prior—saying that they had completely sold out of my books, and asked for more copies. So I gave them ten more signed copies of *Autism ABC*. How totally unexpected, and appreciated!)

> The following story was published In the Orange County Sisters in Crime newsletter (*The Orange Herring*, Issue Vol. 3 No. 4, April, 1994). It is a tad long (even though I did some cutting), but it gives you an idea of what may be in store for you, when you take part in a book signing event.

THE CASE OF THE SOUR SIGNING

Having participated in several seriously successful book signings, I naturally thought that a signing at the B. Dalton Bookseller in the Lakewood Mall (CA) would be a similar experience. As such, I planned to simply enjoy promoting my first book, *Into the Hornet's Nest*, and held high hopes for the situation.

A mall signing, I found, is an altogether different state of affairs:

Indeed, the experience started out on a pleasant note, when the store manager already had a large sign, a table with books and brochures, and chairs in place when I arrived. She then brought me a large Perrier, with two glasses of ice, and left me with a smile and a wave. She was not only prepared, but was courteous, helpful, and encouraging (which is not always the case).

Even so, I could see from the outset that things were going to be different. Settling in, I glanced at the books on the shelves right behind me, and realized that the Howard Stern books—with his nearly nude body on the cover—were stacked directly over my shoulder. *I don't know if that will help me, or hinder me*, I giggled to myself. A short time later, when the manager waltzed by, she realized that a tattered copy was showing. As she reached to take it down, a young woman in her early twenties, who was just strolling down the mall, shrieked, wide-eyed: "Don't take Howard Stern down! That's a great book!" She looked around for support from others, as a small crowd of strangers gathered to watch the excitement, and then slowly drifted off, when no more was forthcoming. I hope this is not indicative of the way things are going to go, I worried. And rightly so!

First of all, the date was a disaster (being the same Saturday that 1200 teachers in the Long Beach Unified School District were taking the dreaded LDS exam: under duress, I might add. They were so stressed about the situation, they planned to move directly to the bars thereafter, to drown their sorrows. And these are the teetotalers I'm describing! So none of my colleagues would be visiting me in a show of support.

Right off, it was clear that many of the people walking by hadn't one iota of interest in books. Some of the ones who actually wandered into the store seemed to be functioning illiterates. An elderly man—obviously homeless—stood by me for a three-hour period, not moving from "his" spot. He constantly leafed through a book as he talked, gestured, and laughed to himself, throughout the afternoon. It was rather disconcerting. For quite some time, I watched the fashion (or lack thereof) parade, and was truly surprised at what some people considered appropriate attire. I suddenly came to the startling realization that, through the passage of years, I had somehow become an old fuddy-duddy! At least the costumes kept my mind off the fact that *no one was buying my books.*

The first man to approach me asked where the automotive books were shelved. The second man wanted computer information. Then a young woman pleaded, "Is the book about John Kennedy, Jr. in yet? Please say it is! I've been waiting and waiting for a copy!" *Well, I'm sure taking this place by storm,* I concluded.

Another man—whose shirt announced to the world that his name was Vince—walked up to me and grabbed a book. Taking a short glance at the cover, he slammed it back down on the table. "I don't even have to read this book to know that it was written from a liberal point of view!" he shouted, as he charged back into the bookstacks.

A few seconds slipped by, and he was back again. Looking at the cover, he again shouted, "Hah! This is about the inner city, where all the blacks live. I'm from Alabama, and was in the service with about 90 percent blacks. I worked with them, I lived with them, and let me tell you, *they're not human!*" I was shocked by his attitude. He then launched into a diatribe about how the blacks have ruined our country, what with all their demonstrations, Dr. Martin Luther King, Jr., and so on. Having said that, off he stormed (I was thankful that some of my friends who just happened to be African Americans, and had told me they were coming, had yet to arrive.) How embarrassing!

Another man strolled by with his young daughter, and said that his wife was a teacher in Long Beach, and that she was taking some horrible test. I sympathized. He later came back and bought a copy of my book. "To make her laugh," he said.

Vince returned, picked up my book, and read my name aloud: "Dr. Sherry L. Meinberg. Meinberg, *Meinberg!*" His head jerked up, and his eyes bored into mine, as he shouted, scarely containing himself, "Are you *Jewish?!*" (I'm Irish, actually, but didn't feel that my ethnic background was any of his business.) He then launched into a scathing attack, of what he termed, the Jewish situation. "Jews are worse than blacks, because they are the ones that got the blacks all fired up to demonstrate to begin with!" He rattled on and on, from a conspiracy angle, with his eyes seemingly rolling around in their sockets. After venting his thoughts on the subjects, he steamed off down the mall. (I was amazed to see such a vocal outburst in California, and was glad that my Jewish friends did not have to see such a sad display of anti-semitism). But I learned something important: Even though I had worked for the better part of my life in an urban environment, I had never seen such adult hostility before. I always thought it was still a political and social issue for a few pockets of people down South, who clung to the old stereotypes. Boy, was I wrong! It seems that racism is alive and active in the west, as well.

Shortly thereafter, a black man in his early twenties

stopped to discuss the publishing business. He was a struggling poet, who just needed some direction and support. *His timing is great, if nothing else,* I thought, as he just barely missed Vince.

About this time, a striking woman arrived, and slid a large photograph toward me. I didn't recognize her, but I *did* remember the photo. It was a copy of my first grade class's picture, taken when I was five years old. I was standing in the front row, and so was she—right next to me. What fun to reminisce and discuss our youth!

A man sailed by, waved and shouted, "Too bad! My wife just bought your book two weeks ago!" Then a photographer arrived to take my picture for an upcoming newspaper article. Sadly, there were only two fans there at the time.

Another woman came on the scene, and while she was talking to other adults standing around me, her three-year-old daughter climbed up on my lap. She began scribbling a picture, with my red felt pen, on the back of one of my fliers. "What's your name?" she asked conversationally, while continuing her creation. The five-year-old brother, seeing what fun his sister was having, grabbed my ball point pen and told me that he intended to *keep* it. *Isn't it nice that children feel so comfortable around me?* I thought, while trying to unclench my teeth. Their nonstop fussing and fighting definitely impeded any further discussion I might have had with potential customers.

Throughout the afternoon, it did not escape my attention that whenever a *man* seemed to overstay his welcome, my husband (who had planted himself in the middle of the mall directly across from me), felt duty bound to move in. He acted in a very official capacity, by straightening up my table area, pouring me water, and discussing my book, while standing as close to me as possible. If that didn't convey his intended "territorial rights" message, his deliberate stare (used as a last resort) did. I found it terribly amusing, but oddly comforting, at the same time, considering the fact that we'd been married for twenty-three years (at the time). His stance, however, did *not* help me sell books.

A number of young teenage girls were causing quite a noisy spectacle. It turned out that they were all excitedly discussing *me* (a real live author!). I was the subject of a lot of interest and commotion, but again, I sold no books.

Vince returned. He showed me the stub of his paycheck ($127.00 for a two-week period), and said that was the reason he hadn't bought my book to begin with. But he had thought better of it—after all, I had listened to him (*Did I have a choice?* I mused)—so he'd come back for a copy. When I didn't offer to give him a copy, he finally paid for one. I signed it, and he left, while I mentally dusted my hands of him.

A constant ebb and flow of people passed by me, and I chatted for the whole three-hour session, but only sold a total of eleven books. I did, however, get a job offer (from a private school in town), touched bases with several old friends, and happily discussed "growing up" and "changes" with three former students, who just happened by. Happily, the manager of the local Marie Callendar's Restaurant dropped over to invite my husband and me to "dinner on the house." I couldn't believe that I was finally getting a *perk* from all this publishing business. Wow!

As I was starting to pack up and leave for the restaurant, Vince returned. He managed to change his whole delivery, focus, and facial and body language, as he *pleaded* with me to help him get a job as a *teacher!* He grabbed one of my business cards, as he exited, stage right. My husband's response was, "You always did attract the weird ones!" (I refrained from responding that I had also attracted *him!* Some things are better left unsaid.)

Unfortunately, my story wasn't over yet. Vince called me twice on Monday, at 8:00 A.M. and again at

11:15 A.M. I began screening my phone calls. I had a sinking feeling that I might remember this particular book signing for a long time to come.

PUBLICITY:

Most new books are unadvertised, ignored, and forgotten. A great book no one knows about does not fulfill its purpose. Publishing Houses will not do any publicity, unless it is for an author in the category of Dan Brown. A book's success depends upon great public relations and marketing. Experts say that 90 percent of what it takes to succeed is publicity, marketing, and promoting. The bottom line is that promotion is a do-it-yourself proposition.

Understand that any time a writer gets any ink or publicity, it's good news, even if you are misquoted, which has been my experience in every print interview of mine. (In fact, in the TV episode about my stalking experiences, I was interviewed over the phone several times, and then in person for four hours straight, and they had the book in their hands, and *still* got a number of facts wrong).

The only thing worse than being talked about—
Is not being talked about.
—Oscar Wilde

It doesn't take a genius to realize that you can't sell your book if people don't know about it. Most authors have to throw their own book parties, or finagle friends into marking the celebration (this is where book clubs are very useful), or schedule and bear the cost of book tours.

Dan Poynter suggests that you don't spend any money on advertising until all the free publicity is exhausted. I contacted local newspapers, and was interviewed and photographed by them, and I later advertised in several, as they were cheaper than the larger newspapers. Within a relatively short period, five articles were written about me, and people were contacting me, saying that I was "everywhere." It was fun to see everyone's reaction.

In fact, Dan Poynter, the self-publishing, cutting-edge guru, has written two books on the subject, that should be in every writer's library: *Dan Poynter's Self- Publishing Manual: How to Write, Print and Sell Your Own Book*, and *Dan Poynter's Self-Publishing Manual: How to Write, Print and Sell Your Own Book Employing the Latest Technologies and the Newest Techniques Vol. 2.*

Without an agent, you must schedule your own radio, TV, and print interviews, as well as bookstore meet-and-greets. (I booked more radio interviews than my agent, which was another concern of mine.) The more you are able to do on your book's behalf, the better. Publicity is key to getting attention for your book. Understand that every time you get any ink or airtime, you're ahead of your competitors. Experts tell us to do *five* things each day to promote our books. Yikes! I'm lucky to do one thing now and then, but I do it as often as I can. And I get results.

TIP: It has been suggested that for every two hours of writing, if you put in 15 minutes of publicity, you would have 50+ hours of promotion per year.

> *Everything comes to him*
> *who hustles while he waits.*
> —Thomas Edison

PUBLICITY STUNTS:

A publicity stunt is a planned event, designed to attract the public's attention. I don't recommend them, as they can backfire. "It's kind of like dating," says Geoff Williams ("Top 10 Successful Marketing Stunts," *Entrepreneur*, 7/20/06). "There's a lot of effort involved, and sometimes, humiliation." However, if you're already a known megastar, or involved with a large company, it can work for you, no matter how shameless.

> Consider comedian Joan Rivers (2012), all dressed up, holding a bullhorn, and shouting both outside and inside a Costco in Burbank (because they didn't carry her book!), as she handcuffed herself to

a shopping cart in protest. Police were called. Her team sold 150 books out of a box in the parking lot. Cash only. She received major exposure to millions of people (via TV news, follow-up talk shows, newspapers, and cell phones), and it didn't cost her even one thin dime.

Kristina Reed, a Disney producer, was removed from the Dolby Theatre by security, during the Oscars event (2013), after she was caught throwing paper airplanes from the balcony. Newspapers around the world blared the news that she was kicked out, thrown out, tossed out, or booted from her seat. Her paper airplanes had lipstick kisses on them, as did those thrown by the male character in her film (which won the Oscar for Best Animated Short), who used paper airplanes to get the attention of a girl. After arguing with security, Ms. Reed was finally escorted back to her seat, within ten minutes time. Whether it is viewed as a blatant publicity stunt, or a cute, clever way for harmless fun and self-promotion, Ms. Reed received a great deal of free international press, as a result.

PUBLICISTS:

Hiring a publicist isn't a vanity,
it's a realistic commercial decision.
—Paul Cowan

Your book promotion is up to you. If you have neither the time, expertise, nor the inclination to promote your book, you may feel the need to hire your own professional publicist or marketing service. A publicist's job is all about going the extra mile for pitching your title with reviewers, but they rarely do more than send out the book, and make follow-up calls. Know up front that hiring an independent publicist may not yield further public notice or press, and you won't know if it is a lack of effort on his/her part, or simply that reviewers are uninterested. Unless, of course, you make it known that you expect specific feedback. Some publicists and marketers specialize in certain genres (science, cookbooks, Christian, computers, etc.), so you might want to search for them. With or without a publicist, however, you need to roll up your sleeves, get busy, and apply your own elbow grease.

Even if you're being published through a major publishing house, their promotion is now next to nil (since they no longer support the majority of their authors), so you may want to hire your own publicist, for a short period of time (say a two to six months contract). Publicists generally put together a press kit and marketing materials, place news releases, obtain reviews, place strategic ads, set up radio, television, and print interviews, organize autograph parties and book tours, and send media alerts. Some build websites, juggle social media campaigns, and supervise blogging and webcasting: whatever you want. Know up front that publicists are expensive. The monthly retainer is somewhere between $500 and $8,000, depending on your needs. You can do-it-yourself, of course (Check out Dan Poynter's *Self-Publishing Manual: How to Write, Print and Sell Your Own Book*, and *The Self-Publishing Manual, Volume II*. Also, *Sell Your Book on Amazon, Second Edition*, by Brent Sampson), and you can hire a publicist for a couple of specific functions.

For instance: Irwin Zucker's Promotion in Motion firm will book you with radio interviewers (all over the nation) for only a nominal fee per show. He is the founder of Book Publicists of Southern California (1976), which prints a glossy bi-monthly newsletter, *Know Thy Shelf*, that keeps readers up-to-date with member, local, and national book public relations news. The dues are only $40.00 a year (the lowest of all similar organizations). The meetings are a good place to schmooze with authors and media personalities, and publicize your book, as you listen to informative speakers and celebrities. Many members live in other states, and are unable to visit the meetings, but enjoy the newsletter, and the networking interaction and advice among authors, publicists, publishers, and suppliers, in both print and broadcast media. All find the member directory useful, and enjoy the prestigious annual IRWIN Awards. Check out their meetings and membership:

Book Publicists of Southern California
714 Crescent Drive, Beverly Hills, CA 90210
(323) 461-3921 Cell (323) 497-4001
website: www.bookpublicists.org

PART IV

WRITER'S HELPERS

WRITER'S HELPERS

The difference between winning and losing
is often . . . not quitting.
—Walt Disney

SELF-CARE:

Self-caring is being responsible
and not allowing any excuses.
—Alexandra Stoddard

Tend to yourself first (fasten your seatbelt, and as the airlines direct, apply the oxygen mask to yourself before helping others). Attend to your joy. Focus on taking great care of yourself. Stop abandoning yourself. Treat yourself as the most important person in your life.

If we don't take care of our bodies
where will we live?
—Louise Hay

Pay attention to your health needs. Writers need to pay attention to eyestrain, headaches, neck aches, backaches, and carpal tunnel syndrome. Good health is a prerequisite for tackling your writing challenges. Take care of yourself *first*. Involve your whole being in the idea of being healthy. See yourself as healthy, regardless of circumstances. You can improve your health in simple ways. Do some good self-mothering (feed yourself, drink more water than sodas or coffee, pace yourself, nurture yourself, protect yourself, rest, and get some fresh air).

"Even the smallest amount of self-nurturance will have an immediate and beneficial impact on your writing," says Julia Cameron. Pamper yourself. Experts say that the more you love and nurture yourself, the better you are able to love and nurture others. Engage in more self-care activities (hair, manicures, pedicures, massages, facials, fun stuff, meditation, sleep). "Whatever minor indulgences you choose, their payoff is more energy, both physical and emotional," Victoria Moran assures us. Compassion starts with you. Treat yourself with love. As Louise Hay says, "Loving ourselves works miracles in our lives." She further adds, "When we really love ourselves, everything in our life works."

Write when you are ready. Be gentle and patient while you're learning to write. Expect both peaks and valleys in the writing process, and don't let them throw you.

Being good to oneself
is not selfish,
it is self-preserving.
—Robert S. Cowles III, M.D.

EXERCISE/MOVEMENT:

Those who think
they have no time for bodily exercise
will sooner or later
have to find the time for illness.
—Edward Stanley

There is nothing that is more consistently prescribed by doctors than to exercise regularly. It is the best-known, scientifically-proven method to significantly reduce stress. Actually, any kind of activity that gets you *moving* is good for you: exercise, yoga, belly dancing, Tai Chi, aerobics, martial arts, bicycling, skating, sports, and so forth. You don't need to invest in a gym membership or expensive equipment. "Doing anything physical is much better than remaining inactive," says Deepak Chopra, M.D.

Andrew Weil, M.D., recommends that people make walking their primary form of exercise. Many experts—in various fields—suggest walking for health. They recommend walking for at least 20 minutes, three times a week, or ten minutes each day. In addition, you think better on your feet, and exercise feeds your brain. Gary Small, M.D. says that "Physical exercise appears not only to keep brain cells alive, but also to grow new neurons." Dharma Khalsa, M.D., agrees, making a strong case that a regular exercise program can slow the aging of your brain, defend against the loss of memory, and prevent Alzheimer's disease. Plus, as Dan Millman says, "Getting in touch with the earth and growing things, can help you reconnect with your own nature."

Know that: "All practice is mental as well as physical. And the reverse is also true: movement in the body brings movement in the mind," says Carolyn Scott Kortgeln, in *The Spirited Walker*. As an added bonus, you may find a number of things to write about, just by taking a walk in your local park or mall.

> (I shared this story with others via email, and it wound up in the *Beachcomber* newspaper, by Steve Propes, news reporter.)
>
> At 5:30 AM, 2012 Amazing Woman winner, Dr. Sherry L. Meinberg, was out "walking up the middle of Stearnlee towards the park, with no cars or people out and about yet, when, I swear, a coyote ran across in front of me, by maybe three feet. I could've reached out and touched it. I was astounded, as it zoomed back down the street. It didn't even glance at me,

as it was so focused on something else. It was very weird—and scary—because I knew I had to walk back in that same direction. So much for my resolve to start walking again."

Walkers are known to be people who step out with purpose, step forward, and make a move. Stephen King says that the secret of his success is that he stayed healthy, he walked daily (until his accident), and he stayed married. Something to think about.

REST/RELAXATION:

There is never a reason
not to relax.
—Kedar Harris

Slow down, let go, unwind, put your feet up, and relax. You need to factor in some down time. There is a difference between being busy and being driven. You can't keep your nose to the grindstone and your shoulder to the wheel all the time. Give your overworked brain and body a rest. Relaxation is vital to ensure your health and well-being. Allowing stress to affect you can lead to depression, illness, weight gain, and such. Get your anxiety under control by relaxing. Have plenty of interludes in which to do nothing but putter, wander about, and be totally unproductive. Cuddle up with a good book (on a different subject than your manuscript!), or unwind with a hobby, or spend time with your pet. Don't plan on the *when* and *how* of your leisure time, just do what comes to mind, when it comes to mind. Your body knows when it needs a break.

Strive, persist—
and then relax.
—Alexandra Stoddard

BREATHING:

We live our lifetime
one breath at a time.
—Alexandra Stoddard

Catch your breath! Start where you are. It doesn't take a high IQ, or education, or talent, to take that first step. It has been said that writing is like breathing. It's possible to do it well, but the point is to *do it no matter what.* (For instance, I am a shallow breather, but I'm still here. Inhaling and exhaling *is* my exercise. Granted, I can't do yoga or some types of meditation—due to allergies—but I can still do *some* things well.)

As good as your mind is, it's not at its best
unless you get the circulation going,
the oxygen flowing, the blood flowing.
—Joan Price

Experts say that the easiest way to self-calm, is to

slow down your breathing and concentrate on it. Breathe in through your nose, and out through your mouth. Inhale deeply and count to five, hold your breath for five seconds, then exhale slowly, counting to five. It is suggested that you do this ten times, to relax your muscles and nerves.

Visualize the stress and tension leaving your body. Brian Weiss, M.D., suggests, "Breathe out stress and tensions, breathe in beautiful energy." Victoria Moran advises: "Tell yourself as you inhale that you are breathing in life and strength and glorious possibilities. When you exhale, know that your are expelling the mental pressures, aggravations, and limitations that may have held you back."

Dan Millman suggests that you take at least one slow, deep, deliberate breath every hour, for the rest of your life, and relax as much as you can in everything you do.

> *You ain't living*
> *if you ain't breathing hard!*
> —Mac Eakin

Every time you breathe in, thank a tree. Trees are the longest-living organisms on Earth. They beautify and protect our environment by adding color, shelter, and shade. They renew our air supply by soaking up carbon dioxide and producing oxygen.

Plant trees, under whose
shade you do not expect to sit.
—Nelson Henderson

SIDEBAR: It takes six trees to replace the consumption of 100 reams of copy paper. When each book of mine is published, I always donate money to local (city and county) tree organizations. Won't you join me?

SIDEBAR: Combat deforestation! Note that there are many national tree organizations that would gladly accept author donations: The Arbor Day Foundation, Trees for the Future; Save the Redwoods; The Nature Conservancy, American Forests, Conservatree, Tree Neutral, Archangel Ancient Tree Archive, and so forth. If you would prefer to actually help plant trees, there are many tree projects, as well: One Million Trees Project, ABA Seer's Planting Project; Tree Bank; TreeLink, and so on. Consider replenishing the stock.

The clearest way
into the Universe
is through
a forest wilderness.
—John Muir

INTENTIONS:

Keep your thoughts
on what you intend to create.
—Dr. Wayne Dyer

Anyone who has been paying attention during the last couple of decades, realizes that physicists and metaphysicians have arrived at the same conclusion: *Form follows thought.* Todd Michael, M.D. talks at length, in his fascinating book, *The Twelve Conditions of a Miracle*, about the translation of the phrase in John, "In the beginning was the Word . . . " He states that because the original Greek contains layers of highly subtle innuendo, it does not readily translate into English. As such, he suggests that a more accurate translation would be along the lines of, "In the beginning was a thought with a powerful potential, a creative intent . . . ," and so on.

You, too, can turn your hazy thoughts and wishful desires into strong intentions. Set your writing goals, and work toward them, without wavering. According to Dr. Abraham Maslow, a sense of purpose is at the very top of the pyramid of self-actualization. And Stanford University physicist William Tiller, through various experiments, has concluded that directed thoughts produce demonstrable physical energy. Other scientists agree, showing that changes can occur simply through the act of intention. "Your imagination is your preview of life's coming attractions," said Albert Einstein. And still other scientists (compiled in *The Intention Experiment*, by Lynne McTaggart) have shown that attention, belief, motivation, and confidence are important in the process of intention. Philosophers and historical figures are also mentioned in Dr. Wayne Dyer's colorful book, *The Power of Intention*, showing that intention determines everything. And *The Amazing Power of Deliberate Intent*, by Esther and Jerry Hicks, emphasizes the importance of harnessing the power of your thoughts and intentions.

> *Every intention is*
> *a trigger for transformation.*
> —Deepak Chopra

Intent is the mother of creation. The clearer you are about your writing, the easier it will be to reach your goal. Your desire to write "does not elevate to the level of intent until there is a commitment to bring that desire into fruition," says the Reverend Deborah L. Johnson, in *Your Deepest Intent*. You must have a Yes! in your heart, stake your claim, and keep your eye on the end result, to keep your writing flame burning.

> *Intention rules the earth.*
> —Oprah Winfrey

Your writing is all about an "ongoing, never-ending refocusing," as Esther and Jerry Hicks remind us. "Whenever you take the time to focus on something and write it on paper, your focus (and power) increases." So send your intentions out into the Universe. "Your intentions are your Universal order forms," says Sandra Anne Taylor, so you must be specific. Persistence counts. Determination counts.

BREADCRUMBS FOR BEGINNERS

When you set clear intentions, focusing on them with strong emotion, and take action, you are setting up a self-fulfilling prophecy.

> *All we really need*
> *is clarity of intent.*
> —Deepak Chopra

BELIEF:

> *If one is lucky, a solitary fantasy*
> *can totally transform*
> *one million realities.*
> —Maya Angelou

Certainty, belief, and faith, are necessary and powerful forces for creating your goals. Gregg Braden clearly shows that scientists are now telling us how "everything we experience as 'life' is directly linked to what we believe," and that, "Experiments show that the focus of our attention changes reality itself." Your thinking and the belief you hold shapes your reality and creates matter. Braden further states that we're limited only by our beliefs.

Hold good thoughts about your manuscript. Believe in yourself as a writer. You must think, speak, and act with confidence. Push and persist. Totally believe. As David Spangler says: "The 'magnet' of manifestation pulls to us whatever corresponds to the images and beliefs we hold in our minds." The key element here is the directed and focused use of your mind. Todd Michael agrees, saying, "Over and over, reprogram your mind at the deepest possible level to believe and receive."

Hundreds of books by past and present-day authors (Louise Hay, Mike Dooley, Esther and Jerry Hicks, Ernest Holmes, and the like) agree with Frank Lloyd Wright's statement: "The thing always happens that you really believe in, and the *belief* in a thing makes it happen." David Cameron Gikandi concurs: "Everything is possible to the extent that you are certain." Believe, know, and *feel*. Expectation is a powerful force. Gregg Braden sums it up by saying, "It's our power of belief that creates the actual fact." Confidently believe that your manuscript will be successful.

> *To accomplish great things*
> *we must not only act, but also dream;*
> *not only plan, but also believe.*
> —Anatole France

CHALLENGES:

> *I had become an armchair warrior*
> *whose battles were championed*
> *by alter egos*
> *on TV or at the movies.*
> —Dan Millman

Know upfront that there may be uncertainty, delays, and detours, in your writing project. There will be periods of adjustment and discomfort. (Three men quit the four-year BYU doctoral program at the outset—one on the second day, and two others within two weeks, before we barely got started. They didn'l even give themselves a chance to succeed.) Know that all accomplishments require effort, courage, and will. If you handle what's in front of you now, the future will take care of itself. Don't let challenges knock you off balance, or discourage you. When you get stuck, and feel like you're getting nowhere, stagnating, or slipping backward, Dan Millman says that you may actually be backing up to get a good running start. Let neither loss, lack, or adversity stop you in your tracks. Don't cave into setbacks. Think of them, Mike Dooley says, as only "steps in the mambo, tango, and the cha-cha-cha." Don't stop dancing.

Challenges are part and parcel of any all-encompassing, worthwhile adventure, like writing. It is said that they will come when you are ready to grow, overcome, and be more than you are now. If it were too easy, everyone would write a book. (Many say they can, but they can't, they don't, and they won't.) So, Tom Dooley further suggests that, "when you're facing a challenge, rise up, don't back down. See it as a stepping stone, not a wall; a valley, not an abyss." Hold good thoughts in your mind. Find the positive in all situations; see the best. Keep generating positive changes. Dwell on the end result, not the cursed hows. Focus on your *feelings*, and forge ahead.

A ship is safe
in harbor—
but that's not
what ships are for.
—John A. Shedd

AFFIRMATIONS:

An affirmation is a statement
that is true
in the grand scheme of things,
but that may not be
an observable fact
in our lives right now.
—Victoria Moran

Affirmations are conscious autosuggestions. Written, silently read, said aloud, or sung, this technique produces extraordinary results. You are reminding yourself over and over of what you want to achieve. "You are retraining your thinking and your speaking into positive patterns," says Louise L. Hay. There will always be peaks and valleys in your writing, and affirmations can help in that regard. They do not deny the reality of your concerns, but they provide something stronger and more powerful than your worries to think about. Affirmations keep you on track. They counteract any negative self-talk, or self-sabotaging behaviors. "As you think, so shall it be."

According to Dr. Eric Maisel, a psychotherapist who has authored 40 books: "To affirm is to declare positively, solemnly, and formally that one is equal to a challenge, or growing equal to that challenge, that one is on the track, that one is consciously and forcefully attempting to better oneself and grow in a certain direction."

Start working with one affirmation. For it to make a difference in your life, you must get past your brain's built in bias. To counteract this, you need to not only repeat the sentence over and over again, but you must *believe* it. ("I am a writer." "I am a professional writer.")

Dr. Fred Alan Wolf, a quantum physicist, explains in *The Secret*, that the words *I am* are powerful. "When you say *I am*, the words that follow are summoning creation with a mighty force, because you are declaring it to be fact. You are stating it with certainty."

David Cameron Gikandi wrote a whole book, *A Happy Pocket Full of Money*, around three short sentences: "I am wealth. I am abundance. I am joy." Create your own affirmations, starting with "I am . . . " to help you feel happy and successful as a writer.

Take care what words
you speak that follow "I am."
In so speaking
you create your life.
—Alan Cohen

Sandra Anne Taylor says to " . . . keep repeating your affirmations—even hundreds of times a day—until you feel a shift in your attitude." Say them aloud in the privacy of your home, in front of your mirror, while in the tub or shower, while doing the dishes or any other mundane task, or driving your car. Taylor continues: "When you say them right out loud, your acoustic energy amplifies your electromagnetic vibrations and doubles their power."

Get in the habit of silently saying affirmations (hypnotic routine repetitions) to keep you on target, when you're standing in a long line at the bank, grocery store, or post office, or you're waiting in the doctor's or dental office, or when you're stuck in traffic. To affirm is to state something positively and persistently ("I am a wonderful writer. I contribute positive change in the world.").

"Neuroscientists have proven over and over again," says Brendon Burchard, "that new neural pathways can be formed (and old ones strengthened) by the conscious focus of our attention, and deliberate practice." Affirmations are used by those in the business world, the sports world, the entertainment world, education, health, and service organizations, as well as by writers (Esther and Jerry Hicks, Dr. Doreen Virtue, Dr. Wayne Dyer, Gregg Braden, David Spangler, Alan Cohen, Catherine Ponder, Dr. Norman Vincent Peale, and so on). As you say your positive statements, *feel* as if the outcome has already happened.

TIP: Stick Post-its all around your house, and in your car, or calendars. Place them in your wallet and pockets. You can even record affirmations for easy listening, while you're walking, jogging, running, or driving. Affirmations are self-affirming, and keep your attention on your goal.

TIP: Make a stack of 3x5 affirmation cards, which you can read through each day, at the beginning of a writing project. Much later, you need only to flip through the cards, reading a few at a time, when you need a boost.

Later, your affirmations will become longer, and more specific, to fit your writing needs.

ACTIVITY: Use blank 3x5 cards. Write:

- *Every day, in every way, my writing is getting better and better.* (To paraphrase Emile Coue (1857-1926) the French pharmacist—who first discovered the placebo effect). On the flip side, write:

- *My ideas come faster than I can write, and they're all good ideas. (Thanks to Carolyn See.)*

- *I have an endless stream of green lights before me! (To paraphrase Dr. Wayne W. Dyer.)*

- *I have all the time I need, to write what I want to write.*

- *Everything I read, learn, and experience, helps to better my writing skills.*

Insert the <u>title</u> of your book into your affirmations, wherever possible:

- *<u>My book</u> is wildly successful, and helpful in every way.*

- *I experience a bigger, brighter, bolder future through <u>my book</u>.*

- *The information and joy I bring to others via <u>my book</u>, is a gift I give to myself. Each reader finds something of import.*

- *I am a happy, well-respected author, both nationally and internationally known. <u>My book</u> generates ripples of influence. I have it all!*

BREADCRUMBS FOR BEGINNERS

- *I am energized, engaged, and enthusiastic about supporting my book, and getting it out into the world.*

MANTRAS:

> *Keep writing. Keep writing.*
> *Keep writing.*

While you're at it, you might think about mantras, which another form of autosuggestion. A mantra can be a sound, a syllable, a single word, or a short group of words that are considered capable of creating a transformation.

When I ingest my meds, vitamins, and food, I mentally chant: *Transform, regenerate, renew.* When Terry L. Neal takes his daily walks, he chants: *Wisdom, health, wealth, and happiness.* Sandra Anne Taylor repeats: *Choose love, choose love, choose love.* Whenever there is a problem, Louise L. Hay suggests that you repeat, "All is well." Many are those who chant *Peace, peace, peace, peace,* or *Joy, joy, joy.* If you want to kick-start your efforts, chant, *"I can do it! I can do it!"* over and over again. Dr. Wayne Dyer suggests that you "Shout yes to everyone as often as you can." *Yes, yes, yes, yes!* He advises: "Making yes your inner mantra allows you to extend yes outside of yourself, and attract more of yes into your own personal intending." Try it. What have you got to lose?

Thank you, Thank you, Thank you . . .

A mantra is the silent repetition of a specific word or message, such as Thank you, Gracias, Merci, Danke schoen, in whatever language you choose. "Simply by taking the time to focus on what you already have in your life, recognizing your great fortune and appreciating it, will automatically put you in a great mood," says Sonia Ricotti. You don't have to be specific about any one thing you are grateful for—just lump them all together in your mind. Offer a general Thank You to the Universe, as you are being grateful for your entire writing experience. You may want to show your gratitude for:

- The time you have found to write;

- Your ability to focus on writing;

- Your efforts (good, bad, indifferent) at writing;

- Your memories as fodder for writing;

- Your daily observations as fodder for writing;

- Your imagination and creative ideas;

- The lessons you've already learned;

- Your ability to overcome writing challenges;

- Your openness and awareness of situations; and,

- Your joy in the process of writing.

All the above, and more, can be enfolded in your simple chant of: *Thank You, Thank You, Thank You* . . .

> *If we chant while*
> *simultaneously holding an idea,*
> *the mental picture manifests*
> *into physical form rapidly.*
> —Doreen Virtue

VISUALIZATIONS:

> *Everyone visualizes.*
> *Losers visualize the penalties of failure.*
> *Winners visualize the rewards of success.*
> —Dr. Rob Gilbert

To visualize merely means to picture something, to form an image, or paint a portrait in your mind. You simply focus on that photo in your brain. You mentally see what you want, as if it were physically present. Use your imagination, and picture yourself writing easily and effortlessly, and enjoying it. Take some time each day for a mental rehearsal or some imagery practice. Mentally see yourself doing what you want, having what you want, and feeling the way you want. Visualizing the end result of your writing (a manuscript, a published book, copies of your book flying off the shelves, a congratulations party) helps you achieve publication. By visualizing, you will be developing a subconscious blueprint for your future.

Shift from a linear mindset to a cyclical mindset, by joining the beginning of your writing project with the end, via visualization. Experts (Mike Dooley, Dan Millman, Todd Michael, Louise Hay, Dr. Wayne Dyer, Dr. Alberto Villoldo, Ernest Holmes) agree that visualizations are the best thing you can do to improve your performance in any area. Consciously cultivate a clear mental picture of your book's successful completion.

Get in the habit of using visualizations. Alexandra Stoddard urges: "Before you get out of bed in the morning, stretch your legs and arms, yawn, and then visualize an ideal day." To visualize is to spark great changes in your life.

Visualizing is much more powerful than affirmations...a picture is worth a thousand words. Sports professionals (Tiger Woods), business executives (Oprah Winfrey), celebrities (Jim Carrey), and politicians (Arnold Schwarzenegger) do this on a daily basis. Once a day for five or so minutes is sufficient. That's it! How easy can anything get? You are simply seeing—in your mind's eye—the end result you want.

Imagine what you want to happen with your book. Vividly focus on the details (sights, sounds, colors, textures, people). Put yourself in the scene. *Feel* your emotions, as if it were happening now. See yourself enjoying the writing, the publication, and the promotion of your book. See your book enjoyed by readers, and talking about it. See your book critically and commercially received.

Dwell only on the positive end result. Positive visualization lifts your consciousness from thoughts of fear and failure to happiness and success. Never spend any time agitating over *how* it's going to happen. Dwell only on the end goal, where you have already arrived! Set the stage for your grand event! In your imagination, see yourself deliriously jumping up and down, whooping with joy. You could even throw in a ticker-tape parade, while confetti swirls around you and your book, with pyrotechnics exploding in the background. Seeing is believing. Believe that this final state has already come to pass. Produce what you want to happen. Simply close your eyes for a short time every day, and visualize your goal, as if it has already been achieved. See yourself having the feelings and experiences your really seek for your book.

DECLARATION:

As God is my witness,
I'll never be hungry again.
—Scarlett O'Hara

The above declaration was made famous through both the Pulitzer-winning book (1936) and the ten Academy Awards movie (1939) of *Gone with the Wind*, by Margaret Mitchell. There is tremendous energy in your spoken words. Once you declare that something is so, you send a signal into the Universe that moves that something toward you. You attract it. You magnetize it. Decide and declare. State your declaration aloud, and with feeling, and *allow* it to come into you life. Intention rules.

Betsy Lerner invites you to "Come out of the closet, and announce yourself as a writer." Be bold. Declare it. This takes courage, at first. All you have to do is decide, and say, with *feeling*: "Yes! I can write. *I am* a writer!" Shout it into your mirror. When you get used to that, you can add, "I am an *excellent* writer." Later, you might add a phrase, "I am an *excellent* writer; readers *love* my books." And later, still, you might combine other sentences into an affirmation: "I am an excellent writer; readers love my books. I am a bridge. I light the way."

We are what we repeatedly do.
—Aristotle

So if you are always writing, you are a writer. Declare yourself to be a writer; the very act of writing makes it so. Jack Canfield said, "I'm going to declare that, I'm going to believe it, and I'm going to act as if it's true."

Like attracts like and . . .
we attract just what we are in mind.
—Ernest Holmes

ACT AS IF:

The only way
we truly make a decision
is by acting.
—Dan Millman

Your beliefs are powerful. Believing in yourself as a writer is a large part of making the transition to *being* a writer. As has been said by others, thinking big but acting small, is the same thing as thinking small. Imagine. Make believe it is so, with a total lack of doubt. Keep your sights on the goal. Persistence can compensate for many shortcomings. Go for it!

If you want to be enthusiastic,
act enthusiastic.
—Dale Carnegie

Act as if your writing dreams have come true. Act as if it's a done deal. Act as if you are already a published writer (think letters, blogs). Act as if you're writing a real page-turner. Think, speak, and act "as if" without hesitation. Writing is belief in motion. Conduct yourself with concrete confidence.

> *Act as if what you do*
> *makes a difference.*
> *It does.*
> —William James

CELEBRATE:

> *There are some days*
> *when I think I'm going to die from*
> *an overdose of satisfaction.*
> —Salvador Dali

Become your own cheering section! Rarely does the writer congratulate herself. She doesn't see the long goal she set for herself, and that she stayed the course, or the courage it took. Each step along the way is cause for excitement. Celebrate each and every one of your accomplishments, changes, and breakthroughs. Acknowledge your achievements and success. Even if the world isn't noticing you, notice yourself. Pat yourself on the back. Recognize all that you've learned along the way. Enjoy seeing your dream come true. Give yourself an award of some kind for all your hard work. Buy yourself a guilt-free gift, or send yourself flowers, or eat out at a fancy place, or go someplace you've always wanted to go. Splurge. Indulge yourself. Pull out all the stops. Do something to mark the occasion by treating yourself to fulfilling experiences. Give yourself time to sparkle, shimmer, and shine. Feel special.

PART V

FINAL WORDS

END REMARKS:

Every end is a new beginning.
—Proverb

Everyone knows that writing is a low-paying, thankless field. Even so, the only thing most authors want more than getting into print is *staying* in print. They don't want to be akin to a One-Trick Pony. They want to have staying power. Others are satisfied with writing only one book. They successfully got it out of their systems. Just as some individuals are satisfied by climbing one mountain, or running one marathon. That's all they signed up for, that's all they want to accomplish. It was simply on their bucket list of things to do, and they are happy they reached their goal, and feel fulfilled and complete, and are now free to work toward other objectives.

Talent is no guarantee of success, anyway. Always remember: If you want to be a writer, you must read a lot, and you must write a lot. And, for every person who writes a book, there are thousands who believe they could—but *don't*. Consider yourself a success. Most people die with their stories still within them. If you have anything to say, say it now.

Write what you want to write, because it pleases you, and for no other reason. If you write for the joy of it, you can write forever. To paraphrase J.D. Salinger, you should get very quiet, and ask yourself what kind of writing you would most like to read, and then sit down and write it for yourself. Know that if you care enough to write it, someone will care enough to read it. Writers and readers are a comfort to each other. Commit to writing no matter what. Commit to finishing, no matter what. Commit to sharing, no matter what. Follow the breadcrumbs of those who have gone before you. Live the literary life of reading, writing, and corresponding. WRITE!

> *When I am dead,*
> *I hope it may be said:*
> *"His sins were scarlet,*
> *but his books were read."*
> —Hilaire Belloc

Remember the first tip I shared with you? Writing is just talking on paper. Chant: "I am unique, I am creative, and I have something important to say!" You can do this!

As you more than likely have heard before: We are

all works in progress. We are all rough drafts. None of us are finished, final, *done*. It is never too late to find your writing voice. Have faith and confidence in yourself as a writer. Follow the breadcrumbs, the trail that authors have left for you to follow. **You can do this!**

*Writing is about
enriching the lives
of those who will read your work,
and enriching your own life, as well.*
—Stephen King

Now is the time to celebrate and cheer the end of this book. You've read it all the way through. Break out the noisemakers and silly hats! Dance to the music, blow bubbles, and party on!

*One might take children's philosophy to heart.
They do not despise a bubble
because it burst:
They immediately set to work to blow another one.*
—EDGE Keynote

Now, please, go. Write your asses off.
—Natalie Goldberg

*If my doctor told me
I only had six minutes to live,
I wouldn't brood.
I'd type a little faster.*
—Nathaniel Hawthorne

BIBLIOGRAPHY

Armstrong, Lance & Sally Jenkins. *It's Not About the Bike: My Journey Back to Life*. New York: Putnam, 2000.

Armstrong, Lance, Sally Jenkins, & Donna Sinisgalli. *Every Second Counts*. New York: Broadway, 2003.

Atchity, Kenneth. *A Writer's Time: A Guide to the Creative Process, from Vision through Revision*. New York: Norton, 1986.

Ballon, Rachel Friedman. *Blueprint for Writing: A Writer's Guide to Creativity, Craft, and Career*. Los Angeles, CA: Lowell House, 1994.

Baldacci, David (editor). *No Rest for the Dead*. New York: Simon & Schuster, 2011.

Bartlett, Pam. *WomenConnected*. Greenbank, WA: Glenmore Press, 2007.

Baum, L. Frank. *The Wizard of Oz*. New York: Barnes & Noble Classics, 2004 reprint from 1865.

Benchley, Peter. *Jaws*. New York: Doubleday, 1974.

Block, Lawrence. *Telling Lies for Fun and Profit: A Manual for Fiction Writers*. New York: Quill/ William Morrow, 1994.

Braden, Gregg. *The Spontaneous Healing of Belief: Shattering the Paradigm of False Limits*. Carlsbad, CA: Hay House, 2008.

Braden, Gregg. *The Divine Matrix: Bridging Time. Space, Miracles, and Belief*. Carlsbad, CA: Hay House, 2007.

Burchard, Brendon. *The Charge: Activating the 10 Human Drives That Make You Feel Alive*. New York: Free Press, 2012.

Burkeman, Oliver. *The Antidote: Happiness for People Who Can't Stand Positive Thinking*. U.K.: Faber & Faber, 2012.

Byrne, Rhonda. *The Secret*. New York: Atria Books, 2006.

Cameron, Julia. *The Right to Write: An Invitation and Initiation into the Writing Life*. New York: Tarcher/ Putnam, 1998.

Canfield, Jack, Mark Victor Hanson, Patty Hanson, & Irene Dunlap (editors), *Chicken Soup for the Kid's Soul*. Deer Beach, FL: Health Communications, 1998.

Chandler, Raymond. *The Big Sleep*. New York: Barnes & Noble, 2011 reprint from 1930.

Child, Lee. *Jack Reacher's Rules*. New York: Delacorte Press, 2012.

Child, Lee. *A Wanted Man*. New York: Delacorte Press, 2012.

Child, Lee. *One Shot*. New York: Delacorte Press, 2005.

Chopra, Deepak, M.D. *Ageless Body, Timeless Mind: The Quantum Alternative to Growing Old*. New York: Harmony Books, 1993.

Clarke, Sir Arthur C. *2001: A Space Odyssey*. New York: New American Library, 1968.

Cochrane, James. *Between You and I: a little book of Bad English*. Naperville, IL: Sourcebooks, Inc., 2004.

Crais, Robert. *Suspect*. New York: Putnam, 2013.

Dickens, Charles. *A Tale of Two Cities*. New York: Barnes & Noble, 2003 reprint from 1859.

Dickens, Charles. *A Christmas Carol*. New York: Barnes & Noble, 2003 reprint from 1843.

Dillard, Annie. *The Writing Life*. New York: Harper & Row, 1989.

Dooley, Mike. *Even More Notes from the Universe: Dancing Life's Dance*. New York: Atria, 2005.

Dooley, Mike. *Notes from the Universe: New Perspectives from an Old Friend*. New York: Atria, 2003.

Dyer, Wayne, Ph.D. *The Power of Intention: Learning to Co- create Your World Your Way*. New York: Hay House, 2010.

Evanovich, Janet. *Notorious Nineteen*. New York: St. Martin's Griffin, 2013.

Evanovich, Janet. *How I Write: Secrets of a Bestselling Author*. New York: St. Martin's Griffin, 2006.

Evanovich, Janet. *Hot Six*. New York: St. Martin's Griffin, 2000.

Evanovich, Janet. *High Five*. New York: St. Martin's Griffin, 1999.

Faulkner, William. *As I Lay Dying*. New York: Norton, 2009 reprint from 1930.

Frank, Anne. *The Diary of Anne Frank*. New York: Random House, 1956.

Frey, James. *A Million Little Pieces*. New York: Random House, 2003.

Gerke, Jeff. *The First 50 Pages: Engage Agents, Editors, and Readers, and Set Up Your Novel for Success*. Cincinnati, OH: Writer's Digest, 2011.

Gikandi, David Cameron. *A Happy Pocketful of Money: Your Quantum Leap into the Understanding, Having, and Enjoying of Immense Wealth and Happiness*. Bloomington, IN: Xlibris, 2008.

Goldberg, Natalie. *Writing Down the Bones: Freeing the Writer Within*. Boston, MS: Shambhala, 2005.

Gulli, Andrew F. & 26 writers. *No Rest for the Dead*. New York: Touchstone, 2011.

Gutkind, Lee. *You Can't Make This Stuff Up*. Boston, MS: DeCapo Press/Lifelong Books, 2012.

Halpern, Justin. *Sh*t My Dad Says*. UK: It Books, 2010.

Hay, Louise L. & Mona Lisa Schulz, M.D., Ph.D. *All is Well: Heal Your Body with Meditation, Affirmations, and Intuition*. Carlsbad, CA: Hay House, 2013.

Hay, Louise L. *You Can Heal Your Life*. Carlsbad, CA: Hay House, 2004.

Hay, Louise L. *The Power is Within You*. Carson, CA: Hay House, 1991.

Hemingway, Ernest. *A Farewell to Arms*. New York: Scribner, 2006 reprint from 1929.

Hemingway, Ernest. *The Sun Also Rises*. New York: Scribner, 2006 reprint from 1926.

Hicks, Esther & Jerry Hicks, *The Amazing Power of Deliberate Intent: Living the Art of Allowing*. Carlsbad, CA: Hay House, 2004.

Holloway, Monica. *Driving with Dead People*. New York: Simon & Schuster, 2008.

Irving, Clifford. *The Autobiography of Howard Hughes*. New York: McGraw-Hill, 1971.

• Johnson, Rev. Deborah H. *Your Deepest Intent*. Boulder, CO: Sounds True, 2007.

Joyce, C. Alan & Sarah Janssen. *I Used to Know That Literature*. New York: Reader's Digest, 2012.

Kagawa, Julie. *Summer's Crossing*. Buffalo, NY: Harlequin Teen, 2011.

Khalsa, Dharma Singh, M.D. *Brain Longevity: The Breakthrough Medical Program that Improves Your Mind and Memory*. New York: Warner, 1997.

King, Stephen. *On Writing: A Memoir of the Craft*. New York: Scribner, 2000.

King, Stephen. *The Stand*. New York: Barnes & Noble, 2011 reprint from 1978.

Kortge, Carolyn Scott. *The Spirited Walker: Fitness Walking for Clarity, Balance, and Spiritual Connection*. San Francisco, CA: Harper, 1998.

Kozak, Ellen M. *From Pen to Print: The Secrets of Getting Published Successfully*. New York: Henry Holt, 1992.

Lamott, Anne. *Bird by Bird: Some Instructions on Writing and Life*. New York: Anchor Books/ Random House, 1994.

Leonard, Elmore. 10 Rules of Writing. New York: William Morrow, 2001.

Lerner, Betsy. *The Forest for the Trees: An Editor's Advice to Writers*. New York: Riverhead Books, 2001.

Maisel, Eric, Ph.D. *Affirmations for Artists*. New York: Putnam, 1996.

Mallon, Thomas. *Stolen Words: Forays into the Origins and Ravages of Plagiarism*. New York: Penguin, 1989.

Mansbach, Adam. *Seriously, Just Go to Sleep*. Brooklyn, NY: Akashic Books, 2012.

Mansbach, Adam. *Go the F**k to Sleep*. Brooklyn, NY: Akashic Books, 2011.

Marrero, Frank. *A Crisis in Inner City Educaton*. Text of Speech, sponsored by John F. Kennedy University: In Motion Magazine.com, 4/25/06.

Masello, Robert. *Robert's Rules of Writing: 101 Unconventional Lessons Every Writer Needs to Know*. Cincinatti, OH: Writer's Digest, 2005.

Max, Tucker. *Assholes Finish First*. New York: Gallery Books/Simon & Schuster, 2011.

McCarry, Charles. *The Secret Lovers*. New York: Overlook Press, 1977.

McCourt, Frank. *Angela's Ashes*. New York: Scribner's, 1996.

McTaggart, Lynne. *The Intention Experiment: Using Your Thoughts to Change Your Life and the World*. New York: Free Press, 2007.

Meinberg, Sherry L., Ed.D. *Diabetes ABC*. Parker, CO: Outskirts Press, 2013.

Meinberg, Sherry L., Ed.D. *Imperfect Weddings are Best*. North Charleston, SC: CreateSpace, 2012.

Meinberg, Sherry L., Ed.D. *Recess is Over! No Nonsense Strategies and Tips for Student Teachers and New Teachers*. Charleston, SC: Booksurge, 2010.

Meinberg, Sherry L., Ed.D. *Autism ABC*. Charleston, SC: Booksurge, 2009.

Meinberg, Sherry L., Ed.D. *The Bogeyman: Stalking and its Aftermath*. New York: iUniverse, 2003.

Meinberg, Sherry L., Ed.D. *Toxic Attention: Keeping Safe from Stalkers, Abusers, and Intruders*. Lincoln, NE: iUniverse, 2003.

Meinberg, Sherry L., Ed.D. *Be the Boss of Your Brain: Take Control of Your Life*. Minden, NV: Ripple Effect, 1999.

Meinberg, Sherry L., Ed.D, *Into the Hornet's Nest: An Incredible Look at Life in an Inner City School*. Saratoga, CA: A & E, 1993.

Meloy, J. Reid (editor). *The Psychology of Stalking: Clinical and Forensic Perspectives.* San Diego, CA: Academic Press, 1998.

Michael, Todd, M.D. *The Twelve Conditions of a Miracle: The Miracle Worker's Handbook.* New York: Tarcher/Penguin, 2004.

Millman, Dan. *Living on Purpose: Straight Answers to Life's Tough Questions.* Novato, CA: New World Library, 2000.

Millman, Dan. *No Ordinary Moments: A Peaceful Warrior's Guide to Daily Life.* Tiburon, CA: H.J. Kramer, 1992.

Millman, Dan. *Sacred Journey of the Peaceful Warrior.* Tiburon, CA: H.J. Kramer, 1991.

Mitchell, Margaret. *Gone With the Wind.* New York: Macmillan, 1936.

Moran, Victoria. *Creating a Charmed Life: Sensible, Spiritual Secrets Every Busy Woman Should Know.* San Francisco, CA: Harper, 1999.

Moran, Victoria. *Lit from Within: Tending Your Soul for Lifelong Beauty.* San Francisco, CA: Harper, 2001.

Moran, Victoria. *Living a Charmed Life: Your Guide to Finding Magic in Every Moment of Every Day.* San Francisco, CA: Harper, 2009.

Morgan, Marlo. *Mutant Message Down Under.* New York: Harper/Collins, 1991.

Myss, Carolyn. *Invisible Acts of Power: Personal Choices that Create Miracles.* New York: Free Press, 2004.

Neal, Terry L. *The Search for Zarahemla.* North Charleston, SC: CreateSpace, 2012.

Norwood, Eric. "A Page Without Punctuation is a Life Without Spaces." *Living Well Journal,* March 16, 2012.

O'Conner, Patricia T. *Woe is I: The Grammarphobe's Guide to Better English in Plain English.* New York: Riverhead Books, 2003

Palahniuk, Chuck. *Diary: A Novel.* New York: Anchor Press, 2004.

Parker, Dorothy. *The Collected Dorothy Parker.* UK: Penguin Modern Classics, 2007.

Patterson, James. *Merry Christmas, Alex Cross.* New York: Little, Brown, 2013.

Poynter, Dan. *Self-Publishing Manual: How to Write, Print, and Sell Your Own Book*. Santa Barbara, CA: Para Publishing, 16th edition, 2007.

Poynter, Dan. *Self-Publishing Manual, Volume II: How to Write, Print, and Sell Your Own Book Employing the Latest Technologies and the Newest Techniques*. Santa Barbara, CA: Para Publishing, 2009.

Rasberry, Salli & Padi Selwyn. *Living Your Life Outloud: How to Unlock Your Creativity and Unleash Your Joy*. New York: Pocket Books, 1995.

Ricotti, Sonia. *The Law of Attraction Plain and Simple: Create the Extraordinary Life That You Deserve*. Charlottesville, VA: Hampton Roads, 2008.

Robbins, Anthony. *Awaken the Giant Within: How to Take Immediate Control of Your Mental, Emotional, Physical, and Financial Destiny!* New York: Free Press, 1991.

Salinger, J.D. "Seymour: An Introduction," *The New Yorker*, June 6, 1959.

Sampson, Brent. *Sell Your Book on Amazon, 2nd Edition*. Denver, CO: 2010.

Santoso, Alex. "The Naked Truth: Authors Who Write in the Buff," *Neatorama*, January 30, 2007.

See, Carolyn. *Making a Literary Life: Advice for Writers and Other Dreamers.* New York: Ballantine Books, 2002.

Schwalbe, Will. *The End of Your Life Book Club.* New York: Knopf, 2012.

Sluyter, Dean. *The Zen Commandments: Ten Suggestions for a Life of Inner Freedom.* Tarcher/ Penguin, 2001.

Small, Gary, M.D. *The Memory Bible: An Innovative Strategy for Keeping Your Brain Young.* New York: Hyperion, 2002.

Smith, James V. *The Writer's Little Helper: Everything You Need to Know to Write Better and Get Published.* Blue Ash, OH: Writer's Digest Books, 2012.

Spangler, David. *Everyday Miracles: The Inner Art of Manifestation.* New York: Bantom, 1996.

Stoddard, Alexandra. *Living Beautifully Together: How to Live Graciously in a Hectic World by Finding Time to Love Your Family, Your Friends, and Yourself.* New York: Doubleday, 1989.

Strunk, Jr., William, and E.B. White. *The Elements of Style.* Needham, MS: Allyn Bacon, 1979.

Taylor, Sandra Anne. *Quantum Success: The Astounding Science of Wealth and Happiness.* Carlsbad, CA: Hay House, 2006.

Tiberghien, Susan M. *One Year to a Writing Life: Twelve Lessons to Deepen Every Writer's Art and Craft.* Pennsylvania, PA: Da Capo Press, 2007.

Tolstoy, Leo. *War and Peace.* Cambridge: Cambridge World Classics, 2010 reprint from 1869.

University of Chicago Press, *The Chicago Manual of Style, 14th Edition.* Chicago, IL: The University of Chicago Press, 1993.

Villoldo, Alberto, Ph.D. *The Four Insights: Wisdom, Power, and Grace of the Earthkeepers.* Carlsbad, CA: Hay House, 2006.

Viorst, Judith. *Alexander and the Terrible, Horrible, No Good, Very Bad Day.* New York: Antheneum, 1972.

Viorst, Judith. *The Tenth Good Thing About Barney.* New York: Atheneum, 1987.

Virtue, Doreen, *The Lightworker's Way: Awakening Your Spiritual Power to Know and Heal.* Carlsbad, CA: Hay House, 1997.

Vitale, Joe. *The Attractor Factor: 5 Easy Steps for Creating Wealth (or Anything Else) from the Inside Out.* Hoboken, NJ: John Wiley & Sons, 2005.

Weil, Andrew, M.D. *Spontaneous Healing.* New York: Ballentine, 2000.

Weiss, Brian, M.D. *Messages From the Masters: Tapping into the Power of Love.* New York: Warner, 2,000.

Williams, Geoff. "Top 10 Successful Marketing Stunts." *Entrepreneur,* July 20, 2006.

Winthrop, Elizabeth. *Tough Eddie.* New York: Penguin, 1989.

Zolotow, Charlotte. *William's Doll.* New York: Harper Collins, 1985.

CREDITS

Atchity, Kenneth. *A Writer's Time: A Guide to the Creative Process, from Vision through Revision.* [pp. 22, 23, 48, 66, 110.]

Ballon, Rachel Friedman. *Blueprint for Writing: A Writer's Guide to Creativity, Craft, and Career.* [pp. 52, 53, 76, 82, 103, 140.]

Bartlett, Pam. *WomenConnected.* [pp. 129, 132.]

Block, Lawrence. *Telling Lies for Fun and Profit: A Manual for Fiction Writers.* [pp. 30-31, 33, 37, 39, 43, 47, 49, 198, 219.]

Braden, Gregg. *The Spontaneous Healing of Belief: Shattering the Paradigm of False Limits.* [pp. ix, x, 4, 74, 75.]

Braden, Gregg. *The Divine Matrix: Bridging Time, Space, Miracles, and Belief.* [p.114.]

Burchard, Brendon. *The Charge: Activating the 10 Human Drives That Make You Feel Alive* [pp. 7, 8, 21, 22, 25, 42, 196.]

Byrne, Rhonda. *The Secret.* [pp. 93, 96, 117, 119, 168.]

Cameron, Julia. *The Right to Write: An Invitation and Initiation into the Writing Life.* [pp. 1, 3, 4, 7, 10, 13, 14, 19, 20, 23, 26, 38, 42, 50, 64-68, 128.]

Child, Lee. *Jack Reacher's Rules.* [pp. 2, 107.]

Chopra, Deepak, M.D. *Ageless Body, Timeless Mind: The Quantum Alternative to Growing Old.* [pp. 103, 201.]

Dillard, Annie. *The Writing Life.* [pp. 13, 39.]

Dooley, Mike. *Even More Notes from the Universe: Dancing Life's Dance.* [pp. x, 15.]

Dooley, Mike. *Notes from the Universe: New Perspectives from an Old Friend.* [pp. 9, 25, 31, 136 149, 150, 185, 210.]

Dyer, Wayne, Ph.D. *The Power of Intention: Learning to Co-create Your World Your Way.* [pp. 3, 8, 102, 103, 155, 177-178].

Evanovich, Janet. *How I Write: Secrets of a Bestselling Author.* [pp. 3, 8, 11, 23, 24, 39, 66, 78, 95-96, 97, 100, 102- 3, 177, 192-3, 200.]

Gerke, Jeff. *The First 50 Pages: Engage Agents, Editors, and Readers, and Set Up Your Novel for Success.* [pp. 71, 73,

Gikandi, David Cameron. *A Happy Pocket Full of Money.* [pp. 16, 102.]

Goldberg, Natalie. *Writing Down the Bones: Freeing the Writer Within* [pp. xiv, 1, 3, 5, 7, 25.]

Gutkind, Lee. *You Can't Make This Stuff Up* [pp. 7, 37, 44, 45, 47, 52, 53, 57, 230, 231.]

Hay, Louise L. *You Can Heal Your Life.* [pp. xiii, 17.]

Hay, Louise L. *The Power is Within You.* [pp. 22, 33-47.]

Hicks, Esther & Jerry Hicks, *The Amazing Power of Deliberate Intent: Living the Art of Allowing.* [p. 7, 181.]

Johnson, Rev. Deborah H. *Your Deepest Intent.* Boulder, CO: Sounds True, 2007. [pp. 26, 27, 28, 225.]

King, Stephen, *On Writing: A Memoir of the Craft* [pp. 57, 116, 118, 144, 148, 153, 154, 161, 165, 174, 176, 177.]

Kortge, Carolyn Scott. *The Spirited Walker: Fitness Walking for Clarity, Balance, and Spiritual Connection.* [pp. xvii, 9.]

Kozak, Ellen M. *From Pen to Print: The Secrets of Getting Published Successfully.* [pp. 6, 8, 16, 18, 23, 75, 77, 125.]

Lamott, Anne. *Bird by Bird: Some Instructions on Writing and Life.* [pp. xii, xxii, 21-22, 25-26, 28, 45, 54-55, 59, 62, 227, 230.]

Lerner, Betsy. *The Forest for the Trees: An Editor's Advice to Writers.* [pp. 57, 67, 69, 70, 166, 178, 208, 221.]

Leonard, Elmore. *10 Rules of Writing.* [pp. 33, 75.]

Maisel, Eric, Ph.D. *Affirmations for Artists.* [p. viii.]

McTaggart, Lynne. *The Intention Experiment: Using Your Thoughts to Change Your Life and the World.* [pp. 24, 57, 61.]

Masello, Robert. *Robert's Rules of Writing: 101 Unconventional Lessons Every Writer Needs to Know.* [pp. 1-2, 3-4, 5-6, 42.]

Michael, Todd, M.D. *The Twelve Conditions of a Miracle: The Miracle Worker's Handbook.* [pp. 15-18, 71, 103, 118, 138.]

Millman, Dan. *No Ordinary Moments: A Peaceful Warrior's Guide to Daily Life.* [pp. 20, 80, 85, 115, 175.]

Millman, Dan. *Living on Purpose.* [p. 140.]

Millman, Dan. *Sacred Journey of the Peaceful Warrior.* [pp. 25, 63, 72, 82.]

Moran, Victoria. *Creating a Charmed Life: Sensible, Spiritual Secrets Every Busy Woman Should Know.* [pp. 75, 156, 164, 201.]

Moran, Victoria. *Lit from Within: Tending Your Soul for Lifelong Beauty.* [pp. 15-19.]

Moran, Victoria. *Living a Charmed Life: Your Guide to Finding Magic in Every Moment of Every Day.* [pp. 21-24.]

Myss, Carolyn. *Invisible Acts of Power: Personal Choices that Create Miracles.* [p. 257.]

Poynter, Dan. *Dan Poynter's Self-Publishing Manual: How to Write, Print, and Sell Your Own Book.* [pp. 57, 93-95, 342.]

Poynter, Dan. *Dan Poynter's Self-Publishing Manual, Vol. 2: How to Write, Print, and Sell Your Own Book Employing the Latest Technologies and the Newest Techniques.* [pp. 41, 52, 74, 75, 83, 109.]

Rasberry, Salli & Padi Selwyn. *Living Your Life Outloud: How to Unlock Your Creativity and Unleash Your Joy.* [pp. 99- 105.]

Ricotti, Sonia. *The Law of Attraction Plain and Simple: Create the Extraordinary Life That You Deserve.* [p. 69.]

Robbins, Anthony. *Awaken the Giant Within: How to Take Immediate Control of Your Mental, Emotional, Physical, and Financial Destiny!* [pp. 86-87.]

See, Carolyn. *Making a Literary Life: Advice for Writers and Other Dreamers.* [pp. xx, xxi, 4, 5, 16, 23, 24, 53, 78, 91, 118, 129, 137, 143, 147, 160, 168, 219, 225, 250.]

Small, Gary, M.D. *The Memory Bible: An Innovative Strategy for Keeping Your Brain Young.* [p. 167.]

Spangler, David. *Everyday Miracles: The Inner Art of Manifestation.* [p. 46.]

Stoddard, Alexandra. *Living Beautifully Together: How to Live Graciously in a Hectic World by Finding Time to Love Your Family, Your Friends, and Yourself.* [pp. 27, 28, 35, 39. 110, 130]

Taylor, Sandra Anne. *Quantum Success: The Astounding Science of Wealth and Happiness.* [pp. xiii, xiv, 93-101, 105, 106, 135, 140.]

Virtue, Doreen, *The Lightworker's Way: Awakening Your Spiritual Power to Know and Heal.* [pp. 102, 126.]

Vitale, Joe, *The Attractor Factor: 5 Easy Steps for Creating Wealth (or Anything Else) from the Inside Out.* [pp. 142- 145.]

Weiss, Brian, M.D. *Messages From the Masters: Tapping into the Power of Love.* [p. 14.]

ABOUT THE AUTHOR

"Books are my life!" says Dr. Sherry L. Meinberg, a recognized bookaholic. "I read books, I write books, I edit books. I share books. I eat, sleep, and breathe books."

A mishmash of books are stacked in every room of her home. A voracious reader, she generally devours a book a day, usually with three to five books being read at the same time. As such, she regularly donates books to individuals, libraries, schools, and shelters. Even her car license says: READ4ME, and the license plate holder reads: SO MANY BOOKS, SO LITTLE TIME.

Dr. Meinberg has spent over 50 years in the educational world, as a teacher (elementary, middle school, high school, and university), mentor, reading specialist, language arts specialist, literacy specialist, librarian, co-author of district guides, core adjunct university professor, and a supervisor of student teachers.

In addition to an academic life, she has corporate and nonprofit experience. She now teaches creative writing classes for OASIS, a national educational organization for mature adults. She founded and supports the Autism Honor Library in conjunction with the Autism in Long Beach foundation. She is a speaker on a variety of subjects, for various groups, conferences, and conventions, and has been interviewed on numerous radio and television shows. She absolutely loves storytelling, and has carried on a lifelong love affair with the printed word. She is a true bibliophile.

Dr. Meinberg has been honored with numerous city, county, and state accolades, and alongside her books, she has garnered over 70 local and national awards. *Breadcrumbs for Beginners: Following the Writing Trail* is her eleventh nonfiction book. She is all about getting the word out.

Dr. Sherry L. Meinberg
encourages your feedback.
Your comments, stories, and questions
are most welcome.

<sherrymeinberg@verizon.net>

*Will you succeed? Yes, you will indeed!
Ninety-eight and three-quarters percent,
guaranteed.*
—Dr. Seuss

INDEX